TEARING THE WORLD APART

ADVISORY BOARD

David Evans, General Editor
Barry Jean Ancelet
Edward A. Berlin
Joyce J. Bolden
Rob Bowman
Susan C. Cook
Curtis Ellison
William Ferris
John Edward Hasse
Kip Lornell
Bill Malone
Eddie S. Meadows
Manuel H. Peña
Wayne D. Shirley
Robert Walser

TEARING THE WORLD APART

BOB DYLAN AND THE TWENTY-FIRST CENTURY

EDITED BY
NINA GOSS
AND **ERIC HOFFMAN**

University Press of Mississippi / Jackson

www.upress.state.ms.us

The University Press of Mississippi is a member of
the Association of American University Presses.

Copyright © 2017 by University Press of Mississippi
All rights reserved

First printing 2017

∞

Library of Congress Cataloging-in-Publication Data

Names: Goss, Nina. | Hoffman, Eric R.
Title: Tearing the world apart : Bob Dylan and the twenty-first century /
  edited by Nina Goss and Eric Hoffman.
Description: Jackson : University Press of Mississippi, [2017] | Series:
  American made music series | Includes bibliographical references and index. |
Identifiers: LCCN 2017011365 (print) | LCCN 2017013224 (ebook) | ISBN
  9781496813336 (epub single) | ISBN 9781496813343 (epub institutional) |
  ISBN 9781496813350 (pdf single) | ISBN 9781496813367 (pdf institutional)
  | ISBN 9781496813329 (hardcover : alk. paper)
Subjects: LCSH: Dylan, Bob, 1941-—Criticism and interpretation. | Popular
  music—History and criticism.
Classification: LCC ML420.D98 (ebook) | LCC ML420.D98 T43 2017 (print) | DDC
  782.42164092—dc23
LC record available at https://lccn.loc.gov/2017011365

British Library Cataloging-in-Publication Data available

CONTENTS

Introduction 3

CHAPTER ONE   Visions of the Flood: *Masked and Anonymous* between *"Love and Theft"* and *Modern Times* 13
Alberto Brodesco

CHAPTER TWO   Dylan's *Together Through Life*: Rolling in Places 28
James Cody

CHAPTER THREE   Down the Foggy Ruins of Time: Bob Dylan and the Performance of Timelessness 45
Andrea Cossu

CHAPTER FOUR   *Tempest*, Bob Dylan, and the Bardic Arts 63
Anne Margaret Daniel

CHAPTER FIVE   You Can't Repeat the Past? Bob Dylan's *"Love and Theft"* and the Events of 9/11 73
Jesper Doolaard

CHAPTER SIX   A Sudden Blow: The Story of Violence in *"Love and Theft"* and *Modern Times* 85
Nina Goss

CHAPTER SEVEN   Narrative in *"Love and Theft,"* *Modern Times*, and *Tempest* 103
Jonathan Hodgers

CHAPTER EIGHT Dylan's Direction Home through the World's Mighty Opposites 117
Jamie Lorentzen

CHAPTER NINE Performative Lyric Voice and the Refrain as an Architectonic Element in Bob Dylan 134
Fahri Öz

CHAPTER TEN The Last Bob Dylan Record 151
Nick Smart

CHAPTER ELEVEN "Everybody Got to Wonder What's the Matter with This Cruel World Today": Social Consciousness and Political Commentary in *"Love and Theft"* and *Modern Times* 158
Thad Williamson

Works Cited... 177
Contributors 185
Index... 189

TEARING THE WORLD APART

INTRODUCTION

On November 18, 2015, five days after the Paris bombings, Bob Dylan performed in Madrid; armed guards were posted at the venue. News accounts reported that Dylan had insisted on this increased security; Dylan offered a public statement explaining that he had not personally requested armed protection. Also in November, Sony released several iterations of a treasure chest: the heretofore-unreleased tapes of Dylan's 1965–66 recording sessions, the twelfth volume of the voluminous *Bootleg Series*. This hoard of hoards comprises eighteen compact discs and has been offered in an extravagant limited edition package for a list price of US$599.

Thus, in less than one month, Bob Dylan's actions are commented on in the context of today's grievous world, and Bob Dylan's fifty-year-old recording detritus is avidly consumed and examined. Go back a couple of months and Bob Dylan is in the running for the Nobel Prize for literature,[1] and selling half a minute of charm to IBM for use in a television ad, the latest in an ongoing, perhaps entirely cynical late-career flirtation with the lucrative world of advertising. Musicians selling products became commonplace by the 1980s; even Willie Nelson was doing it—though admittedly he owed money to the IRS (and anyway, comedian Bill Hicks, who otherwise declared that musicians who deigned to whore themselves to commercial advertising were immediately "off the artistic roll call," was all too willing to give Willie a pass, given the circumstances). "I used to care," Dylan sings in his sole recorded Y2K output, a contribution to the soundtrack for Michael Douglas film *Wonder Boys* (2000), which concerns an aging Boomer staring down mortality, "but things have changed."[2]

In fact, once a counterculture icon, Bob Dylan has a long and storied history as a corporate shill, licensing his 1964 song "The Times They Are a-Changin'" to an accountancy firm (1994), Canada's Bank of Montreal (1996), and insurance conglomerate Kaiser Permanente (2005). More recently, he's sold the rights to such iconic songs as 1973's "Forever Young" to Pepsi in a reprehensible 2009 Super Bowl ad that used a horrendous will.i.am rap sampling of Dylan's song played over a predictable montage of 1960s Dylan footage. Dylan has also made appearances in commercials, including Cadillac in 2007, selling environmentally unfriendly, Boomer-marketed Escalades no less, and, notoriously, in a 2004 Victoria's Secret commercial that made use of Dylan's song of romantic defeat, "Love Sick" from *Time Out of Mind* (1997), made all the more interesting due to a comment Dylan made nearly forty years earlier during a widely seen, lengthy 1965 television conference—filmed during the height of Dylan's countercultural relevance—where Dylan jokingly told one interviewer that someday he would like to sell women's underwear.

Thus, what began in the 1960s as a bit of surrealistic, Allen Ginsberg–inspired irony, apparently transformed into a resigned, post-9/11 cash grab, a cynicism that is difficult to reconcile with the sincerity and authenticity of his recorded music during this era, with its tangible reverence for that "old, weird America" (in Greil Marcus's phrase). As ever with Dylan, it remains difficult to determine if this recent willingness to participate in corporate America, an institution which he once decried as an affront to the authenticity of the American tradition, is in fact a tongue-in-cheek critique of the times in which we live, that the Boomers who once so tenaciously clung to his every word as a new gospel meant to free them from the chains of oppression were now willing participants in their own oppression, if not actively responsible for it. Is Dylan in his own not-so-subtle way criticizing or chastising his generation for their apparent hollow, self-centered idealism, their empty rhetoric of free love? Is this the same irony and surrealistic jest that infused his mid-1960s persona? Was he saying that the Cultural Revolution failed, crushed under the weight of its own hubris and smug self-satisfaction? That Dylan's "The Times They Are a-Changin'" played over a commercial for a bank and an insurance company seems almost to be a slap in the face to these so-called "flower children," a final rejection of a culture which long misunderstood him, and had wrongly claimed him as a spokesperson, whose ideals he perceived as fake, unconvincing, self-absorbed, self-serving, and self-aggrandizing. Seen in this light, Dylan's embrace of capitalist culture is perhaps not so much a resignation as it is a final rejection of a generation whose voice he did not want to represent. For, as the essays in this present volume argue, Bob Dylan's voice is not the voice of a single postwar American generation, but rather a voice that is in many ways outside time, an American voice that derives from a rich musical tradition, from folk music to rock and roll, from Tin Pan Alley to bluegrass, from jazz to Western swing, from blues to ballads. It is, moreover, a uniquely poetic voice, and one that brings with it a lyrical tradition that stretches back to the French *trouvère*s, forward to the Beats and beyond.

A decisive turn in Dylan's career, a moment perhaps as important as Dylan plugging in at the Newport Folk Festival on July 24, 1965, was his December 14, 1963, acceptance speech for the Tom Paine Award, a largely symbolic award given by the Emergency Civil Liberties Union (ECLU), a group of moneyed, well-intentioned Old Left liberals. Dylan presented this speech just three weeks after the assassination of US President John F. Kennedy, and in it compared himself with presidential assassin Lee Harvey Oswald, figuring that confused lone drifter to be the harbinger of a new era; that the world did not belong to the old. There was no need to "look back," he declared (a subsequent documentary film on Dylan would be titled *Dont Look Back* [1967]), as the past offered only the illusion of progress; there was still much work to be done. The previous generation—meaning the Old Left liberals in attendance—had confused the timelessness and natural inclination of the youth culture to reject the culture of their forebears as merely another example of the infiltration of that political bogeyman communism, when in fact rebellion has no political window dressing. Instead, the current youth culture was more interested in, say, the sexual opportunities afforded by the automobile, with recreational drugs, with reading existentialist texts by Sartre and Camus then proliferating in paperback, with their disposable incomes, drive-in movie theaters, science fiction, cheap gasoline, fast cars, and leather jackets. Dylan's arrival in New York City just two years previous had seen the waning of the folk scene, and the rise of rock and roll heralded by the Beatles and Elvis Presley seemed to indicate that, if one wanted to develop as an artist and to remain relevant, the transition to electric rock 'n' roll was the only viable alternative. Those who later derided Dylan's decision to "go electric" in 1965 lacked vision, calling into question his sincerity as a folk artist. Yet Dylan was eager to disassociate himself with what he perceived as an antiquated artistic expression of interest mostly to hobbyists and anthropologists.

Indeed, one can best describe Dylan's trio of mid-1960s albums (*Bringing It All Back Home* [1965], *Highway 61 Revisited* [1965], and *Blonde on Blonde* [1966]) as playful and experimental; in fact, he was inventing a new art form. These albums were also surprisingly personal and vengeful; for example, they lack the self-referential irony of later efforts. In these seminal works, Dylan plays against his own image; their acid visions turn from society at large to personal relationships, as in *Highway 61*'s "Like a Rolling Stone," "Ballad of a Thin Man," or the Beat-inspired surrealism of *Bringing It All Back*'s "Mr. Tambourine Man" and *Blonde*'s "Sad-Eyed Lady of the Lowlands." More importantly, these albums involve a renewal of American music, a freewheeling interpretation of the American songbook, infusing it with substance, originality, and relevance, a startlingly engaging output that remained largely unmatched until nearly forty years later in the three major albums under consideration here: *"Love and Theft"* (2001), *Modern Times* (2006), and *Tempest* (2012), each released in roughly six-year intervals.

What we see in the mid-1960s Dylan is an artist all too willing to feed the fires of his own artistic exploration and to fan its flames. That he was mistaken for a "voice of a generation" was an unfortunate and unintended consequence, one that largely crippled his creative output for the next three decades. What was revolutionary in 1965, two years later became a burden. Though the 1960s counterculture was just a single, transitory moment in time, encompassing only a few short years in Dylan's now fifty-plus-year career, it is a moment with which, like a mosquito trapped in amber, Dylan has become inextricably associated, much to his apparent consternation. (This period is notably absent in the first volume of his decidedly non-chronological 2004 autobiography, *Chronicles, Volume One*, hereafter referred to as *Chronicles*).

Following an unruly, emotionally exhausting tour of Europe in the spring of 1966, culminating in a venomous response at Manchester, England's Free Trade Hall on May 17, where he was famously decried by one attendee as "Judas," Dylan retreated into the New York woods following a July 29 motorcycle accident. He was later joined by members of his touring group, the Hawks, and together they made a series of lo-fi recordings in the basement of a house just outside Woodstock. There, Dylan began the slow and still ongoing deconstruction of his Rimbaud-like mid-sixties persona, a persona he has since replaced numerous times yet which both Dylan and his critical and cultural interpreters continue to find inescapably iconic and seductive. See, for example, the number of his *Bootleg Series* recordings devoted to his 1960s output, the Martin Scorsese documentary *No Direction Home* (2005), which ends in 1966, or the non-linear 2007 Todd Haynes film *I'm Not There*, which, together with its inspiring text, poet Stephen Scobie's groundbreaking *Alias: Bob Dylan* (1991), in many ways mythologizes the concept of these "many faces" by casting six separate individuals as Dylan: a poet named Rimbaud (a play on Rimbaud's *Je est un autre*, or "I is another"); an eleven-year-old African American boy named Woody Guthrie, an interpretation of Dylan as a young Guthrie enthusiast; folk musician Jack Rollins, embodying Dylan's early sixties folk output, and an actor playing Jack Rollins in a film-within-a-film entitled—after the 1980 Dylan song—*Grain of Sand*; outlaw Billy McCarty, an amalgam of Dylan's late sixties, early seventies folk revivalism of *The Basement Tapes*, *John Wesley Harding* (both 1967), and Alias, Dylan's on-screen character in Sam Peckinpah and Rudolph Wurlitzer's acid western *Pat Garrett and Billy the Kid* (1973); Father John, a depiction of Dylan's late seventies/early eighties incarnation as a Christian rock singer; and, most prominently, a woman (Cate Blanchett) playing Jude Quinn, Dylan's mid-sixties "goes electric" persona.

The past half century in which Dylan has been an actively creative force has been a tumultuous era: things *have* changed. The hydrogen bomb, civil rights, feminism, Vietnam, Nixon, Watergate, secret bombings, the oil crisis, Iranian hostages, Reaganomics and the dismantling of the middle class, Iran-Contra, the war in Iraq, the Clinton scandal, the impeachment, the conflicts in Israel-Palestine and the Middle East, 9/11. To some degree, we are all hemmed in by the historical and political present, and are therefore products of our times—the people, places, objects, and events around us—and this is what is examined in this volume: how modern times have changed and how Bob Dylan as an artist has responded to those times and changed with them, utilizing a distinctly American idiom as a kind of connective tissue.

Numerous critics have noted that Dylan's *"Love and Theft"* was released on September 11, 2001, and the coincidence does provide a convenient if somewhat simplistic illustration of the way Dylan continues to be relevant, if not by design then at least by chance. At times this relevance is forced upon us and him: tastemakers in the media and in the universities consist largely of middle-aged, well-to-do white males who grew up listening to Dylan in their parents' dens and in dorm rooms. Scholarly essays and articles on Dylan continued to proliferate; classes are taught on his life and music. That he ranked number one in the charts for *Modern Times* in 2006 is not so much a testament to the continued relevance of his music so much as it is proof that the audience still buying compact discs largely consists of aging Boomers, the same audience that buys the Escalades he now sells.

Bob Dylan is of course aware of how much things have changed. After all, in December 1963, he saw through the smugness of those well-to-do upper-class liberals who awarded him the Tom Paine award, quoting to them from *Macbeth* ("out, out brief candle"), a line deriving from the speech where Macbeth describes life as being full of sound and fury, signifying nothing. Indeed, much of Dylan's post-1960s output, arguably from *Self Portrait*

(1970) forward, represents an active non-signification. In fact, it is only when Dylan resigned himself to his canonization as a Voice of a Generation (ca. the late 1980s, while touring with counterculture icons the Grateful Dead, no less) that he was finally able to free himself from a decade-long creative lull, marked on one end by his embrace of Christian rock (1979–81) and the other with his release of the three worst albums of his career (*Knocked Out Loaded* [1986], *Down in the Groove* [1988], and *Dylan and the Dead* [1988]). In the years following, Dylan released the inspired *Oh Mercy* (1989), two albums of traditional covers (*Good As I Been to You* [1992] and *World Gone Wrong* [1993]), and performed a series of electrifying live shows—the yet-to-be-professionally-released 1993 Supper Club performances, widely circulated on bootleg, and probably an inevitable future installment of Dylan's *Bootleg Series*—followed by his critically and commercially celebrated final work of the twentieth century, the Grammy Award–winning *Time Out of Mind*, an award also bestowed on his single "Things Have Changed," "*Love and Theft*," and *Modern Times* (both, conspicuously, as best contemporary folk record).

Shadows in the Night (2015), his studio recordings of fastidious and intimate renditions of songs familiarized by Frank Sinatra, was also nominated for a Grammy. Together with the public reception of this Sinatra album, the release of the massive twelfth *Bootleg Series*, and news of heightened security at a Dylan concert following the Paris bombings, the items in this very short time frame testify first to the truism of Bob Dylan's enduring relevance, and, second, to the discord of his relevance. Arguing about the urgent necessity of a deceptively mundane image in "Desolation Row" (1965)—tweaked, as Dylan so often does, in live performance—and in the same hour relishing Dylan's smooth and salty delivery of Irving Berlin's pensive trifle, "What'll I Do?" are two fine pleasures that have almost nothing but Bob Dylan in common. And the bewitching incongruities that range over his fifty-year recording and performing career coexist with demands from a portion of his listeners for a peculiar, fixed moral standard: when Bob Dylan does ads for IBM or Cadillac, or ostensibly requires men with guns to protect him, he commits special hypocrisies.

For example, Dylan's performing life and original studio work since his first millennial release, "*Love and Theft*," is its own species of contrarianism. His restlessness is now a legend of its own as he continues to tirelessly bring his no-frills intensity to small venues in any country that will have him and his band. Restless and also antiquarian: while Dylan's work post-2000 has repeatedly captivated listeners and refreshed interest in his development as an artist, the songs are at home in bygone worlds. In an unrefurbished voice, millennial Dylan sings of old wars, old cars, old places, old desire, old living. Dylan's current composition method recalls Dr. Frankenstein and his creature: he consistently poaches used bits and pieces from other writers and tunesmiths—including, among many others, Peter Green's translations of Ovid and Henry Timrod, Ma Rainey and Charley Patton, Japanese novelist Junichi Saga—sewing them together and transforming them into something that shouldn't walk on its own yet so often does.

Tearing the World Apart is a rare collection of essays whose exclusive focus is Dylan's output in the new millennium. This project initially took the studio releases *"Love and Theft"* and *Modern Times* as the objects of study, yet soon enough Dylan outstripped us and the collection felt incomplete without attention paid to *Together Through Life* (2009), *Tempest*, and the 2003 film *Masked and Anonymous*, which Dylan starred in and largely wrote.

Fortunately, in this collection of essays you'll find justice done to contrarianism. You won't find forced resolutions of Dylan's contradictions, or misguided apologetics for his ventures. These are eleven writers with disparate personal and academic relations to Dylan's work. We propose that the combination of Dylan's bountiful capacity to inspire and/or vex his listeners, in tandem with all the disparity and contradiction, does great service to academic inquiry: consider each essay as a showcase for its author's academic focus or writerly concern.

Attempts to arrange the essays into thematic sections repeatedly failed to serve the range of topics, which in turn failed to serve Dylan's tendency to inspire promiscuously. The result is alphabetical by author, and we hope you will use the table of contents as a menu and not a syllabus.

- Film and film studies: Jonathan Hodgers uses the discourse of film studies to frame his discussion of narrative and identity in Dylan's recent lyrics. Alberto Brodesco, also concerned with narrative identity, takes on the much-neglected film, *Masked and Anonymous*, and finds a deep playfulness in Dylan's masking himself as composer, performer, and personae.
- [The] *Tempest*: Nick Smart reads *Tempest* by focusing on the homonym lurking in "Bob Dylan's last album." And while so many reviewers questioned en passant a connection between Dylan's most recent collection of original songs and Shakespeare's last play, Anne Daniel leads us on a comprehensive and also delightful journey through the places where the Bard and Bob meet.
- We offer another intertextual exploration with Jamie Lorentzen's conversation between Dylan and Kierkegaard. Lorentzen's inventive juxtaposition illuminates the synthetic nature of Dylan's millennial work.

- Even on ostensibly familiar ground, songwriting and performing, one will find challenges to the conventional appraisals of Dylan's achievements. Using "High Water (For Charley Patton)" (2001) as his centerpiece, Fahri Öz looks at performativity in Dylan's millennial career and helps put to rest philistine scuffles between songwriting and poetry.
- Three essays recharge the timeworn story of Bob Dylan, legend and icon. Andrea Cossu explores ways Dylan has been trapped by public "memorialization." Portions of his audience, reinforced by corporate and institutional eagerness to benefit from Dylan's unique cultural status, insist that Dylan's "timelessness" is the indestructible patina of his reign in the 1960s. Cossu directs us to Dylan's challenges to his own image. The volume's coeditor, Nina Goss, uses *"Love and Theft"* and *Modern Times* to tell a story of Dylan's meaning and mattering to a member of his audience with no roots in the sixties origin story. And Jesper Doolaard takes on the appalling uncanniness of the release date of *"Love and Theft"* with discretion and insight that makes a unique contribution to the general study of relevance and art.
- Perhaps finish with James Cody's lyrical and astute ode to *Together Through Life*, a record too often overlooked when considering Dylan's millennial output. Cody reminds us why we do this work in the first place—because of the pleasure that is the byproduct of Bob Dylan scholarship.

For the purpose of this text, we have decided not to include any essays specifically addressing Dylan's album of Christmas songs, *Christmas in the Heart* (2009), or his selection of Sinatra-related standards, *Shadows in the Night* and its follow-ups *Fallen Angels* (2016) and the three-CD collection *Triplicate* (2017), not because of any lack of quality or relevance but because they consist of covers, as opposed to the creative alchemy apparent on other recordings. The non-twenty-first-century work *Time Out of Mind* receives more attention here, in part because of its position as a transitional album that in some ways announced the critical and creative resurgence Dylan continued with albums released after the turn of the century, and the tendency of critics to—wrongly, in our opinion—view the album as the first of a trilogy that continues with *"Love and Theft"* and *Modern Times*. (These three albums have been subsequently [2008] packaged as such by Sony Records for an overseas release; and *Tell Tale Signs*, a collection of Dylan "bootlegs"—many of them never previously released—collects songs ranging from *Oh Mercy* to *Modern Times*.) As Dylan himself has noted, *Time Out of Mind* is also more of a piece with *Oh Mercy*, if only by virtue of both albums featuring production by Daniel Lanois. In any event, we do not believe Dylan is generally all that intentional; like most great artists, he works intuitively, in order to lend his music dynamism and spontaneity, as opposed to cementing his work with a strictly procedural interpretation, programmatically linking one effort to the next with some linear progression. Somewhat after the fact, Dylan came to see a greater similarity between *"Love and Theft"* and *Modern Times*. "I would think more of *Love and Theft* as the beginning of a trilogy, if there's going to be a trilogy," Dylan told author Jonathan Lethem in a 2006 *Rolling Stone* interview, shortly after the release of *Modern Times*.[3] Seen from this perspective, Dylan clearly considered his initial twenty-first-century efforts as yet another advance, another chapter in his continually unraveling, fascinating, singular career.

NG
EH

Editors' note: As you read these essays, you will notice that some passages of lyrics from Bob Dylan's songs will read in context as abridged. Lyrics to Bob Dylan's songs through *Together Through Life* can be found at http://bobdylan.com/songs/. The editors claim responsibility for these abridgements.

NOTES

1. Dylan was eventually awarded the Nobel Prize for Literature in 2016. The Nobel Committee received much criticism for awarding him the prize, as did Dylan in his delayed response and his refusal to appear at the award ceremony, though he did pen an acceptance speech read in his absence. "Bob Dylan's Nobel Prize Speech," *New York Times*, December 10, 2016. www.nytimes.com/2016/12/10/arts/bob-dylan-nobel-prize-acceptance-speech.html.

2. Quotations from Dylan's songs are identified by song titles within the text and are quoted either from his lyrics located online at bobdylan.com or from Bob Dylan: *Lyrics, 1962–2001* (New York City: Simon & Schuster, 2004).

3. Jonathan Lethem, "The Genius and Modern Times of Bob Dylan." *Rolling Stone* 1008, www.rollingstone.com/music/news/the-genius-and-modern-times-of-bob-dylan-20060907.

CHAPTER ONE

VISIONS OF THE FLOOD: MASKED AND ANONYMOUS BETWEEN "LOVE AND THEFT" AND MODERN TIMES

Alberto Brodesco

ALIAS

In a bar, somewhere in the United States, Bob Dylan and his band are playing a Bob Dylan song, "Down in the Flood (Crash on the Levee)" (1967). We are not watching a YouTube clip, a documentary, or a filmed concert but a feature film, *Masked and Anonymous*, co-written by Bob Dylan and director Larry Charles. In the film, the singer's name is not Bob Dylan but Jack Fate. Tony Garnier, Larry Campbell, Charlie Sexton, and George Recile (Dylan's 2003 touring band) are introduced as the Simple Twists of Fate, a Jack Fate cover band that Fate himself joins on stage. Moreover, the bar is geographically in the United States, yet the America in this film's narrative is a very different place, a merciless dictatorship. As writer and actor Bob Dylan can play two of his favorite games: assume a mask and shadowbox with an alias; and, continuing to skip from the real world to an imaginary one, portray a world bound for apocalypse.

The plot follows a has-been singer, Jack Fate, freed from prison by promoter Uncle Sweetheart (John Goodman) to hold a music performance intended for a nationwide broadcast. The concert is set up for the benefit of the orphans of the opposing riots of governmental, revolutionary, and counterrevolutionary forces that are devastating the country in a civil war. Fate is the rejected son of the country's president-dictator. Fate was in prison because many years before he was caught in bed with his father's mistress. The long-ill president dies at the precise moment when Fate starts to sing the first and subsequently only song of the benefit concert. The president will be succeeded in power by the wicked, Shakespearean-named Edmund (Mickey Rourke), who immediately gives a terrifying speech whose broadcast obscures the concert's transmission.[1] The television screen goes blank. A gang of government thugs bursts into the studio to stop the music. Accused of the murder of a journalist, Fate is led back to jail.

Jack Fate both is and is not Bob Dylan. He *is not* because he has a different name and because in the film's diegetic universe a rock star named "Bob Dylan" does not exist (while Billy Joel, Paul McCartney, Bruce Springsteen, Sting, and others are named). At the same time Fate *is* Bob Dylan: the character is played by Bob Dylan, sings Dylan's songs, and plays with Dylan's band. Furthermore, the depiction of Jack Fate as a washed-out star is evidently tailored on Dylan's career and personal idiosyncrasies. These involve some of the most common charges addressed to Dylan's artistic choices and ideological turns. Journalist Tom Friend (Jeff Bridges) asks: "You remember Hendrix at Woodstock? I'm just curious, you weren't there were you?"—an allusion to Dylan's absence from the Woodstock stage in the summer of 1969.[2] In *Masked and Anonymous*, the journalist—a profession often seen with distrust by Dylan—plays the part of the evil character. The assistant to Fate's manager, Nina (Jessica Lange), tells Uncle Sweetheart: "Are his songs going to be recognizable? That's what I want to know"—a reference to the alleged difficulty to spot the songs rewritten live by Bob Dylan on his so-called Never Ending Tour (1988–present). Sweetheart's reply works as an ironic self-defense for Dylan himself: "All of his songs are recognizable, even if they are not recognizable." Also, the scene in which a mother approaches Fate and tells him "my daughter has memorized all of your songs" seems to portray Bob Dylan's daily nightmare when on tour, with obsessed fans willing to show him their love and blind devotion. Fate asks: "Is that so? Why'd she do that?" The honest but lamentable answer is "'Cause I made her, that's why." The interpretation of Fate's song lyrics is also essentially a Bob Dylan auto-exegesis. Listening to "Drifter's Escape" (1967), Tom Friend's lover, Pagan Lace (Penelope Cruz), comments: "I love his songs 'cause they're not precise. They're emotionally ambiguous. Nobody else will do that. They invite different interpretations." Even Uncle Sweetheart proposes his reading of "Drifter's Escape": "What strikes you about the song is the Jekyll and Hyde quality."

Jack Fate is doubtlessly Dylan's alias. Leaving aside concert footage and filmed interviews, Bob Dylan's cinematographic presences involve a disguised self-portrait: either in documentaries: *Dont Look Back* (D. A. Pennebaker, 1967), *Eat the Document* (Bob Dylan, 1972); in fiction: *Hearts of Fire* (Richard

Marquand, 1984), *Catchfire* (Alan Smithee [Dennis Hopper], 1990), *Dharma & Greg* episode "Play Lady Play" (1999); or in documentary-fiction: *Renaldo and Clara* (Bob Dylan, 1978).[3] Even an "expository documentary"[4] like Martin Scorsese's *No Direction Home* communicates the idea of an unachievable portrait: facts, witnesses, interviews, concert footage are just pieces of a broken mirror. In Sam Peckinpah's *Pat Garrett and Billy the Kid*, Dylan plays the role of an outsider in Billy's gang. Here is the dialogue between Dylan and two other gang members when his character is introduced:

GANG MEMBER ONE:—What's your name, boy?
ALIAS:—Alias.
GANG MEMBER ONE:—Alias what?
ALIAS:—Alias anything you please.
GANG MEMBER ONE:—What do we call you?
ALIAS:—Alias . . .
GANG MEMBER TWO:—Hell, let's call him Alias.
ALIAS:—That's what I'd do.
GANG MEMBER ONE:—Alias it is.

Dylan seems to use cinema to play hide-and-seek with his multiple identities. In front of the request for truth made by the film medium, all that Dylan can do is wear a mask. Questioned about his participation in *Hearts of Fire*, he confirmed how problematic he finds the referential nature of the photographic medium, the ontological connection between the sign and the represented object: "When I asked, 'What am I supposed to do in this scene?' the director would say, 'Just be yourself.' Then I'd have to think, 'Which one?' Nobody ever explained it to me."[5] Surrendering to the multiplicity of Dylan's identities characterizes Todd Haynes's anti-biopic *I'm Not There*, where the character of Bob Dylan is interpreted by six different actors, including an African American boy and a woman (Cate Blanchett).

Masked and Anonymous certainly does not mark a peak in Bob Dylan's long artistic journey. Precisely set between *"Love and Theft"* and *Modern Times*, however, it is an important key to understanding his commitment and intention in the first decade of the twenty-first century. Like the two albums, the film is built on lyrical images, trademarks, obsessions, counterpositions, remote visions, and narrative dead ends.[6] Also in the film are plenty of what Dylan calls "appropriations"[7] from a large spectrum of sources. Intertextuality is indeed a major attribute of Bob Dylan's work, particularly from *"Love and Theft"* onward. *Masked and Anonymous*'s references go from the speeches of

US presidents (John Quincy Adams; Andrew Jackson's Farewell Address)[8] to novels (*Naked Lunch* by William Burroughs; *The Big Money* by John Dos Passos; *The Journal of Albion Moonlight* by Kenneth Patchen; *Death Is My Dancing Partner* by Cornell Woolrich; *Moon Palace* by Paul Auster),[9] plays (*Agamemnon* by Aeschylus, *Easter* by August Strindberg),[10] sports books (*Ball Four* by Jim Bouton),[11] and religious texts (the Gospel of Matthew; *Letter to Donatus concerning God's grace* by Saint Cyprian).[12]

As I have already mentioned, the film also permits Dylan to dedicate space to one of his favorite topics. If *Masked and Anonymous* is, as many critics have noted, a Bob Dylan song in film form,[13] it is certainly an "apocalypse song," a sort of sub-genre in Dylan's songwriting at least since "A Hard Rain's A-Gonna Fall" (1963).[14] As David Janssen and Edward Whitelock write, "apocalypse is Dylan's muse.... Apocalyptic aesthetic ... is perhaps *the* defining element of both the content and style of Dylan's own songs."[15] In *"Love and Theft"* and *Modern Times* we hear allusions to the end of time in "Mississippi," "High Water (For Charley Patton)," "Sugar Baby," "Thunder on the Mountain," "The Levee's Gonna Break," and "Ain't Talkin'," songs filled with figures of inundations, deluges, thunders, skies on fire, and blowing horns. All of these signs are intended as warning messages from Nature or God. *Masked and Anonymous* is a bridge between the two albums and a lightning rod for Dylan's apocalyptic obsession.

DOWN IN THE FLOOD

Joining the Simple Twists on stage, Jack Fate picks up the guitar and sings these verses: "Crash on the levee, water's gonna overflow / Swamp's gonna rise, no boat's gonna row."[16] Two years before the production of *Masked and Anonymous*, Bob Dylan recorded for *"Love and Theft"* "High Water (For Charley Patton)," another song about the flood. A few years later, in *Modern Times*, we find one more major water problem in "The Levee's Gonna Break"—a kind of remake of "Down in the Flood." Floods are prominent in the musical culture of the American South. The image, which has obvious similarities with the Genesis deluge, allows Dylan to cross and condense references to black music and the biblical tradition.[17]

The first song performed in *Masked and Anonymous* sets the frame for the whole film, inscribed in an apocalyptic outline. Most of the songs featured in the movie come from the apocalyptic repertoire. Other than "Down in the Flood," Jack Fate sings, at the film's climax, "Cold Irons Bound" (1997). The apocalyptic playlist on the soundtrack also includes the condemned land mentioned in "Blind Willie McTell" (recorded 1983; released 1991), the black shadows of "Not Dark Yet" (1997), the mysterious valley below of Sertab Erener's cover of "One More Cup of Coffee (Valley Below)" (1976), and the road to Armageddon in Jerry Garcia's cover of "Señor (Tales of Yankee Power)" (1978).

If the apocalypse can be evoked in songs by a few inflamed, biblical lyrics, a film has to face the difficulty of visually creating this same imagery. As Bob Dylan himself said about *Masked and Anonymous* ten years after its release, "whatever vision I had for that movie, that never could've carried to the screen."[18] What can be portrayed in a film is instead the *descent* toward the apocalypse. This is the domain of dystopian fiction. *Masked and Anonymous* does not literally show the apocalypse, yet is set in a dystopian country and depicts a political world and its distortions. Like all dystopian narratives, it assumes the ethical role of a warning: to avoid ending up like that in the future we have to take action to modify our present. Dystopia can be read *a contrario* as the only possible manifestation of utopia in contemporary society.[19] Dystopian literature and art focus on possible futures, faraway planets, afterlife visions. In these representations the reader or viewer is invited to find possibilities of resistance to the apparently inexorable progression that leads to the apocalypse.

In *Masked and Anonymous* we hear the following news on the radio: "Geologists in Trenton are digging the world's deepest hole and have reached the depth of thirty miles. Scientists have measured the temperature down there as up to 3,000 degrees. They have lowered microphones into the pit and heard the sound of millions of suffering souls." In the world of *Masked and Anonymous* Hell is a real place, whose existence is confirmed by science. This allusion works as a mise en abyme, a small insert that has a relation of similarity with the larger text in which it is embedded.[20] This radio-announced Hell recalls *Masked and Anonymous*'s dystopia. The shocking news on the radio, however, is received with general indifference. Even the scientific proof of the existence of Hell is not enough to produce a change in human behavior. Given that the insert *en abyme* summarizes the whole text, the capacity of dystopian art to awaken people's consciousness is therefore radically questioned. If the existence of Hell cannot affect people, neither will dystopian fiction. This nihilism, we may add, can be attacked only by an apolitical or a different political approach to history and social change.

HISTORY, DYSTOPIA, SMITHSVILLE

"If I know nothing else, I know at least one thing is true: that the sacred is in the ordinary, the common things in life." In *Masked and Anonymous* Jack Fate's voice-over mumbles presumed great thoughts in a very naïve way. Such candor makes *Masked and Anonymous* a particularly revealing work. Dystopia is presented as a consequence of the distance we took from "the sacred ... in the ordinary." The return to roots, the ideal of simple living is a recurrent theme of Bob Dylan by the time of *"Love and Theft"* and *Modern Times*.[21] Nonetheless, the memory of the past is not a nostalgic experiment but expresses "the necessity to find an acceptable perspective in front of reality";[22] it is the logical product of Dylan's career-long devotion to American folk, country, and blues tradition, the cultural heritage in which Dylan retrieves the sense of sacred for which he longs.[23]

The confrontation between dystopia and musical tradition is represented in *Masked and Anonymous* with essential traits. In the film we eventually witness an encounter of three different universes that coexist, overlap, and superimpose each other. The first universe is the domain of history: *Masked and Anonymous* makes reference to historical events like Woodstock and historical figures like Richard Nixon or Bruce Springsteen, while on the soundtrack we hear songs written by the real-life Bob Dylan. The second universe is the dystopian/apocalyptic one, depicting a country in war, ruled by a president-dictator. In this world Jack Fate (not Bob Dylan) is a well-known rock star. The third universe is an imaginary or mythical one, this time not dystopian but utopian. We could call it, following Greil Marcus, "Smithsville," the "Invisible Republic" captured and created by Harry Smith's *Anthology of American Folk Music* (1952): "What is Smithsville? It is a small town whose citizens are not distinguishable by race. There are no masters and no slaves.... There is a constant war between the messengers of god and ghost and demons, dancers and drinkers, and, for all anyone knows, between god's messengers and god himself.... This is Smithsville. Here is a mystical body of the republic, a kind of public secret: a declaration of what sort of wishes and fears lay behind any public act, a declaration of a weird but clearly recognizable America within the America of the exercise of institutional majoritarian power."[24]

In *Masked and Anonymous* the symbol of this third universe is Blind Lemon Jefferson's ancient guitar, "one of the guitars that started it all," "the one that played 'Matchbox Blues,'" brought to Fate by his pal Bobby Cupid (Luke Wilson). In a Christ-like sacrifice, the guitar will be smashed on journalist Tom Friend's back to prevent him from killing Jack Fate.

Each of the three universes—History (I), Dystopia (II), and Smithsville (III)—are in dialogue with the other two:

- In the dystopian universe portrayed in *Masked and Anonymous* we find many features of our real, historical universe (Nixon, for example, had been president either in history or in the film's world). Dystopia just emphasizes the decaying signs already readable in History, in the actual contemporary society. History and Dystopia are in an osmotic relation (I↔II).
- Blind Lemon Jefferson, Blind Willie McTell, and all the musicians of the Invisible Republic are of course historical persons and creators of a minoritarian history, an "America within America." That produces the second relation between History and Smithsville (I↔III).
- Apocalyptic and dystopian images abundantly flourish in Smithsville, creating the third connection (II↔III). To experience the proximity of the two universes it is sufficient to listen to a few traditional songs: "High Water Everywhere" by Charley Patton (1929), "John the Revelator" by Blind Willie Johnson (1930), "The World Is Going Wrong" by the Mississippi Sheiks (1931), "If I Had Possession Over Judgment Day" by Robert Johnson (1936), "This World Can't Stand Long" by Roy Acuff (1948).

If History actually "feeds" both Smithsville and Dystopia, we can also observe an action produced by Smithsville that moves toward History and works against the realization of Dystopia. Smithsville fights Dystopia to bring History in a different direction. The Invisible Republic can give hope or salvation, as is stressed in *Masked and Anonymous* by the sacrifice of Blind Lemon's guitar. In the lyrics of "Blind Willie McTell," as featured on the soundtrack, we find an allusive formulation of this belief: "Well, God is in His heaven / And we all want what's His." As Janssen and Whitelock comment, "in the midst of the Wasteland, [the singer] [gives] his listeners a gleam of hope in the resonant ideal of Blind Willie McTell's voice."[25]

Particularly after the recording of *Good As I Been to You* and *World Gone Wrong*, Bob Dylan devoted himself to dismissing the importance of his own figure and affirming the value of his original "prophetic" sources. His fortune—he declares—derives from the chance he had to get in direct contact with the tradition, to be there "to see the end of traditional people,"[26] while the immediately following generation of musicians was not.[27]

In its limpid exposition of the worlds of History, Dystopia, and Smithsville, *Masked and Anonymous* reveals a frame, an imagination, and a philosophy common to *"Love and Theft"* and *Modern Times*, where "in a less straight, less accusative way with respect to the topical songs of the Sixties, but not more tender in the analysis of the surrounding context, Dylan directly confronts a reality less and less human with the founding assumptions of a country born from the utopian intentions of the Pilgrim Fathers."[28] In the 2006 songs "Workingman's Blues #2," "Nettie Moore," and "Ain't Talkin'," we detect the same vision of three universes that overlap: Dylan reads the signs of the apocalypse present in contemporary society and yet at the same time finds space for utopian thought in the "religion of folklore."[29] "Ain't Talkin'" clearly shows how this altarless religion is a saving force able to hold back from the apocalypse the world "filled with speculation," its "hog-eyed" towns, its "cities of the plague": the speaker's companions "approve of me and share my code . . . / I practice a faith that's been long abandoned." The code and the faith of the much-loved companions from Smithsville offer an ethical vision opposing the current dystopia.

THE CARNIVAL

As a sideshow to Jack Fate's concert, Uncle Sweetheart (described in the script[30] as a "combination of John the Baptist and P. T. Barnum") proposes a crew of "freaks and weirdos" that includes Ella the Fortune Teller, the Rubber Girl, the Magician Jean Darkness, a Ventriloquist and his Dummy, the masked wrestler El Mundo, and the likenesses of Abraham Lincoln, Mahatma Gandhi, and Pope John Paul II. Again, *Masked and Anonymous* acts as a naïve confession of Bob Dylan's sources. The Invisible Republic, the world where the voice of Blind Willie McTell spreads, is populated by circuses, carnival shows, and freaks. Let us read an extract from a 2009 interview, in which Dylan depicts—or mythologizes—his early years:[31]

> People have different emotional levels. Especially when you're young. Back then I guess most of my influences could be thought of as eccentric. Mass media had no overwhelming reach so I was drawn to the travelling performers passing through. The sideshow performers—bluegrass singers, the black cowboy with chaps and a lariat doing rope tricks. Miss Europe, Quasimodo, the Bearded Lady, the half-man half-woman, the deformed and the bent, Atlas the Dwarf, the fire-eaters, the teachers and preachers, the blues singers. I remember it like it was yesterday. I got close to some of these people. I learned about dignity from them. Freedom too. Civil rights, human rights. How to stay within yourself. Most others were into the rides like the tilt-a-whirl and the rollercoaster. To me that was the nightmare. All the giddiness.

The artificiality of it. The sledgehammer of life. It didn't make sense or seem real. The stuff off the main road was where force of reality was. At least it struck me that way. When I left home those feelings didn't change.³²

Much earlier in his career, in a 1962 radio interview with Cynthia Gooding, Bob Dylan gives shape to his artistic character by saying he used to "travel with the carnival . . . off and on for about six years," working as clean-up boy and running rides.³³ When Gooding asks him, "At the carnival did you learn songs?" Dylan answers: "No, I learned how to sing though. That's more important." Yet carnival freaks are also a presence in his songs, from *Highway 61 Revisited*'s "Ballad of a Thin Man" and "Desolation Row" to *"Love and Theft"*'s "Honest with Me" ("the Siamese twins are comin' to town"). As stated in the above interview, the freaks' dignity affects the young Dylan. Along with the great singers of the popular tradition they are prominent and legitimate citizens of the Invisible Republic.

The carnivals brought around some other kind of weird performers, the blackface minstrels that constitute an additional influence on Bob Dylan. He declared that "Desolation Row" is "a minstrel song through and through. I saw some ragtag minstrel show in blackface at the carnivals when I was growing up, and it had an effect on me, just as much as seeing the lady with four legs."³⁴ The blackface minstrelsy was a show tradition in which, mostly because of racial segregation, white vaudeville artists with their faces painted black performed music in front of a white audience, caricaturing the stereotypes of African Americans and their musical tradition. Minstrelsy is a major source for understanding *"Love and Theft"* and *Modern Times*. For French critic Louis Skorecki, *"Love and Theft"* is the only Dylan album "to have a title in quotation marks, because it is entirely under the influence of Emmett Miller/*black minstrels. Love and Theft* is in fact the title of a scholarly book, an academic study on the blackface phenomenon in the popular culture of the 19th century."³⁵

Masked and Anonymous, as if it was a list of credits, also acknowledges this reference in a specific scene. Just before the concert Jack Fate runs into a blackface minstrel named Oscar Vogel (Ed Harris). He plays a strategic part in the plot, being the last person Fate meets before jumping onstage. Oscar says to Jack that he once was "the star of the show," the president's favorite performer: "Everything was going great, as long as you kept your mouth shut. But he was doing things that were wrong, your father. . . . I was the only one who was in any position to say anything. Everybody else was too scared. I had the show, I had a forum, so I spoke out. . . . They said it was an accident. Some even said it was a suicide. Some people choose to die in all kinds of ways. Some people jump out of buildings and slit their wrists on the way down. Some fall on their own swords. I opened my mouth." Vogel, the only character who does not bend in front of power, is a ghost, a jokerman, the symbol of the uncompromising dignity of the people from Smithsville.

The most atypical choice of Jack Fate's repertoire is the most typical number from blackface minstrelsy music. The third piece Fate performs in *Masked and Anonymous* is "Dixie" (ca. 1850s), the controversial song about a former slave who is homesick for the cotton plantation of the old times. Jack Fate seems untouched by its undeniable racist connotations, as apparently, on his side, is Bob Dylan himself, whose anti-racist belief is possibly the only certainty we have about Dylan's ideology. The performance of this song in *Masked and Anonymous* is of course meaningful. In the film context "Dixie" could allude to the dystopic nation that Fate finds getting out of jail: "there's no south and north anymore, just this weird, corrupt government where all that is left of America is kitschy debris."[36] In such a land, power demands people be happy with their slavery. Another possible interpretation is that this song puts together and demolishes the three spheres of History, Dystopia, and Popular music. "Dixie" is a melodically beautiful traditional song loaded with history that talks positively about slavery, which Dylan considers the original sin of the United States and eventually the origin of the current dystopia.[37] Louis Skorecki recalls the Rolling Thunder Revue in 1975–76, when Dylan went onstage with his face painted *white*, in a kind of parody of the blackface minstrelsy. Skorecki suggests that this was a way for Dylan to try to hide his whiteness by disguising it under white makeup.[38] Singing "Dixie" obeys the same (quite paradoxical) logic. It is just another way to appear masked and anonymous. Dylan's disguises cannot be simple and change frequently. As a citizen of the Invisible Republic, Dylan knows that Smithsville is a place where a "mask never stays on for long."[39]

ALONE

A particularly crucial moment in *Masked and Anonymous* happens when Jack Fate, with tears in his eyes, visits his father on his death bed. On the soundtrack we hear Jerry Garcia's rendition of Bob Dylan's "Señor (Tales of Yankee Power)," which opens with these lines: "Señor, señor, do you know where we're headin'? / Lincoln County Road or Armageddon?" As Adam Griffey notes, Bob Dylan has indeed been down the path of the apocalypse many times before.[40] Here there are two different possibilities, Armageddon or Lincoln County Road. The choice is between a minor fight, the historical Lincoln County War of 1878, a range war involving Billy the Kid, and the final battle on the Mount of Megiddo. Yet Lincoln County Road may also refer to the place "off the main road, where force of reality is,"[41] inhabited by Billy the Kid and his pals. Bob Dylan seems at ease in that universe, if we take as proof his participation in *Pat Garrett and Billy the Kid*. Following this reading, the choice is again between Armageddon and the proximity with a gang of outlaws who are, without any doubt, rightful citizens of Smithsville.

Masked and Anonymous's plot is built around a phony benefit concert. This performance is not conceived for a real audience but is to be broadcast on television by the government. The concert is presented as a "media event,"[42] a "world ritual," a memorable live broadcast. But nobody except the concert crew is watching when the show begins with "Cold Irons Bound." Jack Fate seems to comment on that situation when he sings: "I'm beginning to hear voices and there's no one around." This supposedly great event unfolds to total indifference of the audience. There is no expectation for this show: nobody is watching it on TV, and in front of the stage there are just a couple of electricians, a bunch of freaks, and the manager's entourage. Who is to blame for this failure? The lack of appeal of the has-been Jack Fate? The organizational incompetence of Uncle Sweetheart? The president's death? The fear of political riots following Edmund's rise to power? Or is television as a medium ultimately culpable, ineffective as it is at really connecting people? What is certain is that the performance remains audience-less. In the context of Bob Dylan's "performing art,"[43] the absence of listeners is an element of major importance. The physical aloneness of Jack and the few people attending the concert assumes political consequences. The only oppositional act of which Jack Fate is capable is, in fact, to warn of the perils of dystopia by singing his apocalyptic songs live—from the first, "Down in the Flood," to the last, "Cold Irons Bound"—or to show a glimpse of the Invisible Republic by playing songs like "Diamond Joe" and "Dixie." Deprived of an audience, Jack's voice falls literally unheard. The only people around Jack Fate and his band are a bunch of freaks. Once again the people from Smithsville are left alone.

NOTES

1. A transcript from the film: "We are giving people a new identity, erasing the collective memory. We are rewriting the history books.... Peace, a lasting peace, can only be achieved

through strength. So, in my first act as the new President . . . we will begin immediately to deploy troops in the southern regions. We will resume the bombing in the jungle. . . . Furthermore, we will alert the rebel leaders that the negotiations have ended. There will be no more compromises, no more concessions, just complete and utter unequivocal surrender." *Masked and Anonymous* (Sony Classic Video, 2004).

2. Dismissed in Dylan's autobiography with a simple: "I missed out on Woodstock—just wasn't there. Altamont—sympathy for the devil—missed that, too." Bob Dylan, *Chronicles, Volume One* (New York: Simon & Schuster, 2004), 122.

3. We might add to this list his quite weird appearances in television commercials: the voyeur/seducer in Victoria's Secret or the tireless rambler in the Cadillac Escalade ad. See Theresa Howard, "Dylan ad for underwear generates lingering buzz," *USA Today*, May 16, 2004, http://usatoday30.usatoday.com/money/advertising/adtrack/2004-05-16-victoria-secrets-dylan_x.htm; and Andrew Adam Newman, "Hey, Mr. Escalade Man," *New York Times*, November 4, 2007: www.nytimes.com/2007/11/04/automobiles/04DYLAN.html/partner/rssnyt?pagewanted=print&_r=0.

4. Bill Nichols, *Introduction to Documentary* (Bloomington and Indianapolis: Indiana University Press, 2001), 105.

5. Edna Gundersen, "Edna Gundersen interview with Dylan," *USA Today*, November 13, 1990, 5; quoted in Vince Farinaccio, *Nothing to Turn Off: The Films and Video of Bob Dylan* (n.p., 2007), 151.

6. "One can play an endless game of connect-the-dots with the film ideas, themes, clues, assertions." Lucas Stensland, "Scatter Shots: Reading *Masked and Anonymous*," *Montague Street: The Art of Bob Dylan* 1 (2009): 82.

7. Mikal Gilmore, "Bob Dylan on His Dark New Album, *Tempest*," *Rolling Stone*, August 1, 2012, www.rollingstone.com/music/news/bob-dylan-on-his-dark-new-album-tempest-20120801.

8. I present only a few examples here in the footnotes (all of these references are taken from "scottw"'s post on the Expecting Rain message board: http://expectingrain.com/discussions/viewtopic.php?f=6&t=34593). Edmund in *Masked and Anonymous* says: "It is from within amongst ourselves, from cupidity, corruption, disappointed ambition, and inordinate thirst for power that factions will be formed and liberty engendered"; and here is the quotation from Jackson's Farewell Address: "It is from within, among yourselves – from cupidity, from corruption, from disappointed ambition and inordinate thirst for power – that factions will be formed and liberty endangered." Andrew Jackson, Farewell Address, March 4, 1837, quoted from www.presidency.ucsb.edu/ws/?pid=67087, par. 21.

9. Ella the Fortune Teller in *Masked and Anonymous*: "You are living in a world where all the jewels, diamonds, pearls, and rubies have been replaced by queer replicas"; Burroughs: "So all that winter, one after the other, the diamonds, emeralds, pearls, rubies and star sapphires of the haut monde go in hock and replaced by queer replicas," William Burroughs, *Naked Lunch* (New York: Grove Press, 2009), 108.

10. Tom Friend in *Masked and Anonymous*: "Once when I was passing a cathedral, a white dove came flying by and dropped a twig it was carrying in its beak at my feet"; Strindberg: "Just now as I was passing the cathedral, a white dove came flying by. It swooped down to the pavement and dropped the twig it was carrying in its beak right at my feet." August Strindberg, *Easter* (Chicago: Aldine, 1962), 288.

11. Crew member in *Masked and Anonymous*: "When I was in welding school, just for kicks, we would heat a steel bar until it was red hot, let the color cool out of it, and then ask the new boy to bring over the metal bar. All it would cost him is the skin off his hand"; Bouton: "And for kicks, they heat a steel bar until it was red hot, let the color cool out of it and then ask the new boy to bring over the metal bar. All it would cost was the skin off his hand." Jim Bouton, *Ball Four Plus Ball Five* (New York: Stein and Day, 1984), 194.

12. Fate in *Masked and Anonymous*: "The way we look at the world is the way we really are. See it from a fair garden, everything looks cheerful. Climb to a higher mountain, and you see plunder and murder. Truth and beauty are in the eye of the beholder"; Saint Cyprian: "It seems a cheerful world, Donatus, when I view it from this fair garden under the shadow of these vines. But if I climbed some great mountain and looked out over the wide lands, you know very well what I would see; brigands on the high road, pirates on the seas, in the amphitheaters men murdered to please the applauding crowds, under all roofs misery and selfishness." Quoted in Thomas S. Kepler, ed., *The Fellowship of the Saints: An Anthology of Christian Devotional Literature* (Nashville: Abingdon-Cokesbury Press, 1948), 8.

13. In *D'où viens-tu Dylan?* (2012), Louis Skorecki writes: "If this film is a flop, it is because it is not a film. What then? A song. As filmed song, *Masked and Anonymous* is worth it" (76); "*Masked and Anonymous* . . . has become a Bob Dylan song, Bible and political fiction all mixed up" (78).

14. See Frances Di Lauro, "Living in the End Times: The Prophetic Language of Bob Dylan," in *Buddha of Suburbia: Proceedings of the Eighth Australian and International Religion, Literature and the Arts Conference*, ed. Carole M. Cusack, Frances Di Lauro, and Christopher Hartney (Sydney: RLA Press, 2005), 186–202.

15. David Janssen and Edward Whitelock, *Apocalypse Jukebox: The End of the World in American Popular Music* (Berkeley: Soft Skull Press, 2009), 101. See also Michael J. Gilmour, *Tangled Up in the Bible: Bob Dylan & Scripture* (New York: Continuum, 2004), 71–90.

16. "Down in the Flood (Crash on the Levee)" is a song from *The Basement Tapes*, the album that includes "the clearest examples of a natural, immanent and imminent, apocalyptic condition" (Janssen and Whitelock, *Apocalypse Jukebox*, 104). All song lyrics are cited from the bobdylan.com database (in the case of "Down in the Flood," with small adaptations to account for the lyrics as sung in the film).

17. See Alessandro Bratus, *Bob Dylan. Un percorso in sedici canzoni* (Milano: Carocci, 2011), 128.

18. Mikal Gilmore, "Bob Dylan: The Rolling Stone Interview," *Rolling Stone*, October 27, 2012, 80.

19. See Francesco Muzzioli, *Scritture della catastrofe* (Roma: Meltemi, 2007), 16.

20. See Lucien Dällenbach, *Le récit spéculaire. Essai sur la mise en abyme* (Paris: Seuil, 1977).

21. One can read this passage from *Chronicles Vol. One* where Dylan rejects the prophetic role he was assigned in the sixties: "I don't know what everybody else was fantasizing about but what I was fantasizing about was a nine-to-five existence, a house on a tree-lined block with a white picket fence, pink roses in the backyard." Dylan, *Chronicles*, 117.

22. Bratus, *Bob Dylan*, 135. See also Gregg M. Campbell, "Bob Dylan and the Pastoral Apocalypse," in the *Journal of Popular Culture* 4 (1975): 696–707.

23. The religiousness with which Bob Dylan looks at the world of traditional music is recorded in the many interviews: "Those old songs are my lexicon and prayer book. All my

beliefs come out of those old songs, literally, anything from 'Let Me Rest on that Peaceful Mountain' to 'Keep on the Sunny Side.' You can find all my philosophy in those old songs. I believe in a God of time and space, but if people ask me about that, my impulse is to point them back toward those songs. I believe in Hank Williams singing 'I Saw the Light.' I've seen the light, too." Interview with John Pareles, *New York Times*, September 28, 1997, quoted in Michael J. Gilmour, *The Gospel According to Bob Dylan: The Old, Old Story for Modern Times* (Louisville: Westminster John Knox Press, 2011), 46.

24. Greil Marcus, *Invisible Republic: Bob Dylan's Basement Tapes* (London: Picador, 1997), 125.

25. Janssen and Whitelock, *Apocalypse Jukebox*, 121.

26. Marcus, *Invisible Republic*, 195. Also this 1993 interview: "These people who originated this music, they're all Shakespeares, you know. They're Thomas Edison, Louis Pasteur. . . . The people who played that music were still around then, and so there was a bunch of us, me included, who got to see all these people close up—people like Son House, Reverend Gary Davis or Sleepy John Estes. Just to sit there and be up close and watch them play, you could study what they were doing, plus a bit of their lives rubbed off on you. Those vibes will carry into you forever, really, so it's like those people, they're still here to me. They're not ghost of the past or anything, they're continually here." Quoted in Andrew Muir, *Troubadour: Early and Late Songs of Bob Dylan* (Bluntisham, UK: Woodstock Publications, 2003), 280.

27. In these stages of rock 'n' roll history, generations succeed each other quickly: Johnny Cash was nine years older than Dylan; Bruce Springsteen is eight years younger.

28. Bratus, *Bob Dylan*, 117.

29. See Alessandro Carrera, *La voce di Bob Dylan. Una spiegazione dell'America* (Milano: Feltrinelli, 2001), 205–49.

30. Available online at http://maskedandanonymousdatabase.blogspot.it.

31. Bill Flanagan, "Interview with Bob Dylan," *Mojo* 189 (August 2009): 51–52.

32. An analysis of this interview and its references (dating back to Latin poet Juvenal) can be found in http://swarmuth.blogspot.it/2009/04/together-through-life-dispatch-7.html.

33. Cynthia Gooding, "Folksinger's Choice," New York, WBAI–FM, March 11, 1962, transcription available at expectingrain.com/dok/int/gooding.html.

34. Edna Gundersen, "Dylan is positively on top of his game," *USA Today*, September 10, 2001, www.usatoday.com/life/music/2001-09-10-bob-dylan.htm.

35. Louis Skorecki, "dylan, emmett miller et moi (2002)," http://skorecki.blogspot.it/2010/12/im-56-dylans-not-60-yet.html. The book is Eric Lott's *Love and Theft: Blackface Minstrelsy and the American Working Class* (Oxford: Oxford University Press, 1993).

36. David Yaffe, *Bob Dylan: Like a Complete Unknown* (New Haven, CT: Yale University Press, 2011), 54.

37. "The United States burned and destroyed itself for the sake of slavery. . . . This country is just too fucked up about color. . . . It's the height of insanity, and it will hold any nation back—or any neighborhood back. Or any anything back. . . . It's doubtful that America's ever going to get rid of that stigmatization. It's a country founded on the backs of slaves. . . . It's the root cause. If slavery had been given up in a more peaceful way, America would be far ahead today." Gilmore, "Bob Dylan: The Rolling Stone Interview," 48.

38. Skorecki, D'où viens-tu Dylan?, 88.

39. Marcus, *Invisible Republic*, 125.

40. Adam Clay Griffey, "Dylan's Apocalypse: Country Music and the End of the World" (master's thesis, Appalachian State University, 2011), 12. Available at http://libres.uncg.edu/ir/asu/listing.aspx?id=8227.

41. Flanagan, "Interview with Bob Dylan," 52.

42. "A . . . narrative genre that employs the unique potential of the electronic media to command attention universally and simultaneously." Daniel Dayan and Elihu Katz, *Media Events: The Live Broadcasting of History* (Cambridge, MA: Harvard University Press, 1992), 1.

43. Paul Williams, *Bob Dylan, Performing Artist* (London: Omnibus Press, 3 vol., 2004–2005).

CHAPTER TWO

DYLAN'S *TOGETHER THROUGH LIFE*: ROLLING IN PLACES

James Cody

Dylan's places confound. They go everywhere and nowhere, and the songs on *Together Through Life* may be the collection that best exemplifies such assertions. His songs have brought us worldwide to Italy, Spain, Mozambique, Tangier, Mexico, the Liverpool docks, and to all across the United States down Highway 61, to the Black Hills of Dakota, that little Minnesota town, Red Hook in Brooklyn, Oxford Town, inside Mobile, Alabama, and outside of Delacroix. More specifically, they take us to Bear Mountain picnics, a topless place to get a beer, to a Dixie band where a woman's hand's outstretched, a Princeton University graduation ceremony, inside the walls of Red Wing and a Buick 6, and even more specifically, 56th and Wabasha. We also are taken to mythical and Biblical places like an immortal shrine in "Golden Loom" (1975) and the gates of Eden. Dylan brings us places where we can see shooting stars, watch rivers flow, and even nights come falling from the sky. He offers us the lowlands and the highlands, shelter from storms, and places from his imagination like desolation row, watchtowers where princes keep view, and some place that could be Lincoln County Road or Armageddon. Even many of his album titles denote or connote places: *Highway 61 Revisited*, *Bringing It All Back Home*, *Nashville Skyline* (1969), *Street-Legal* (1978), *Blood on the Tracks* (1975), and *Under the Red Sky* (1990).

Dylan has mapped out the world for us, and the creation of an interactive map indicating all the places his songs bring us awaits the inspiration of some technologically hip go-getter. But such an invention would not capture what happens when we enter the places to which Dylan summons us through song, which includes not just the lyrics but voice, instruments, and performance.

What is it like to be in the places Dylan has us inhabit? As with most literary questions on Dylan, the answer is complicated. Dylan's places are ephemeral, partly due to being places that "don't make sense no more." They are like riding down the Niagara Falls of someone's skull. They are there and not there, vibrantly here and nowhere, penetrating and elusive at the same time. But the place of the song, the landscape of it, or more exact, the soundscape created by lyrics, voice, instruments, and performance are habitable, even if only for the duration of the song, habitable in the sense of where listeners can be carried if they are open to what Dylan demands.

In "Shelter from the Storm" (1975), Dylan asks us to "Try imagining a place that's always safe and warm." Dylan songs have always demanded of us that we imagine places. The collection of songs on *Together Through Life* is no exception. Arguably, they may be the most demanding in this regard. The recording brings listeners in and out of landscapes. Some are desolate, barren, nowhere lands, others filled with people, activity, and life. Some are real places we recognize and can visit, such as Houston or whatever is conjured by a wife's hometown. But most of them are extensions of an inner world, worlds collapsed upon them and affected by loss, abandonment, or desperation. Landscapes are shaded by emotions that keep us "together through life" experiencing what binds us and what haunts and stalks us. The places that we are tethered to from memories and at the same time can never be the same, and the concerns that shrink our active participation in the present to an unknowable future are evoked in the places mentioned in these songs, songs that compel us to acknowledge that geography binds us psychologically and emotionally. We are forever caught in its thrall, Dylan seems to be calling us to grasp.

The cover chosen for the album, a photograph by Bruce Davidson, also used for the cover of Larry Brown's short story collection, *Big Bad Love* (1990), is emblematic of absence, place, displacement, and togetherness. Davidson, referred to by the *New York Times* as "one of the most influential photographers of the last half century" is a member of Magnum Photos, an international photographers collective, and in 2010 had a collection of his photography published by Gerhard Steidl in a three-volume box set suitably entitled *Outside Inside* (2011).[1] In the photo chosen for *Together Through Life*, what is perhaps noticeable is Dylan's absence. Lovers are together in a place within a place, in back of a vehicle in full embrace, erotically united, on a road, or as Sean Wilentz describes it, "a serious make-out session in the backseat of a speeding car: love and sex."[2] The view of the lovers is from the front seat with the road, a divider, and another car on the other side of it clearly in view. It is a built-in place with a deeply personal intimate experience on display situated on a manmade space, with the expanse of open sky in the background.

The album cover invites us to be alert to how Dylan uses place to bring us together and set us apart. And how place is affected by inner worlds that cannot be controlled but are all we are capable of controlling. This is no slapdash, twilight-of-one's-career compilation. It is an album that explores place seriously, with mockery, heartbreak, and warning.

When I first heard *Together Through Life* I was teaching *King Lear*, a play in which Shakespeare uses the word "nothing" twenty-nine times, the most in any of his plays. "Nothing will come of nothing: speak again," Lear speaks to his most beloved daughter Cordelia. Her reply, "Unhappy that I am, I cannot heave my heart into my mouth: I love your majesty / According to my bond; nor more nor less," sets off a chain of events that spiral out of Lear's control. When Lear banishes her he banishes love; "Cordelia" means heart.

A consistent theme in Shakespeare is chaos assuming reign upon the earth when love leaves. Othello's words hold sway with this idea when he says, "Perdition catch my soul / But I do love thee! And when I love thee not / Chaos is come again." The negation of love is chaos. The barren landscapes, namely those on the heath in *King Lear* prior to, during, and after the penultimate storm scene, are illustrative of what the absence of love looks like. "Beyond Here Lies Nothin'," the first song on *Together Through Life*, suggests or threatens bleak desolation. Dylan seems to be saying that here, in this place, with me, is where love is; beyond here, well, that's another story; there is "Nothin' we can call our own." Lear will find out that beyond his kingdom, which he thoughtlessly divides to have his ego stroked before he dies, there will be nothing he can call his own. He is stripped down to the state of unaccommodated man, the primitive self, living only to survive. If not for experiencing *Together Through Life* for the first time while teaching *Lear*, I may never have caught these associations.

Dylan creates the feel of *King Lear* in this first song, and the title of the album reflects the need for place to be defined by lovers staying together. He does not know what to do without love; alone is "boulevards of broken cars." Projected onto place is the speaker's emotional state, as is so with Lear, who experiences the great storm scene mostly if not entirely in his mind. A performance with Simon Russell Beale in the lead role portrayed the storm scene as only part of Lear's increasing madness. Dylan's speaker sits in a throne when his love is present with him. The whole world is his throne when with her. Such is the case when Lear was with Cordelia. When they are finally united, just before their deaths, he pleads for them to just live in a world of their own:

> No, no, no, no! Come, let's away to prison:
> We two alone will sing like birds i' the cage:
> When thou dost ask me blessing, I'll kneel down,
> And ask of thee forgiveness: so we'll live,
> And pray, and sing, and tell old tales, and laugh
> At gilded butterflies, and hear poor rogues
> Talk of court news; and we'll talk with them too,
> Who loses and who wins; who's in, who's out;
> And take upon's the mystery of things,
> As if we were God's spies: and we'll wear out,
> In a wall'd prison, packs and sects of great ones,
> That ebb and flow by the moon.³

This pining to live only in a world inhabited with one other found both in Lear's words and in the voice of "Beyond Here Lies Nothin'" has much to do with an inability to live with one's self outside a lover's radius. One's identity is contingent on the lover's presence. The speaker knows or rather accepts no other version of himself without the beloved controlled within the space of his environment. The concept of love exists in the world of other Dylan songs, but it is rarely a romantic love, especially (and fittingly) from *Desire* (1976) on. The image is almost cloyingly romantic. The "prison grasp of his own self-love" that he claims in the liner notes of *Another Side of Bob Dylan* (1964) to want to avoid placing someone in is exactly what "Beyond Here" conjures. If we can rely on Dylan's own approved video interpretations of his songs, even one quick peek at the video for "Beyond Here" lets us know that nothing may very well be a lot better than what's going on "here." Violence dominates the video. It is a terrifying depiction of dependence gone so wrong that each person in the relationship lives only to survive the other's attacks, to kill or be killed by the other. Splashed from scene to scene are moments of eroticism tied to lust and hatred and several attempts at murder. The video ends with the lovers bloodied and scarred but clearly aroused as seen from the culminating kiss.

What Dylan allows us to see in "Beyond Here" is a patriarchal view of landscape. Barrenness abounds out there; here is fertility, or at least what creates a fertile mind, or one that senses it cannot live without love. Judith Fryer, whose book *Felicitous Space* delves into the relationship between place and the imagination, observes that "[c]ontemporary perceptions of the American landscape as 'pastoral' are rooted in a projection of male fantasies upon the land"—ones that necessitate the view of the landscape as a mother figure abolishing "threatening, alien, and potentially emasculating" forces.[4] But Dylan writes of the converse of the pastoral—the pastoral as a place of mind. Place is fantasy, a male projection of being womanless, even emasculated. In the video, Dylan undercuts the notion of togetherness negating "the threatening, alien, and potentially emasculating forces."[5] The brutal fight almost to the finish witnessed in the song only serves to make the "mountains of the past" of the "beyond here" longed for again. A question worth asking in a Dylan song is, "What am I witness to?" Dylan lets his speakers witness so much. What listeners witness is the sometimes overwhelming scope of emotions that subdue the speaker driven to escape reality through psychological projections upon space and even beyond. Just as Dylan escapes the here that confronted him on that Princeton graduation stage recounted in the song "Day of the Locusts" (1970), for the romantic pastoral Black Hills of Dakota, the mountains of the past have an allure.

In "Beyond Here Lies Nothin," however, the "beyond here" is where there are mountains of the past. Yet these are not mountains past and gone. Instead, these mountains monstrously demonstrate just how pregnant the past can be. As William Faulkner wrote, "The past is never dead. It's not even past." The love in this song is fixated, obsessive, cloying; but either here or there it remains a fabrication or creation in the mind of the speaker. Painting life as nothingness without her is a lie to both the singer and his object of desire. For him it's delusion, for her, freedom. We only get one side of the story here, but of course that is intentional; Dylan's writing is not proof of his patriarchal allegiances. He is aware of what the word "throne" denotes in the context of this song, for instance, and so he presents part of what love is and does. Love means being possessed in both senses of the word. Yet we're not safe from either. In fact, the song is a mirror held up to every listener. As Dylan says to Bill Flanagan about "This Dream of You," the seventh track on *Together Through Life*: "if you have those kinds of thoughts and feelings you know where the guy is. He's right where you are. If you don't have those thoughts and feelings then he doesn't exist." The operative word with regard to the study of Dylan is "where"—you know where he is because he's you, and he's Dylan, too. In that same interview, Dylan says, "The people in my songs are all me."[6]

"Beyond the Horizon," from *Modern Times*, presents the pastoral opposite of what we experience in "Beyond Here Lies Nothin'." What's beyond the horizon is where romance and a valued life based on togetherness exists. But the longing to be somewhere beyond present circumstances or settings is dangerous. This is where modern feminist literary critics have particular relevance to the study of millennial Dylan. Over time, Dylan's treatment of women has changed. This perhaps is a subject best left for another essay, yet in the context here my conjecture is that Dylan has progressed from naïve misogyny to lyrics that deliberately express misogynistic leanings. Dylan does so intentionally, and this is where a modern study of the pastoral becomes relevant.

Hermione Lee identifies two kinds of pastorals, both with potentially harmful grappling hooks that reduce meaning into unreliable binaries. She defines the "soft pastoral" as "a romance, a dream of celebration, carnival, song, and love: guiltless, prelapsarian gratification, innocent hedonism, to which tender feelings of nostalgia are attached." Yet, it "has the death's head within it." So while fecundity, restoration of community, and life-giving forces abound in the soft pastoral, at the same time it contains an elegiac presence. Lee uses as illustration the coexistence of Jaques and Orlando in *As You Like It*.[7] One leaves that play content with what is restored by its end, but the existential presence of Jaques and his "All the world's a stage" monologue lurks and perhaps even outlasts the blissful outcomes of fathers, daughters, and lovers' relationships reconciled and restored. Likewise, long after hearing it one may be pleasantly aroused by an image of Dylan's from "Beyond the Horizon" such as "At the end of the rainbow, life has only begun / In the long hours of twilight 'neath the stardust above," but what should not be overlooked or forgotten either is the pain from yearning that creates it. What is cast comes from a wretched heart, drowning memories, darkness, dreariness, weakness, weariness, and the worst of what the prison grasp incites: building one's whole world around someone else. This is where the death's head that Lee mentions can be found. In "Beyond Here" it resides not beyond anywhere, but in the "here," which makes it even more disturbing.

In her book *Willa Cather: Double Lives* (1991), Lee cites Willa Cather's penchant for "doubling" or revealing opposition within her work that gets its energy from contraries." I contend that Lee's study effectively fits the study of recent Dylan. Lee describes the contrary to the soft pastoral as the "hard pastoral." In it we see "a realist narrative of labor and endurance," contained within a golden age, "recalled as an idyllic, vanished period of harmony between man and nature." Though nature and man are severed, the value and rewards of hard work and the dignity it provides are fondly recalled and their values sustained. Things that endure referred to in "Beyond Here" are mountains, the moon, and stars. But they are there, not here. Lee's theory of the severance between nature and mankind is also evident in Dylan's song. Dylan upsets the conventions of the hard pastoral by separating what endures in nature from the promise of fulfillment gained by lovers whose loving will endure as long as love does: "We'll keep on lovin' pretty baby / For as long as love will last." It is interesting that Dylan here distinguishes loving from love. There's a hint that neither will last, one tied to the other, even when dependent on the other. Such is the state of the human condition, not so with mountains, the moon, and stars. Ours is an endurance contingent on a concept, a feeling, as fleeting and vanishing as the "harmony between man and nature."[8] It is the false promise of gratification in the here and now that Dylan gets at in this song.

In the *Together Through Life* song "This Dream of You," the theme is the same as in "Beyond Here," yet the opening setting is a "nowhere café." The speaker expresses himself from nowhere; nothingness is again connoted. All or nothing is the seeming message—existence dependent on the loved one's presence even if from a dream. It is only that which keeps the speaker "living on." As Dylan remarks to Flanagan, "There are degrees of happiness. You go from one to the other and then back again. It's hard to be completely happy when those around us are suffering and groaning from hunger."[9] Another kind of hunger is illustrated in "Dream"—one born out of emotional starvation. We witness and hear the voice of suffering in this song. It is hard to be happy when listening to it. Dylan summons the sound of strain produced from suffering. His voice is raspy, sad, laden with whiskey and smoke. It is the sound of resolve and self-pity, as if he is at the end of his rope, but not quite, conversing with a bartender forced to listen while he scrubs the bar, and all tied to being where his beloved is not, which for him is, or might as well be, like being nowhere. Danny Eccleston refers to "Dylan's narrator" as one "tormented by thoughts of a long-gone señorita that stalks the night and haunts the day." And it is this torment that paints the landscape we are forced to confront in this song, one that creates shadows, blindness, and the feeling of being lost in a crowd, a "cheerless room in a curtained gloom," the internal rhyming words accentuating the mood, both cheerless and curtained, cut off, gloom pervading over everything. This is heightened emotional projection, but there is something ephemeral about it all. The feelings in this song are like a short-circuited synapse. Eccleston refers to this pulsating as a "missed opportunity" that "hangs there, agonizingly...."[10] In this song, old things can become new again and a star from heaven can fall. Quicksilver are these moments or sensations. But they weigh heavily, as the voice conveys, because they offer or recall moments of hope. And maybe that's why this nowhere café is one worth defending. Listeners may be reminded of Ernest Hemingway's short story "A Clean, Well-Lighted Place" (1933). Existing as the speaker does carries with it a guarantee of living, a kind reduced to mere endurance or survival, yes, but living on nonetheless. Some things are worth dying over or from, but not this dream.

"This Dream of You" appears to be on the verge of tragedy, the kind gleaned from modernist poet T. S. Eliot. In his exposition of "Not Dark Yet," Christopher Ricks refers to Dylan's penchant for making literary allusions, specifically to the works of Eliot: "Dylan enjoys allusions all right (those lovely mermaids in 'Desolation Row,' where the captain's tower housed T. S. Eliot, are both more and less desolate because they have flowed over from 'The Love Song of J. Alfred Prufrock' [1919])."[11] In "Prufrock" the speaker reveals not shadows but "nerves in patterns on a screen" from a "magic lantern" that can illuminate the speaker's most intimate thoughts, and he wonders what would happen if they were shared; the speaker's yearning to make meaningful human connection is painfully dashed aside by disinterest. It means nothing to her at all. In "This Dream of You," Dylan shape-shifts this direct imagined rejection in Prufrock's mind into the mind of a singer who sees all-knowing shadows that reveal how deeply he misses someone.

Eccleston says that the songs of *Together Through Life* offer "shifting perspectives," alternating between "tragic, comic, satirical."[12] We are brought to a figurative precipice with this song, with a tragedy about to take place or that already has. If sleep can be a temporary death, as Dylan sings on "Workingman's Blues #2," why can't being awake be a temporary life? The speaker feels that everything he touches "seems to disappear," as does night and day. The implication, the tragic one, is that the loved one he touched is now gone. This is packed with things here and then not here and how much such loss hurts, especially when shadows on the wall are constant reminders of what was and what could have been. "Everywhere I turn you are always here."

The feel is similar to that found in Cormac McCarthy's work—specifically, the ephemeral nature of his landscapes, especially those experienced by his picaro characters. These are the ardent-hearted, the ones on a mission. They appear in the form of Billy in *The Crossing* (1994), John Grady in *All the Pretty Horses* (1992), the Kid in *Blood Meridian* (1985), and the boy and his father in *The Road* (2006). And what makes the speaker's landscape ephemeral is the coming and going of the emotional responses to surroundings. As in McCarthy, environments exude indifference. Nature cares nothing for the eyes that rest upon it. Those eyes fixated from emotional inner turmoil airbrush places with meaning that is not there, the mind as a nowhere café–generating machine, nowhere because these places exist only in the mind of those whose eyes are so fixated. As Stephen Tatum says about McCarthy's cowboys, "[H]is characters desire secure foundations; their fate is to traverse a fluid, liminal landscape, usually blinded, confused precisely because their physical abstractions, their schemes, categorizations, and names, and their inherent prejudices and passions prevent them from truly seeing the world as it is, much less their place in it."[13] Likewise, speakers in Dylan's *Together* songs see the world not as it is, but rather the world as tainted by the arrested emotional prisms from which they view the world. In "This Dream of You" the speaker confesses to having no tears left. The mind of the voice we hear has reached a point of emotional exhaustion and can do nothing but cast painful memories upon the places he encounters and shares. The dream that he carries with him destroys while it nourishes. "Quod Me Nutrit Me Destruit" is a Latin phrase that appears under a portrait of Christopher Marlowe, which translates "what nourishes me destroys me." The song exemplifies the going from one to the other and back again that Dylan describes about happiness.

"Forgetful Heart" has a similar speaker with a similar circumstance. A lover he once knew is gone and he pines for the past when they enjoyed each other. This is another pastoral with the death's head. When the beloved was there, life was lived; now that she's gone it is hard to live, and he wonders why they can't be or love the way they used to. The subject is dark, depressing—lonesomeness abounds. And the sound is of pain, whatever that can sound like. What are missing in this song are images of place. Yet this is deliberate. The forgetful heart forgets what things looked like. Places are shadowy at best; "there" is the only reference to where she used to be with him, and again what he hears at night is the vague sound of pain. The last two lines refer to a closed door though that can easily be seen, but then that the door may never have been there at all. There and not there, vanishing, like a hand let go forever, recalling the myth of Orpheus. Dylan connotes the myth with the longing akin to losing a loved one forever but kept present by a constant effort to visit her and bring her back through the powers of memory.

"Tangled Up in Blue" (1975), "Where Are You Tonight? (Journey through Dark Heat)" (1978), and "Nettie Moore" contain Orphic elements as well. The Orpheus myth immediately conjures place, namely the underworld where Orpheus tries to retrieve his beloved Eurydice and, at first, succeeds. It is interesting to note that Orpheus was the greatest mortal musician, and he uses this talent to charm Hades into making a deal with him. Thus, he actually succeeds in this quest, but fails to live up to the bargain made with Hades to refrain from looking back at Eurydice while holding her hand to guide her out of the underworld. The temptation is too strong; he sneaks a peek and she is lost to him forever (she "slipped so far away"). Orpheus lives the rest of his life in misery, only to be torn to pieces by Thracian women who take offense to his indifference at their advances.

The metaphor is clear: you can't go back again. But Dylan wavers on the "can't go back again" directive in his songs. In one, "Summer Days" (2001), he asserts "of course you can"; in "Mississippi" (2001) he agrees "you can always come back" but not all the way. In "Life Is Hard," as in "Forgetful Heart" and "This Dream of You," the going back is through memory. So you can, but . . . "the emptiness is endless." To return to a memory of a loved one gone has a price that is just too costly. As Eric Lott says of the songs on "Love and Theft," "[i]t's the memories that haunt you, things acquired, loved, and lost."[14] But again, they may be the only thing worth living for. Cormac McCarthy has John Grady resist recalling his love in *All the Pretty Horses* for the damage it does to a memory each time it is recalled: "He would not think of Alejandra because he didn't know what was coming or how bad it would be and he thought she was something he better save."[15] In *The Road*, the father believes "each memory recalled must do some violence to its origins. As in a party game. Say the words and pass it on. So be sparing. What you alter in the remembering has yet a reality, known or not."[16] This idea is propelled in "Life Is Hard," a song written to fulfill director Olivier Dahan's quest to find "real songs of the American spirit" for the film *My Own Love Song* (2010),[17] when the singer feels a chill instead of memories by the end of the song. The force of memory is powerful in these lyrics. In the first verse, memories surface from "evening winds," followed by the next three verses that have them aroused from "an old schoolyard," the day she departed, and from just walking down a boulevard. But again, by the last verse, all that remains instead of memories of her is a chill. The damage to the memory is done. You can go back, but not all the way: maybe you can, but after that, memories fade and all that's left is the feeling of what it's like to lose the nearness of someone loved.

Nearness is all that matters to the singer in the song. Place is once again shaped by emotion. The removal of a loved one deprives place of color and life. Togetherness is all that matters. Remember the orgasmic promise in "Lay Lady Lay" (1969): the colors in a loved one's mind can be shown to her by the lover and they can be made to become more intense—vivid even. No color is even hinted at in "Life Is Hard." Instead, emptiness and barren days abound.

Not so coincidentally, *Together Through Life* has a direct reference to the underworld smack dab in the refrain of "My Wife's Hometown." Hell is the singer's wife's hometown. This is perhaps what Eccleston refers to as a comedic shift in perspective, from the tragic, like the Orphic induced ones. Shakespeare could muster the depth of the human condition with comedy as handily as he does with tragedy. The same can be said of Dylan. The song begins with the established place as "here," which we may take as his wife's hometown. Wherever it is, it is not a place the singer wishes to deal with, but he does wish to hear something, a drummer's cymbal specifically. This sounds like the moment when the deal goes down, which on the song of that title on *Modern Times* means death. The song begins outside in the sun, but by the fourth of six verses the singer is inside with "the shutters down," in a place he has been driven to, presumably by that pokey mother-in-law. But the "she" in the fifth verse appears to be the wife, whose love is all he knows. This ties the song to theme of the songs discussed above: the longing, yearning, pining for a loved one. The song is tougher to pin down. It's potpourri-ish, threaded by apparent non-sequiturs. But the confession of losing reason altogether in the fifth verse—a result of knowing only love—resonates with the second verse's claim to know that reasons exist. "Reasons" and "reason" are forced together by similarity of appearance and distinguished by variant meanings. Hell and a hometown are forced together in this way, too—yoked by the mother-in-law variant joke. But it's a mutilation of sorts—an unfair projection upon place that favors only the projector. By the end, we are outside again, trapped in a broken state and a dry county. In this brokenness and barrenness is a warning against an evil eye and advice to just keep walking and not to hang around. This is not the stuff of comedy. It's a surly commentary and uninviting. It's a place that eschews belonging. It's hell; maybe the song wants us to take that more literally.

This song is followed by "If You Ever Go to Houston," the only song on the album with a direct reference to an exact identifiable place. In the song, Houston is a place you don't want to go to unless certain advice is heeded. Dylan even instructs visitors how to walk and where to put their hands. The second verse advises less on the physical and more on the mind: be wary of the police and know what you're doing. Memories of the distant past are reported in the third verse and these memories become associations with place that introduce people, namely women, Mary Anne, Lucy, Betsy. Restlessness is the topic of the fifth verse, but the setting is no longer Houston or so it seems; Houston is not mentioned again until the last verse. The restlessness starts to dominate as the focal point, and the sixth verse gets to the heart of it with dialogue in which either someone who takes the advice from the first verse or the singer himself approaches a policeman about the location (place) of his gal, who was last seen at the Magnolia Hotel. Now we are back in Houston where the Magnolia Hotel is located at 1100 Texas Street. The see-sawing beat to the song underscored by David Hidalgo's accordion makes the gal/pal rhyme comical but not silly as such a rhyme might, especially with the policeman becoming a pal if he finds his gal—such is the proposed bargain.

The song seems all along to be about how to belong somewhere. Being "wedded to geography," as has been said about Willa Cather,[18] is really in many ways about yearning to belong. The belonging in this collection of Dylan songs has all to do with getting place to resuscitate a feeling of belonging once felt when together with someone else. Displacement happens when the beloved is no longer in the same place with the lover. "If You Ever Go to Houston" continues this theme—sneakily, I'd say—until the last verse, when it is more deliberately served up from a range of barrooms throughout Texas, where he asks that the memories he has in them be sent home with the tears from them placed in a bottle. This is the most lasting image in a song that does not preach to its listeners. It is not merely, as Epstein states, "a hip lecture on how to handle yourself in the hot towns of the Lone Star State,"[19] but also a battle between revealing and concealing. The sudden move at the end of the song back to the title's refrain, "If you ever go to Houston," conveys this schizoid narration. But there's no forgetting what was revealed through the painful memories associated with places. Dylan is a master at disguise. He can shift emotional centers as if with a magic wand, hiding them in rhyme and revealing them using the same. He can be deliberate with an emotion through tragedy and still make you feel its pulse within comedy. In "Houston" we are led to believe at first that this is a song akin to "Subterranean Homesick Blues" in which advice pours out line after line. But instead it is just a vehicle for singing the same song about yearning to be together with a loved one as with most of the other songs on *Together Through Life*.

In "I Feel a Change Comin' On," Dylan underscores the album's central theme of togetherness, with an all-encompassing invite to listeners, as in we are all in this together. Note that just about every pronoun is used. They, she, we, you, I ... we're all there. While that is not unique to Dylan's songs, it is to this recording. In addition, each line sounds like the beginning of a new narrative; it has a one-non-sequitur-after-the-other feel to it, or as Eccleston calls it, "a scrapbook of pensées, grouped by themes, not stories as such."[20] There's a line for everyone. So while there is romance and warmth, there is also intrigue and possible betrayal, (verse one), anticipation (verse two), dreams deferred or dashed (verse four), lust (verse five), and self-pity (verse seven): a delectable cherry-picking for everyone whatever mood he or she in. The song offers a place for any listener to feel he or she belongs in it, any particular line a place to project feelings upon. Again, in answer to Bill Flanagan's question, "What are the chances that the guy in 'Feel a Change' is likely to live happily ever after?" Dylan says, "There are degrees of happiness. You go from one to the other and then back again."[21] That response may be the best interpretive commentary I have ever heard Dylan express about any of his own songs, with the exception of the songs from *Oh Mercy* that he thoroughly analyzes in *Chronicles*. When I read that quote, I felt like I got what Dylan was trying to achieve—the sensation of being pulled from happiness while going toward it.

This sensation is mirrored by the in-and-out camera lens perspective we get right from the song's opening. The first line has the singer looking the whole world over, but then the perspective shifts, as if looking east he spotted something from a pair of binoculars he just picked up, and that is his baby, but a quick shift happens. It's not just her; she's not walking alone but with the village priest, which has multiple and multilayered possibilities. Is she confessing something? Having relations with him? Or is he merely a companion with her on a tranquil stroll? Immediately, there's reflection that results in a sudden shot of happiness—seeing his "baby"—that is interrupted by the presence of a village priest (maybe the reason why later she or some other known "object of desire" is referred to as a whore).

The song's warmth overall does win out, from its threaded references to the last or fourth part of the day. Much online debate focused on the origin of this reference. Some say Dylan pulled it from the line of The Prologue to the Man of Law's Tale in David Wright's translation of *The Canterbury Tales*: "the sun / The arc of his artificial *day* had run / The *fourth part* and half an hour and more." However, I think the phrase's allusion to scripture contributes more to the song's ebb and flow. The passage below is taken from the King James Bible, Nehemiah 9:3: "And they stood up in their place, and read in the book of the law of the LORD their God one fourth part of the day; and another fourth part they confessed, and worshipped the LORD their God." The last part or fourth part of the day is 6 p.m., the time of sunset. In the song, this part of the day has transpired. Although not a place proper, the image conjures setting, and all that takes place in the song, all the scraps not stories, take place in this last part of the day. We can all relate to last parts of our days, i.e., our lives, when whatever obligations we have, be it worshipping or others, are over and we settle into what's left. This may be the warmth in the song that Eccleston speaks of, which invites all of us into that place in our lives we call our own—the place where the fade-out is, or always is, the last part of days or all our days, the twilight hours so full of change always felt about to come on, felt from reflection and looking out over the world as the day accomplishes. Perhaps that is why Dylan uses "everybody" three times in the last verse, and fits them/us with money, clothes, and flowers. Yet there is the flitting away from happiness just as we are all in it or invited into it—Dylan is not part of the party. He doesn't have a single rose, this man that some say has "the blood of the land" in his voice. "You go from one to the other and then back again." Dylan as Jaques in *As You Like It* is the presence that snatches happiness away.

"It's All Good" investigates place in a satirical road trip romp. The road has always been an important place for Dylan. His songs abound with its literal and symbolic presence. One could say about Dylan, and really the entire folk tradition, that what is espoused most of all is Michelet's expression *Le but n'est rien; le chemin c'est tout*, "the end is nothing; the road is all." The satire in "It's All Good" is hitched to that idea, a 180-degree spin on it. The disturbing images witnessed in the song are settled by the refrain "It's all good." The intended calming influence when he uses that phrase ameliorates the immorality and destructive forces that propel the compendium of harsh imagery and depictions. The end, then—it will amount to good—is all. It's *all* good. But since we are in Dylan's satirical embrace, there is nothing good about what's seen or described or nothing good that can come of it. Eccleston describes the song as another (the first being "Beyond Here Lies Nothin'") "glimpse of the end of days" song, replete with [m]endacious politicos, starving farmers, widows and orphans swirl[ing] in a fever-dream of the world financial crisis. . . ."[22] The place is one of impending doom, a landscape with a moral breakdown, an interplay of people with places, again, in a crescendo of deterioration and destruction.

Dylan's sarcasm has mostly been deliberate and obvious, e.g., "It Ain't Me, Babe" (1964), "Don't Think Twice, It's Alright" (1963), "Positively 4th Street" (1966), "Is Your Love in Vain" (1978). In "It's All Good," the sarcasm is emphasized with a snide "Oh yeah" that he lets out at the song's end. When asked by Flanagan how that song originated, Dylan replied, "Probably from hearing that phrase one too many times." Yes, as disturbing as one too many mornings. Dylan brings out the ugliness of the phrase—the sinister implications of its use. The cavalier way it is used in everyday conversation suggests being bothered by something is an ill-begotten venture or that to think of what's going on around us as bad is a subversion not to be tolerated. It is best for all that everything from crumbling buildings to killers on the street be interpreted favorably as part of some beneficent plan. This vision is not far removed from the electric shocks people receive in the world created by Kurt Vonnegut in "Harrison Bergeron" (1961). The sweeping cliché "It's All Good" softens or even hides all that's bad and in need of correction, zapping those who think otherwise into a crippling uniformity of thinking. Cruelty, deprivation, waste, and terror ... anything goes and no one is held accountable. This really is one of Dylan's best protest songs. Yet how does it fit into place within this study of Dylan and place? In his interview with Dylan, Flanagan says about "It's All Good" that Dylan "describe[s] a world that gets darker and more miserable with every verse."[23] When I first really listened to the song, I felt that. There's a snowballing effect in the song, an increasing challenge to accept "It's All Good" as a solution to what ails us and the world around us. Here we are together in this place, our place, the world, at times and in many places terrifying and tragic, and all we can say about it is that it's all good?

The song inhabits a post-9/11 world informed by inevitability. It's as if we are all just one more shoe-fall away from having our world, who we are, what we are, where we are, how we are, and why we are taken away from us. The last verse pledges a commitment to violating others and the worst part of it is the implication that there is nothing we can do about it since if the message is that it's all good, very few indeed would change it even if they could. Such a predicament imagined is, as Flanagan says of the song, "kind of funny" (as in this can't happen to me) and "kind of scary "[24] (as in this is already happening).

There is one ray of hope, a silver lining waiting to come down. In the sixth verse the reference to widows and orphans is the only moment when togetherness is urged again: "Come along with me, babe, I wish you would." Despite the mudslinging, dust and dirt heaping between the two that begins the song (shall they be lovers?), there's a wish or invitation to stay together or be together in this. This "beyond here" which in this song is the "here" where all around is nothing, everything is a nowhere café, brings with it a hope that somehow there is a way that the lovers will forge ahead together through this forsaken life. Or maybe the whole song is a cornucopia of idle threats only to keep his babe by convincing her that what's worse is out there but not here with me.

However, I'm not sure I get that in this song. It is too inclusionary, too much of an open invitation. We are all in on this, but not with the "we're all to blame" message of "Who Killed Davey Moore?" (1963) or in "Only a Pawn in Their Game" (1964). No, we are all readied for the role of either victim or victimizer, ready to roll into someone's place. But what if we are together for life in the same place, as in the world, not in some bar, nowhere café, hometown, or Houston, Texas? I can't roll into your world if your world is already mine. In this song, of all songs, I find a kind of reassurance from the album's title. This may be the only song in which the romantic implications of being together through life are not corrupted by a singer motivated to lure his former lover back into his world. There is too much effort by Dylan to raise awareness and social consciousness in this song. The wish for someone else to come with him seems genuine, as it may be the only defense against displacement or being displaced. Similar to the boy and the father in Cormac McCarthy's *The Road*, displacement and pending or real apocalypse are best faced when one's purpose for living is to keep someone else alive, as it is for the father who sacrificed his life to create a meaningful one for his son. This then would be the most memorable and clever way, as Eccleston says, that Dylan "pursues his ancient love through this landscape, full of apocalyptic landmarks...."[25]

"Jolene" and "Shake Shake Mama," the first referred to by Sean Wilentz as a "plain enough sex song,"[26] a description fitting for the latter as well, are good listening tunes but not with any inquiry into the depth of place in our lives and its ties to emotions heightened by loss and yearning for reunion as with the other *Together* songs. These two exceptions may be, as David Dalton refers to all of Dylan's songs from *Time Out of Mind* onward, "ghost stories," as if Dylan "is singing to us from the grave."[27] Dylan is the spook reminding us on "Jolene" and "Shake" that rock 'n' roll is rooted in sex and dance. But the Dylan songs that have always mattered most are the ones that haunt us, either rhythmically or lyrically. In *Together Through Life*, Dylan haunts places with emotional projections and those places come to life, not from the grave but from his mind, into the places that we have projected our emotions. We are together in this, together within and without. No one gets out of these places unscarred.

NOTES

1. James Estrin and Josh Haner, "The Renowned, Unknown Bruce Davidson." *New York Times*, June 28, 2010.
2. Sean Wilentz, *Bob Dylan in America* (New York: Doubleday, 2010), 329.
3. William Shakespeare, *King Lear*. Quoted in *Shakespeare Uncovered: King Lear with Christopher Plummer*. PBS. January 30, 2015.
4. Judith Fryer, *Felicitous Space: The Imaginative Structures of Edith Wharton and Willa Cather* (Chapel Hill: University of North Carolina Press, 1986), 230.
5. Fryer, *Felicitous Space*, 230.
6. Bill Flanagan, "Bob Dylan Interview with Bill Flanagan," *The Telegraph*, April 13, 2009.
7. Hermione Lee, *Double Lives* (New York: Vintage International, 1989), 93.
8. Lee, *Double Lives*, 84, 94.
9. Flanagan, "Bob Dylan Interview," n.p.
10. Danny Eccleston, "New Dylan Album: The First In-Depth Review." *Mojo*, April 17, 2009, n.p.
11. Ricks, Christopher, *Dylan's Visions of Sin* (New York: Harper Collins, 2003), 361.
12. Eccleston, "New Dylan Album," n.p.
13. Megan Riley McGilchrist, *The Western Landscape in Cormac McCarthy and Wallace Stegner* (New York: Routledge, 2010), 187.
14. Eric Lott, "Love and Theft in *'Love and Theft*,'" in *The Cambridge Companion to Bob Dylan*, Kevin J. H. Dettmar, ed. (New York: Cambridge University Press, 2009), 167–73.
15. Cormac McCarthy, *All the Pretty Horses* (New York: Vintage International, 1992), 204.
16. Cormac McCarthy, *The Road* (New York: Vintage International, 1992), 131.
17. Mark Daniel Epstein, *The Ballad of Bob Dylan: A Portrait* (New York: Harper Collins, 2011), 436.
18. Susan Rosowski, "Willa Cather and the Fatality of Place: *O Pioneers!*, *My Antonia*, and *A Lost Lady*," in *Geography and Literature: A Meeting of the Disciplines*, William E. Mallory and Paul Housley, eds. (Syracuse: Syracuse University Press, 1987), 81–94.
19. Epstein, The Ballad of Bob Dylan, 438.
20. Eccleston, "New Dylan Album," n.p.
21. Flanagan, "Bob Dylan Interview," n.p.
22. Eccleston, "New Dylan Album," n.p.
23. Flanagan, "Bob Dylan Interview," n.p.
24. Flanagan, "Bob Dylan Interview," n.p.
25. Eccleston, "New Dylan Album," n.p.
26. Wilentz, *Bob Dylan in America*, 331.
27. David Dalton, *Who Is That Man?: In Search of the Real Bob Dylan* (New York: Hyperion, 2012), 311.

CHAPTER THREE

DOWN THE FOGGY RUINS OF TIME: BOB DYLAN AND THE PERFORMANCE OF TIMELESSNESS

Andrea Cossu

In the 2000s, Bob Dylan and his music have resembled more palimpsest than monument. His past artistic achievements are sculpted in public memory, and are still being reproduced in the present through records, images, the work of critics, and the mythical role Dylan plays for modern popular music. However, so much has gone on since the release of *"Love and Theft"* that it is difficult to connect to the commonplace idea of Dylan as either a prominent rock star or as a troubadour from the foggy ruins of the 1960s. Instead, the modern, contemporary Dylan is a kind of trailblazer. He has moved away from his myth and headed toward other, decidedly subtler musical references, references that are external and sometimes antithetic to the established reputation of Bob Dylan as the source and end of his own genius.

The notion of palimpsest synthesizes many aspects of Dylan's work and artistic *persona*: originally, a palimpsest was a document that was written over, a layer of records and writing, a text that hides the remnants of a text. The concept of palimpsest suggests that there might be something below the surface yet to be discovered, deciphered, and decoded; it suggests also that there exists a temporal distance between two physically inseparable cultural products. If we interpret Dylan's contemporary work since *Time Out of Mind* as a palimpsest, we are left usually with a puzzle: what kind of text lies behind the surface, and what are the directions that one should take in order to reveal what Dylan and his burdensome image and status as a celebrity have hidden, whether consciously or not? The answer goes beyond Dylan's own adoption of a "protean style" of reinvention and self-reinterpretation,[1] and lies more in Dylan's connection with the cultural and musical memories of American vernacular music, to which Dylan points and which are an essential aspect of the definition of his artistic work. The notion of memory, and the way memory are enacted in performance, is a crucial dimension to understand Dylan's role and reputation in the wake of the century.

In this chapter, I will thus expand on ideas I have developed in my previous work on Dylan,[2] with a particular focus on the dynamic relations between collective memory and the making of artistic reputation, which we can understand as representations about an artist that orient public perception and enable expectations about artists and their productions.[3] I will focus especially on the ways Bob Dylan—as an artist, songwriter, and performer—has coped with a double problem of memorialization that seems to have affected him since his renaissance in the late 1990s. On the one hand, the public has been busy memorializing "Bob Dylan," producing an image that has made him timeless while at the same time putting discursive primacy on his role and prominence in the 1960s. A complex network of reputational entrepreneurs (ranging from Columbia executives to several presidents of the United States, who have praised and honored Dylan)[4] have made strategic use of their institutional positioning, their narrative capacity, and their motivations[5] to support a political and aesthetic vision of Dylan as irrevocably linked to the 1960s.[6] On the other hand, it seems that Dylan has tried to escape this fixation on his past-oriented reputation by trying to manage two different sides of collective memory. On one side he has challenged the memory of who "Bob Dylan" is supposed to be (especially when mediated through his work and his songs); on the other he has tried to connect his persona and his work to a wider cultural and musical memory that finds its realization in the vernacular culture of American folk and popular song, seen as a relevant tradition through which the artist is able to reproduce his authenticity. Dylan's agency poses a problem to the discussion on the sociology of the artists, namely to what extent artists can reclaim individuality in the making of artistic moves in a context in which they have become increasingly memorialized, a process that constrains their reputations and puts pressure to act in accordance with expectations produced by past work.

What is interesting in Dylan's response to this puzzle is the centrality of memory work. By this, I mean a collective activity that centers on representations of the past by agents who act as "entrepreneurs of memory," with the goal of making the past relevant in the present through narratives and discourses. In Dylan's case, memory work in the past decade or so has taken two different forms. It is not simply the memory work applied to Dylan himself, as an "object" of collective memory, but most primarily his active role in playing with different memories that transcend the Dylan persona, which have shaped his records, his public image, and his cultural viewpoint about music. As historian Sean Wilentz has written, since *"Love and Theft"* Dylan has "played tricks with the past and present, memory and history,"[7] conjuring up songs from the interplay of different cultural times. On a more lyrical note, Dylan himself has referred to the centrality of American song (a multifarious cultural landscape where everything—folk, country, blues, rock and roll, rhythm and blues, and even Tin Pan Alley—is mixed) not only for his work, but also for the nation itself: "Every one of the records I have made has emanated from the entire panorama of what America is to me. America, to me, is a rising tide that lifts all ships, and I've never really sought inspiration from other types of music."[8]

This vision of America includes Dylan and his songbook, and it reaches well beyond the Dylan we know to include a "lexicon" of songs (again, Dylan's words).[9] Today, an idealized America orients the interpretation of "Bob Dylan" as both star and icon, and his deeper relation to a wider culture inscribed in his work, which has now become the point of entry for endless paths in that musical landscape. For contemporary rock stars the pressure to repeat the past is inscribed in the very logic of the system of stardom, a pressure that puts them on the edge of a nostalgic repetition of their past and their past work.[10] Dylan has countered these pressures by emerging not simply as an *object* of the collective memory of American rock music, but also—and predominantly—as an *entrepreneur* of the memory of American roots music, able to preserve its memory, which modernity and (musically) the rise of rock as a category have somehow erased.

I take "High Water (For Charley Patton)," one of the highlights of *"Love and Theft,"* as a point of departure for this understanding of Dylan as an entrepreneur of different—and sometimes diverging—memories. I pay less attention to the lyrics than to the performative career of the song, particularly how it has been shaped in and through Dylan's performances in the Never Ending Tour. I was drawn to "High Water" originally because the song itself is a palimpsest, and a masterfully crafted one indeed. Yet, putting it into both the context of its performances and the broader musical background against which it is projected, I came to see "High Water" as a peculiar cultural artifact, one that allows Dylan to play with musical memories and in which the past of American music is filtered by Dylan's performance.

MEMORY, NOSTALGIA, AND DYLAN'S PASTS

In Dylan's work since *"Love and Theft,"* there is a sense of longing for the past that makes his work closer to his folk days in the Village, to the world of *The Basement Tapes* and *John Wesley Harding*, and to the acoustic records of the early 1990s, *Good As I Been to You* and *World Gone Wrong*. The musical anachronism[11] of old blues couplets, the revisionism of rock history that Dylan has put in the grooves, defies both rock's progressive narrative and the idea that it has been a great rupture in the history of popular culture. Dylan's approach has been at the same time revisionist, revivalist, and to some extent even reactionary, because it has been aimed at the definition of a musical and cultural lexicon that offers an alternative history of the trajectory of American popular music. This history has deep roots and, as a consequence, downplays the importance of rock's comparatively brief history both for Dylan's own career specifically, and American vernacular music in general. The narratives of rock music's history in which Dylan has been a great protagonist are incorporated in a longer trajectory in which the "streams"[12] that have contributed to the creation of rock come to the surface and become essential for the definition of Dylan as an artist.

This approach is to some extent the opposite of the charismatic narrative that has been historically built around Dylan, according to which he has acted as a pathbreaker in popular music able to create a fracture in its history. This latter vision is consistent with a progressive rock narrative, where the past has been buried by the emergence of rock as a new genre. However, with the passing of generations and the aging of the first generation of protagonists, the issue of the past has returned in full force, because a) rock has generated its own collective memory and b) there has been a deeper attention to continuities and roots rather than to discontinuities and invention.

This change of frame was crucial in the emergence of a competition for the definition of the identity of Dylan as an artist, in which symbolic resources like his perceived status and prestige as a prominent rock musician played a relevant role. Dylan's return to prominence in the field of popular music after the release of *Time Out of Mind* (a comeback that was marked both by new critical success and substantial sales) was the outcome of an arguably quite explicit strategy to reposition the artist vis-à-vis multiple and fragmented pasts, which are however treated in an ambiguous way, as both an element of nostalgia and as a source of artistic legitimation that Dylan has used to promote a new vision of his authenticity as an artist: are these pasts something to regard with regret because they have been lost, or are they pieces that can be reshaped in the present through artistic creativity? If Dylan's comeback has been marked by the relevance of the past, is this a nostalgic past or—on the contrary—some sort of fluid reference that goes through substantial transformation? Does Dylan aim to recreate the past as he perceives it was, or is he rather using it as a "form" that can be made distinctively Dylanesque? In this sense, as Elizabeth Brake has argued in one of the few studies that focus on the relationship between Dylan and the past, "comeback is a figure for escape from nostalgia and overcoming loss, a necessary condition for self-recreation."[13]

At first sight, nostalgia—here defined as the longing for something that has been lost in the past and which can only be partially recreated in the present—is what moves Dylan's modern work, in the form of pastiche and in the form of deliberate allusion in sounds and lyrics: a line from Henry Timrod or F. Scott Fitzgerald, a nod to Chicago bluesman Otis Rush in "Beyond Here Lies Nothin'" (2012), the opening lines from the ballad "Barbara Allen" that change into a much more threatening human carnival in "Scarlet Town" (2012). Yet these reminders of the past work less through the expression of regret and more through active recreation; therefore, the concept acquires a more progressive nuance. In the words of sociologists Michael Pickering and Emily Keightley, "nostalgia can be valued as potentially democratic, opening up new spaces for the articulation of the past and acting as a mode of assimilating this to the rapidly changing modern environment."[14] This kind of productive nostalgia tries to avoid social and cultural amnesia. It does not reach this objective by trying to go back to a past that history has degraded but mainly through the definition of alternative ways of thinking and feeling that, while primarily concerned with the past, seek to contaminate the present with cultural artifacts that connote a sense of "pastness" and, in doing so, to challenge historical and temporal boundaries.

This contamination, however, can present different modalities, from a retreat from the present to revivals that commodify the past. However, nostalgia for the past—insofar as it involves the attempt to reproduce some distinctive features of the past—can only work through "fragments of memory,"[15] because the present cannot be a perfect mirror-image of the past; that would be a utopian endeavor.

Dylan's modern work, if we read it through these lenses, is characterized by the recognition that it is impossible to "repeat the past" as it was, because the past is always a projection conditioned by the ways agents think about the past, made by shattered fragments that are taken out of time and placed—by an act of force and creation—in a time to which they do not belong.

The tension between old musical forms and the image of Bob Dylan embedded in the system of celebrity and rock mythology results from this work on memories pointing to a narrative of American music that cannot be reduced to its more recent history. This narrative comes from the periphery, from forgotten genres and works that have been buried by the affirmation of rock and roll in the 1950s and rock in the 1960s. Dylan has approached the deconstruction of his myth from the periphery, embodying another type of memory-work, one that is able to bypass the Sixties to dive into a more distant past and that resurfaces in the tracks played on his weekly satellite radio show *Theme Time Radio Hour* (2006–2009), or in the covers that Dylan has often performed during the Never Ending Tour,[16] which are in direct connection with the crooning, retro-style that has surprised many who have listened to *"Love and Theft"* or *Modern Times*. At the same time, Dylan has made live performance the center for a transformation of his own work, defining an alternative relationship between the past and the present and in particular between the "recording consciousness"[17] that is constructed by his songs and the "present-oriented" experience of their performance.

HIGH WATER

"High Water (For Charley Patton)" is one of the finest examples of the game of fragments that Dylan has constructed—with increased self-consciousness—in the later part of his career. It is no wonder that it was praised from the beginning as one of the highlights of *"Love and Theft,"* a record that is a pastiche of musical memories, a coalescence of fragments, in a word a palimpsest itself, where any line—original or not, borrowed or reworked—hints at something other than the song itself, and by extension to somebody other than Bob Dylan.

This otherness has been well described by analyses that focus on Dylan's own references to blackface minstrelsy.[18] Despite the explicit references to black blues in the song (Big Joe Turner, Charley Patton, Robert Johnson, and Lightnin' Hopkins), "High Water" is—sonically—an updated minstrel song that evokes other ghosts, like Dock Boggs and Clarence Ashley, banjo virtuoso, singer of "The Coo Coo Bird" and, sometimes, blackface performer in traveling shows. These haunting presences emerge through fragments, explicit or not, as does the presence of Ashley and Boggs, lyrically and in the banjo-driven pattern that haunts and threatens throughout the song.

The fragments, the odd snatches of traditional songs,[19] take the center of the song because they fit so tightly with Dylan's approach to songwriting and performing. In the 1970s, he said that he had had to learn how to do "consciously" what he had done "unconsciously" in the 1960s mixing symbolist verses with folk and rock music. In the 2000s, doing things consciously often leads not to the replication of Dylan-like verses, but to the juxtaposition of Dylan's words with words that come from a distant tradition, as well from other poetic sources that range from the classics to novels about the Japanese mob,[20] a process not limited to songwriting but also encompassing the sound that Dylan has explored. As he told *Los Angeles Times*'s Robert Hilburn in a telltale interview, Dylan uses other musicians' work as a canvas on which he is able to make his own sketch of a song, and then proceed to create a personal landscape of sound and words: "What happens is, I'll take a song I know and simply start playing it in my head. . . . I'll be playing Bob Nolan's 'Tumbling Tumbleweeds,' for instance, in my head constantly—while I am driving a car or talking to a person or sitting around or whatever. People will think they are talking to me and I'm talking back, but I am not. I'm listening to the song in my head. At a certain point, some of the words will change and I'll start writing a song."[21]

There are two very recognizable fragments in "High Water," one coming directly from the blues, the other from the British ballad tradition that found its way to the Appalachians. When Dylan sings "I'm gettin' up in the morning—I believe I'll dust my broom," he faces quite directly the legacy of the dozens of blues singers who, since the 1920s, have made the song "Dust My Broom" popular. He embodies, rather than the despair that the flood brings, the kind of excessive masculinity that is a fundamental part of the blues (and a recurrent theme in "High Water").

The second fragment is even more telltale. At some point, Dylan sings, with a tone that has been seldom heard on his records, "The Cuckoo is a pretty bird, she warbles as she flies." "The Cuckoo" was, like "Pretty-Peggy O" or "House Carpenter," among the many songs that everybody in the folk revival had to play in their process of socialization into the scene, and there is a very early recording of Dylan playing it in the early 1960s. It was first popularized by Clarence Ashley, one of the most prominent voices of Appalachian music.

At first sight, the inclusion of this verse looks like an afterthought. Heylin argues that some of the lyrics sound like filler, particularly those taken from the old Clarence Ashley song: "The cuckoo is a pretty bird, she warbles as she flies." As Heylin writes, "this is one line that smacks of having to find a rhyme, proving that even on this fine song he was sometimes knocking vainly at inspiration's door."[22]

It seems, rather, that the dissonance of those lines brings us closer to the heart of "High Water" than does even the explicit reference to Patton or other bluesmen. There are indeed fewer similarities between Patton's work and Dylan's than there are between the late great banjo players of the Depression era and the haunting tale that is sung in "High Water." Rather than using "The Coo Coo Bird" to find a rhyme, this is where the song begins, a genealogy that has been in Dylan's head and therefore hard to trace. But the song, and the performance, all lead to a reconsideration of the centrality of the "The Coo Coo Bird" as the fragment of musical memory where things started.

Musical memories hold a central position in the experience of songwriting, and Dylan has repeatedly asserted their primacy. Thus, the fragments that are incorporated in his modern work look like what has been left in the song in the process of transformation. This process works through genealogies that link together the past and the present, especially older songs, or artifacts, that are older songs linked to the act of creating a newer song. It is also worth noting, however, that performance plays a role that is not secondary. The fragments are not only lyrical fragments; most of all they are performances brought to a different time by Dylan's activity. The present, the moment of the transformation of a musical item in a Bob Dylan song, is a link in a chain, one that is enriched when the song is projected forward by means of other performances that change it, and in the way it is sung and arranged. It is precisely this dependence on performance (in creation and transformation) that brings Dylan's memory-work to the surface, to the point that timelessness—as a peculiar outcome of memory-work—results as the outcome of performance.

DOWN IN THE FLOOD OF PERFORMANCE: TRADITIONALIZING "BOB DYLAN"

As released on record, "High Water" displays a network of musical references that involve both Dylan's work and America's musical roots. However, as of January 2016 "High Water" has been performed in concert more than six hundred times and has acquired a life of its own in performance. The central position the song has in Dylan's canon derives from these hundreds of performances, which have constructed an alternative context for the song and which have contributed to mutual interactions between "High Water" and other songs. The released version of "High Water" has served rather as a point of departure than as a fixed reference. It stands at the center of a complex network that can be appreciated only in performance. As distant as different songs can seem from each other, the fact that they are performed on the same occasion and on the same night, or that they have similar places in the local economy of a Dylan show, creates similarities and a general convergence between many images and periods of Bob Dylan's career, to the point that they arrange in a non-intuitive way the relationship between different points of Dylan's trajectory (each marked by distinct sounds and visions) and the performance in the present. As performed in concert, songs are freed from the cognitive unity of the albums on which they appeared, and become part of the larger script—the concert—in which they acquire sense as part of a performance that can be experienced only in the moment it is created or, in a mediated way, through bootlegs.

Once they enter into the environment of the Never Ending Tour, Dylan's songs not only acquire a life of their own,[23] in their transformations and deconstructions, they also face the inevitable comparison with an original, a temporally antecedent version, which provides a term for any further evaluation and plays a crucial role in the construction of expectations. The distance between these versions is smaller than might appear at first sight. Dylan does not perform a fixed text which is outside the circle of performance; he refers—sometimes in a faithful, sometimes in a selective and creative way—to another performance, which itself may be an element in the collective memory of the audience. Furthermore, lyrics do not stand alone: they are part of a song, the combination of words and sound in an oral performance.[24] Recorded versions, however, are peculiar performances, because they have a fictitious character[25] and because they are often transformed by multitrack recordings and sound engineers. The sound as it is heard on record is almost never the sound as performed, and indeed many seamless performances are the result of editing and overdubbing (even "High Water" was slightly edited, with the order of the verses changed).[26]

Nonetheless, it is around recorded versions that audience expectations are created. This is a first level of memory work, which affects both the artist and the participants in a show. It is a common ground of reference, to which all the actors involved in the performance react in different ways, especially when Dylan's vocal delivery, and the arrangement, diverge from the canonic version. The memory of the song, in these cases, challenges the moment of performance, by providing an external marker of how Dylan should sound, a marker more recognizable than what happens in the moment. Yet, especially for the hardcore audience, songs have also become available independently of these canonic sources, and have been transformed by the experience of the Never Ending Tour and its performances, to occupy a position which is never close to what is expected, because they are surrounded by other songs, in a process that (especially in its first fifteen years) favored change, unpredictability, and contingency, whether in the arrangement or in Dylan's vocal delivery.

The closed system of references that one could retrieve in the released "High Water" was thus made richer by many other elements that have become available within the history of the song as performed in concert. "High Water" has acquired another life as a central piece of Dylan shows and as a song that could change thanks to subtle changes in the arrangement, in the banjo rolls, or in the way Dylan delivered it.[27] These changes affect—especially for the hardcore fans—the perception of the song, which becomes detached from the perceived original (the recorded version) and is incorporated into a process, i.e., the history of its performance, in which many different versions act as items for comparison.

What is compared, in this case, are other versions of the song. Tempo and lyrics do not change much, but the arrangement does, in a continuum that makes the song oscillate between rock and old-time music, thanks to the prominence of the guitar or the banjo, seen as two markers of different types of musical authenticity, the rock authenticity that Dylan has embodied for a long time, and the more traditional, or traditionalized, authenticity he has advocated for in the past decade.

At the same time, the fact that old-time music features so prominently in the song's themes (the flood) and references (the blues, Appalachian music) is an important aspect in performances "High Water." To some extent, the song is Dylan's manifesto for timelessness, which is achieved by the juxtaposition of contemporary elements that belong to the discourse of rock music as a genre, and musical forms that predate rock. From this point of view, "High Water" stands as a point of departure toward fragments of musical genres, themes, and topoi, to which it points and from which it gains strength and legitimacy. The reconstruction of this network is essential in order to understand how Dylan constructs the timelessness that some authors have identified as one of the peculiar characteristics of his modern work. This timelessness, rather than relying exclusively on the intertextual references of the lyrics, results more from Dylan's ability to trace connections between his song as performed on stage and the two subsectors of American musical memory that he has had to cope with in the Never Ending Tour, namely the memory of his own work (as held by the audience, with all its burden in terms of expectations and pressures to stay close to the record as a primary element of this memory) and the collective memory of vernacular music, which he seems to have explored with increased mastery when he has turned away from the mythic representation as a rock star and adopted the new, and more challenging, persona of an entrepreneur of tradition.

If we take this perspective, "High Water" is not only a song that changes dramatically even when it seems to stay close to the record, but also a song that is central in this process. As performed on stage, "High Water" brings forward memories of two distinct sets of songs, Dylan's and the tradition he has increasingly referred to. These are the two main pillars on which Dylan's contemporary authenticity is built, although they are unequally balanced both in the fans' perception and in the construction of the modern image of "Bob Dylan."

As an item of imagined tradition, "High Water" cannot escape its proximate references that are evident on record and are subject to subtle changes when it is performed on stage. As close as a live performance can be to its imagined or desired original, there have always been fragments that have brought it closer or farther away from its musical references, of which the fragments in the text (most notably, Ashley's) are just a side. Since at least during its first outings it was constructed around musician Larry Campbell's driving banjo, it is worth noting that most of the dialogue with the past is carried out by two actors on the stage, Campbell and Dylan, and by two very distinct, but almost never dissonant, instruments, the banjo and Dylan's voice.

The banjo, the most traditional instrument that can be heard in "High Water," is the door to the world Dylan is trying to bring to life—albeit a desperate life—in the song, as a direct reference to the white blues (again, a blackface trick). Thus, "The Coo Coo Bird" is explicitly mentioned, but sometimes the banjo accompaniment is more reminiscent of "Pretty Polly" than anything Ashley recorded in his life. Not as slow as Dock Boggs's iconic version, and nearly as fast as Ralph Stanley's bluegrass rendition, Campbell's and later Donnie Herron's banjo is able to provide sonic references to both versions, and in so doing opens a new territory of memory, where "High Water" fits not only in the distant tradition, but also in Dylan's canon as a song that reconnects the older Dylan to his first steps in the folk revival.

"Pretty Polly" is a song that Dylan played in his early days in Greenwich Village, and which later served as a source for his own "Ballad of Hollis Brown" (1962).[28] While he has never returned to "Pretty Polly" over the years, "Hollis Brown" has been a favorite of Dylan live sets. He played it frequently during the 1974 tour with the Band, sang it at the controversial Live Aid in

1985, and sometimes with Tom Petty and the Heartbreakers in 1986–87. It is therefore a song to which Dylan has returned several times and with different arrangements, and often has been subject to the Never Ending Tour logic of transformation and deconstruction. It entered the Never Ending Tour as an energetic electric track, but in two decades it has transformed into an electric ballad in a minor tonality that is driven—not surprisingly—by a haunting banjo. In other words, its distance from "High Water" has been reduced to the point that the songs are often interchangeable.

This traditionalization of Dylan's songs has often followed quite recognizable paths, especially when (starting from 1999) he decided to go back for a half-acoustic, half-electric concert (something he had not done since the 1966 tour with the Hawks). The roots of *"Love and Theft"* lie in the crossing of borders (from electric to acoustic) and in the exchange between Dylan's songs and the traditionals he played during that era, a "memory palace"[29] that included authentic singers ranging from Lead Belly to the Stanley Brothers and Elizabeth Cotten. The songs Dylan included in these sets (some of them performed acoustic for decades, others going back and forth from electric to acoustic), provided the ground for *"Love and Theft,"* not simply because the musical roots of the record can be found in these sets, but also because the acoustic sets provided the opportunity to traditionalize Dylan's material, by transformation and juxtaposition.

Dylan's own songs have been malleable and he has stretched their status and their place in his canon, struggling between a categorization in terms of rock pure and simple. "High Water" appeared in the set lists alongside some of the songs that Dylan had first recorded in his folk phase (or at its end) and that had gone through countless transformations during his career. Such is the case of another song that has ended up with changed references, and has been to some extent traditionalized, "It's Alright Ma (I'm Only Bleeding)" (1965).

"It's Alright Ma," like many songs from Dylan's early canon, winks more than once at traditional material, yet it is also perceived as one of the most distinctive among his works, especially because of the power of its lyric and its political, yet not topical, content. In the course of Dylan's career, it has been transfigured by many arrangements, both acoustic and electric. The same oscillation happened in the context of the Never Ending Tour, when it was at first a rarity, performed during the acoustic sets, and then a staple of Dylan's early 2000s shows in a slow, bluesy arrangement that gave less power to the music but was good for showcasing Dylan's phrasing and diction.

Then, for a few years, "It's Alright Ma" was almost overplayed, nearly at every show. In 2008, "High Water" and "It's Alright Ma" were often in the same set lists, even though at that point they were more or less interchangeable because they shared a similar arrangement that was centered on a haunting banjo line and on repetitive riffs played by electric guitar. This similar structure made the songs sound alike even though the differences in their trajectories should not be overlooked. As performed in concert, "High Water" is always reminiscent of its original released version, save for the absence of the banjo in 2003. "It's Alright Ma" is a different matter, though, because using traditional instruments in a central role in the performance served to highlight the song's link to tradition and to bracket its "originality" as a Dylan song. Versions of "It's Alright Ma" from 2008 (an unexceptional year when it comes to Dylan's performances, with the exception of this song) are almost an anachronism in themselves, so closely do they resemble songs that Clarence Ashley himself could have played in the 1920s.

In 2008 it became clear that "It's Alright Ma" is at the same time a different type of folk song and a rock anthem. It is a close relative of "Highway 51," which Dylan recorded early in his career, but also of the Everly Brothers' "Wake Up Little Susie" (1957), with which it shares a guitar riff. In its electric form, it has been a pounding rock number, filled with blues-rock echoes, on which Dylan declaimed the lyrics with a prophetic stance. It thus brings together two different streams of American music: the blues, with its riff on the pentatonic scale; and hillbilly music (itself immersed in the blues at more than one level), with its banjo.

The year 2008 saw the maximum convergence between the two songs, when "High Water" and "It's Alright Ma" were performed with a focus on their similarities and on the traditional roots that Dylan had made emerge as fundamental features of the songs. This type of memory work thus linked sectors of the Dylan canon and sectors of the tradition that he had used for inspiration. After that point "It's Alright Ma" almost disappeared, while "High Water" remains a central song in his shows.

While "High Water" and "It's Alright Ma" belong to different sectors of the Dylan canon, they have converged in performance, one successful in bringing some sense of the musical past to the present, the other crossing eras until a friction is created between its highly symbolist (and therefore modernist) lyrics, and the timeless arrangement of recent years, with echoes of early rock and roll and ancient country blues. Nor was this the only case of convergence and—through convergence—traditionalization. By traditionalizing his repertoire, Dylan has performed his detachment both from the established narrative of the 1960s (with its focus on the double, Janus-like figures of the folk troubadour and the pioneer of rock music) and from the limitations of a narrative that confines him exclusively to the realm inhabited by rock stars, with their global appeal and cross-generational fandom. From "Love and Theft" forward, both the 1960s and rock seem to be inadequate narrative templates when it comes to interpreting Dylan's work and the way he has performed his comeback during the late 1990s and the early 2000s.

The effectiveness of memory work, and the transformations that his own work has gone through when filtered through memory, has contributed to the creation of another side to Dylan's authenticity, which has been shaped mainly in live performance. The authenticity Dylan tried to explore[30] was a "tree with roots," deep in the heart of the "old, weird America." Now that Dylan's songs too belong to the "old, weird America," he can push them closer to the musical coordinates that lie at its foundations. In some cases, this process has involved the discovery of unexpected roots, as in the case of "It's Alright Ma." In others he has pursued pastness and timelessness as a strategy to present his material, to the point that many songs of his catalogue have received the *"Love and Theft"* treatment: jazz has influenced live performances of "If Dogs Run Free" (1970) and "Not Dark Yet"; the blues has come to prominence in many songs; countrified acoustic rock—or is it simply Americana?—has resurfaced in the versions of "The Ballad of Frankie Lee and Judas Priest" (1967) and "Fourth Time Around" (1966). "Desolation Row," meanwhile, has become a carnival bark, less surreal and more ironic. On Dylan's part, these efforts to traditionalize his past through fragments and traces can be less successful than they were at the turn of the century (due to the decline in his voice, but also to imaginative arrangements); yet the project has gone on, defining a more adequate picture of who he has been and is, and how he has achieved his position as a contemporary—and at the same time timeless—artist.

Bob Dylan's efforts in the remaking of a collective memory of American vernacular music lie deep in his logic of performing authenticity. The need to escape the Bob Dylan myth involved primarily a reconnection to the artist's work through the lenses of tradition, in a revisionist attempt to refocus the image of the artist. The diverse memory-projects that found their way in the Never Ending Tour—rearticulating the memory of "Bob Dylan" by the increased visibility of live performing, reworking his songbook, connecting it to other songs and visions of American music—have moved from the periphery of established representations about Dylan, which constitute the core of his artistic reputation. Memory work, in this sense, has often involved a struggle for the definition of the artist, with Dylan reclaiming the centrality of his songs by means of performance, challenging both recorded versions and the audience's expectations that are often constructed with reference to those versions. The project has gone against recorded versions, but also against the stability of the songs themselves as performed, with Dylan exploiting more and more his improvisational ability as a songster, exploring the interactions among these different projects of memory, which rest on the convergence of his traditionalized songs and the actualized tradition from which he has consistently drawn during the Never Ending Tour, even more than in other periods of his career.

This convergence between Dylan's reworked songs (especially those analyzed in this chapter), the fragments he has used as an intertextual and an interperformative *trait d'union* in his songs, and the work of others, contributes in different ways to the performance of authenticity. They highlight different aspects of his claim to cultural authority: the songs he has written are the source of his status for the wider audience; the fragments he incorporates—not considering the tiresome debate about "plagiarism"—connect the modern Dylan to both his roots in the folk revival, and to a broader tradition, which comes to the surface in full force by his ability as a songster who masters at least a hundred years of American vernacular music. Performances, especially in the period until *Modern Times*, act as moments of condensation, where the trajectory of individual songs (regardless of their origin and their originality), detached from the memory of its recording, are tweaked by proximity and similarity. Some of these songs have inhabited the territory of Dylan's performances for decades, like in the case of "It's Alright Ma," or have become staples during the last decade, like "High Water," two songs that—together with "Ballad of Hollis Brown" and the earlier "John Brown" (1962)—constitute a set of songs that contribute to the traditionalization of Dylan and challenge the reproduction of his 1960s image (ironically, three of these songs belong to the folk and acoustic phase of Dylan's career). Other changes have been subtler, because they have regarded the role played by songs in the acoustic set, the moments in the shows in which Dylan was more open to the production of convergence. Many of these songs were either originally solo acoustic and played with the full band during the Never Ending Tour, or "electric" rock tracks that were brought closer to the imagined tradition that has fed Dylan's late career.

Dylan's claims to authenticity have informed these songs, in the arrangements, the instrumentation, and also the performance style. There has been, in other words, a centrality of performance in the production of timelessness (a concept that results from the complex interplay of social times and performative claims about the present and the past) that is an essential part of Dylan's late career. The Never Ending Tour has extended the occasions in which this play was possible, because only during the Never Ending Tour could Dylan's old songs find a new environment. Their references are to be found outside the clichés of rock music, closer to the pre-rock sounds that he cherishes. The interplay between the old and the new, different sides of collective memory (the memory of Dylan for his audience, and the memory of his songs) are reshaped consciously in this project, whose ultimate consequence has been the softening of the boundaries between Dylan and his tradition, and—an important and often overlooked consequence—the shaping of a new Dylan who compresses his songs into the present format of his performance, thus bringing them into a present of anachronistic sound and vision, while at the same time locating his own songs closer to their distant roots.

NOTES

1. Benedict Giamo, "Bob Dylan's Protean Style," in *Refractions of Bob Dylan: Cultural Appropriations of an American Icon*, Eugen Banauch, ed. (Manchester, UK: Manchester University Press, 2015).

2. Andrea Cossu, *It Ain't Me, Babe: Bob Dylan and the Performance of Authenticity* (Boulder, CO: Paradigm, 2012).

3. Howard S. Becker, *Art Worlds* (Chicago: University of Chicago Press, 1982); Tia DeNora, *Beethoven and the Construction of Genius: Musical Politics in Vienna, 1792–1803* (Berkeley: University of California Press, 1995).

4. The notion of entrepreneur as used here is explicitly sociological, and has less to do with patterns of economic accumulation than it has with the establishment of symbolic value and the accumulation of symbolic capital (Bourdieu 1977) in the form of prestige and status. In a sense, reputational entrepreneurs (Fine 1996) are the agents involved in the production of specific representations about historical figures and, in this specific case, artists and artistic work. While they may also have an economic interest in the making of symbolic capital (for example, the role Albert Grossman played in shaping Dylan's early career), their aims are more nuanced. What they hold as a significant stake in the process of reputation making is the establishment and circulation of representation about artists and their work as symbolic resources that can be used in a social context where they resonate with established themes and with a broader culture.

5. Gary A. Fine, "Reputational Entrepreneurs and the Memory of Incompetence: Melting Supporters, Partisan Warriors, and Images of President Harding," *American Journal of Sociology* 101(5) (1996); and *Difficult Reputations: Collective Memories of the Evil, Inept, and Controversial* (Chicago: University of Chicago Press, 2001).

6. Sociologists of artistic reputation often stress the cooperative, networked activity that socially constructs artistic talent and genius. Rather than supporting a charismatic, artist-oriented theory of artistic reputation, according to which the artist is the primary source of his own talent, they focus more on the conditions, the opportunities, and the activities that allow talent and recognition to emerge. Reputational entrepreneurs are crucial figures in this

process, because they are able to intervene in the construction of representations about the artist and broadcasting to a wider audience. Not all these efforts can be successful, however, because the presence of three features is required: the successful reputational entrepreneur must have an interest in shaping a reputation in a certain way (motivation); the reputational account should be "credible" for the entrepreneur and "plausible" to significant audiences (narrative facility); and finally, the reputational entrepreneur must be in a structural position in which those claims "gain credence and are spread by virtue of the placement of their maker" (Fine 1996, 1162–63). Among the relevant "reputational entrepreneurs" who have shaped Dylan's career (especially in its early phase) one needs to mention Albert Grossman, Izzy Young, Pete Seeger, and Joan Baez. Over the past two decades, Dylan's manager Jeff Rosen has risen to prominence as the curator of the majority of Dylan's retrospective releases such as *The Bootleg Series*. See Andrea Cossu, "Poetry, Politics, and America: Awards and the Memorialization of Bob Dylan," *Celebrity Studies* 4(2) (2013): 235–37.

7. Wilentz, *Bob Dylan in America*, 263.

8. Mikal Gilmore, "Bob Dylan" *Rolling Stone*, November 22, 2001.

9. Jon Pareles, "A Wiser Voice Blowin' in the Autumn Wind," *New York Times*, September 28, 1997.

10. Lee Marshall, *Bob Dylan: The Never Ending Star* (Oxford, UK: Polity, 2007).

11. Sean Wilentz, *Bob Dylan in America* (New York: Doubleday, 2010).

12. Philip Ennis, *The Seventh Stream: The Emergence of Rock and Roll in American Popular Music* (Middletown: Wesleyan University Press, 1992).

13. Elizabeth Brake, "You can always come back, but you can't come back all the way: Freedom and the past in Dylan's recent work," in D. Boucher and G. Browning, eds., *The Political Art of Bob Dylan* (Upton Pyne, UK: Imprint Academic, 2009), 185.

14. Michael Pickering and Emily Keightley, "The Modalities of Nostalgia," *Current Sociology* 54(6) (2006): 923.

15. Svetlana Boym, *The Future of Nostalgia* (New York: Basic Books, 2001).

16. Derek Barker, *The Songs He Didn't Write: Bob Dylan Under the Influence* (New Malden, UK: Chrome Dreams, 2008).

17. Marshall, *Bob Dylan: The Never Ending Star*.

18. Eric Lott, "Love and Theft in *'Love and Theft'*" and *Love and Theft*; A. L. Nielsen, "Crow Jane Approximately: Bob Dylan's Black Masque," in *Highway 61 Revisited: Bob Dylan's Road from Minnesota to the World*, C. J. Sheehy and T. Swiss, eds. (Minneapolis: University of Minnesota Press, 2009), 186–96; R. Reginio, "Nettie Moore: Minstrelsy and the Cultural Economy of Race in Bob Dylan's Late Albums," in *Highway 61 Revisited: Bob Dylan's Road from Minnesota to the World*, 213–24.

19. Clinton Heylin, *Still on the Road: The Songs of Bob Dylan Vol. 2: 1974–2008* (London: Constable, 2010), 461.

20. Yaffe, *Bob Dylan: Like a Complete Unknown*.

21. Robert Hilburn, "Rock's Enigmatic Poet Opens a Long-Private Door," *Los Angeles Times*, April 4, 2004.

22. Heylin, *Still on the Road*, 461.

23. Paul Williams, *Bob Dylan: Mind Out of Time, Performing Artist 1986–1990 and Beyond* (London: Omnibus Press, 2004): Andrew Muir, *Razor's Edge: Bob Dylan and the Never Ending Tour* (London: Helter Skelter, 2001).

24. Betsy Bowden, *Performed Literature: Words and Music by Bob Dylan* (Bloomington: Indiana University Press, 1982), 1.

25. S. Frith, *Performing Rites: On the Value of Popular Music* (Cambridge: Harvard University Press, 1996). Recorded versions, as Frith argues, create the impression of a performance, the illusion that what we hear is the faithful recreation of something that has taken place in the studio. On the contrary, songs as they are released are the result of editing, engineering, multitrack recording, and overdubs. As such, they are a constructed "text" more than they are a performance of that text. This point would be worthy of further analysis with regard to Dylan's own disdain for modern techniques of recording.

26. See Damien Love, "Recording with Bob Dylan: Chris Shaw Tells All," *Uncut*, November 2008.

27. In 2013, when Dylan scripted the show including two different sets and an intermission, "High Water" was part of a subset of songs that opened and closed the main sets: "Things Have Changed," "Love Sick," "High Water," and "Long and Wasted Years" (2012). In many cases, these were also the highlights of a show constructed in such a way to showcase the "modern" Dylan, with hardly any songs from the 1960s and 1970s.

28. Todd Harvey, *The Formative Dylan: Transmission and Stylistic Influences 1961–1963* (Lanham, MD: Scarecrow Press, 2001).

29. Robert Polito, "Bob Dylan's Memory Palace," in *Highway 61 Revisited: Bob Dylan's Road from Minnesota to the World*, 140–53.

30. Richard A. Peterson, *Creating Country Music: Fabricating Authenticity* (Chicago: University of Chicago Press, 1997); Cossu, *It Ain't Me, Babe*.

CHAPTER FOUR

TEMPEST, BOB DYLAN, AND THE BARDIC ARTS

Anne Margaret Daniel

It was inevitable, upon the release of a record titled *Tempest*, that Bob Dylan would be likened—yet again—to William Shakespeare. *The Tempest* (ca. 1611) was Shakespeare's last completed play. Would this be Dylan's last album of original songs? Would he now, like Prospero, give up his spells, break his staff, and drown his book? Dylan himself tried to slide out of the comparisons and speculations in his *Rolling Stone* interview, hinging humorously on an article, and telling Mikal Gilmore, "Shakespeare's last play was called *The Tempest*. It wasn't just called *Tempest*. The name of my record is just plain *Tempest*. It's two different titles."[1]

Give Dylan credit, please, for a sense of humor. Not many people do, spending too much time in twitching awe. Like Shakespeare, Dylan inspires such a reaction—yet, like Shakespeare, he can also be funny as hell. Dwelling in the admitted darkness of *Tempest* is romance, good humor, and intricate patterns of both rhyme and sound. The perfect-ten tracks of this record come straight to us from a bard's ear and a poet's pen; I daresay *Tempest* shows Bob Dylan to be every bit a Renaissance man. Just how Shakespearean, in all the multitudinous meanings of the word, is *Tempest*, though?

Dylan's Shakespeare references in the past have ranged from the patent—like Shakespeare in the alley ("Stuck Inside of Mobile with the Memphis Blues Again" [1966]), Ophelia 'neath the window ("Desolation Row" [1965]), and Othello and Desdemona ("Po' Boy" [2001])—to the subtler. A line from *Measure for Measure* (1604) floats into "Mississippi"; Mercutio's "time out o' mind" from his glorious Queen Mab speech in *Romeo and Juliet* (ca. 1592-97) turns into an album title. These shout-outs and quotations have been itemized and chronicled. Additionally, Dylan has been much compared to Shakespeare as a wordsmith, poet, chronicler of his times, and genius.

What interests me more, and particularly in terms of *Tempest*, are those patterns of rhyme and sound I mention in the paragraph above. I would bet that Bob Dylan knows the parts of some of Shakespeare's leading actors by heart—and many of the sonnets, too. In the lyrics of *Tempest*'s songs, his syntax often sounds much like that of Renaissance English. In the melodies, the simple instruments and musical lines could have floated out of the Globe on an afternoon when the flag flew, to let Elizabethan London know the play was about to begin.

This sensibility has been with Dylan a long time. As a young man, he learned folk music and plainsong, ballads and sea chanteys, the plaints of the Appalachians and epics of the Highlands. Read the *Foxfire* books (1972–2004)—the way people talk in Fines Creek, North Carolina; Greeneville, Tennessee; and Big Stone Gap, Virginia, is the closest thing we can hear today to the King's English, or rather to Queen Elizabeth's. The idioms and deliveries, phrasings and syntax of speech dating back to Shakespeare's day are alive and well in Dylan's *Tempest*—to me, a far more interesting link to Shakespeare than the record's title.

Melodically, the sound of the record is unique—thanks, surely, to the musicians on it, headed by Los Lobos musician David Hidalgo, but also to "Jack Frost," Dylan's nom de plume as producer. Dylan has produced his own records as Frost before (*"Love and Theft"* and *Modern Times*), yet none sound like this one. There are no bells and whistles on this record, except for real, old-fashioned ones. Overproduction and electronics are blissfully absent; many of the instruments that sound out on *Tempest* are ones extant for many centuries. Hidalgo, with an accordion in his hands, can sound like a harmonica or a whole horn section. Simple strings propel the songs—a slappy thump of the bass, Donnie Herron's light bright fiddle, the touch of a guitar that sounds like a lute, the plink of a piano more harpsichord than honky-tonk.

The simplicity of the sound of the instruments reflects in every melody. "Duquesne Whistle" showcases a two-note wah-wah rise and fall; "Scarlet Town" and "Long and Wasted Years" make it a three-note rise and fall, minus the wah-wah. Some of the songs are more recited than sung, reminding me that, for all the songs in his plays, we do not know the actual music that accompanied Shakespeare's words. The title track and "Roll On John" conclude *Tempest* with very few notes used indeed.

Moreover, Dylan's use of rhyme enriches *Tempest*; the album resounds with rhyming couplets, internal rhymes, and alliteration; great, snappy, unexpected rhymes; bitter tragic rhymes; elegant baroque rhymes; simple one-syllable unforgettables. The words fit into the music perfectly: two simple notes, two short words, and a rhyme nail you to your seat as surely as do those couplets ending a Shakespearean scene, and yet, Dylan makes the rhyme unpredictable, unexpected. For every bed/head, wrong/long, one/done, Dylan rhymes "God" with "firing squad" or "dancers twirled" with "the underworld." Shakespeare's rhymes are richest in *A Midsummer Night's Dream* (ca. 1590–97), written in verse, and most memorable and sharp in *Hamlet* (ca. 1599–1602) and *The Tempest*, where they are scant and therefore resonant when they occur—chiefly in couplets. In *Hamlet* they mark the end of a speech or scene, and are usually Hamlet's words: "I have that within which passeth show / These but the trappings and the suits of woe,"[2] or "the time is out of joint, O cursed spite / That ever I was born to set it right!"[3] In Shakespeare's *The Tempest*, couplets are almost entirely confined to the songs, from Ariel's lyrics to the sailors' drunken ditties to Caliban's chant of revolt: "'Ban, 'ban, Ca-caliban / Has a new master: get a new man." Prospero's final prologue, too, is in verse, and in it he hands off the power to create, and break, a spell to the clapping hands of his audience. It is important to note that—despite repeatedly saying he intends to—he has not relinquished any of his powers until applause happens, people are leaving the great Globe, and the play is over.

The way Dylan uses words, the command he has over them, and the number of them he knows and deploys to immense effect are all among the things I love most about his songwriting. He's a conjurer with words. At the beginning of *Henry V* (ca. 1600), the Chorus yearns for "a Muse of Fire, that would ascend / The brightest heaven of invention"[4] and brings us, in reality, to witness Henry, his army, the French powers, and the battle of Agincourt. That Muse of Fire is a combination of language and imagination. The poets supply the former, and we the latter—encouraged, in a metadramatic moment, by the language. Shakespeare got it. Dylan gets it.

The first song on *Tempest* conjures up a journey, and doesn't a good journey begin with the whistle of a leaving train? "Duquesne" is an odd name, and fun to say, if you know how to pronounce it. It is also a town that seems to be lost in the middle of nowhere, but that hooks up to anywhere by train. But which Duquesne is it, anyway? They're all over the American map—including one in Arizona that's a ghost town now. As *Tempest* was released, a Pittsburgh, Pennsylvania, newspaper ran an article saying Bob Dylan had written a new song about the Duquesne Steel Works and Andrew Carnegie.

Certainly, there are modern, twentieth-century moments in the song. Yet the archaic phrases, and past-times syntax particularly, are what strike me from the first. The blowing whistle and the repeated blowing echo the raging of *King Lear* (ca. 1605–6) in Act III, Scene 2. Ian Bell had a good point when he said that all the critics looking for Prospero in Dylan's *Tempest* would have found "a better fit" with Lear.⁵ Remember, too, the winter wind blowing in one of the best-known songs from *As You Like It* (1599)—like *The Tempest* a story of a nobleman in exile who returns triumphant. "You old rascal" is a standout line in a play called *Sir John Oldcastle*—published anonymously in 1600, and then, in 1619, as Shakespeare's. Critics are still debating whether or not he had a hand in it. "Break of day," with its singular and unmodern phrasing, isn't from some sentimental song of the early 1900s. Shakespeare loves the phrase, and uses it in his sonnets and his plays—most relevantly in *The Merchant of Venice* and in the context of music:

> And what is music then? Then music is
> Even as the flourish when true subjects bow
> To a new-crowned monarch. Such it is
> As are those dulcet sounds in break of day
> That creep into the dreaming bridegroom's ear
> And summon him to marriage.⁶

Likewise, that beautifully redundant, extra-deadly "kill me dead" is Shakespeare's. The devastated Titus Andronicus from the eponymous play (ca. 1588–93), showing his violated, mutilated daughter Lavinia to the people of Rome, was the first to use the phrase: "he that wounded her / Hath hurt me more than had he killed me dead."⁷ Similarly, in *Hamlet* the Player Queen, asserting her faith to the Player King in the lines Hamlet has written to turn "The Murder of Gonzago" into "The Mousetrap," intones the chilling couplet, "A second time I kill my husband dead / When second husband kisses me in bed."⁸

"Soon After Midnight" is when some people's days begin, true. It is when lovers can meet, at "morrow deep midnight," and it is when ghosts walk, as Hamlet begins with the clock having "now struck twelve." It is also when revelry of illicit sorts ensues: Falstaff and Master Shallow, hearing those chimes at midnight as young men in the company of the "bona-robas." Dylan gives us a whole brothelful of folks, here, and things are sexy at first but bloody later. Both Shakespeare's Titania, the fairy queen, and Edmund Spenser's *Faerie Queene* (1590–96), are recalled as midnight dates as well. What about the old-fashioned "sing your praises"? Yes, it is English Renaissance, first used variously in the King James Bible of 1611, and by Ben Jonson in *The Alchemist* (1610). As the song ends, the ladies may treat him kindly—despite his violent bent—but where the singer really wants to be, "more than ever," ma'am, is with you. That "more than ever" may not sound Shakespearean, but it is, as is the preceding "it's now or never" (first recorded use: 1560). In *A Midsummer Night's Dream*, and in *Much Ado About Nothing* (1598–99), Shakespeare uses "more than ever" in the context of lovers meeting.

The lilt of long-ago language makes Dylan's *Tempest* sound more Elizabethan than do evident individual quotations like "I came to bury, not to praise." In the context of "Pay in Blood," Dylan is not being ironic: he is there to bury, and nowise to praise, unlike Mark Antony. And in "Early Roman Kings" it may not be a terrible stretch to want to find in, say, "distributing the corn" a circumstance crucial to the plot of *Coriolanus* (1605–8), or in the jump from a "blood-clotted rag" to a waving strawberry-spotted handkerchief that seals Desdemona's doom in *Othello* (1603).

The Shakespearean flipping of word order, the loose and easy play of subjects, objects, verbs, adjectives, and adverbs upsets subject-object-verb, with modifying words clinging to the main ones. In this sense, Dylan clearly loves the Renaissance freedom of linguistic inversion and unconstraint. The ballad "Tin Angel" is particularly full of inverted phrases like "onward he went," "never again this world you'll see," and "his blood did flow." This befits a ballad, which is, after all, one of the earliest English song forms—but the same phrasing is among the modern words of the other tracks.

"Narrow Way" begins with a singer trying to get back "in my right mind," or, as King Lear would say, "in my perfect mind." This track, and the ensuing standout song "Long and Wasted Years," are full of the consonant alliterations Shakespeare uses constantly in his plays ("Seems, Madam! Nay, it is. I know not seems"[9]) and poetry ("sessions of sweet silent thought"[10]). Dylan clearly relishes the "s"es in "Long and Wasted Years" these days, as he half sings, half chants the lines—with increasing variation—in concert. There are zinger couplets and patterned internal rhymes, a trail of linguistic breadcrumbs to a rocking gritty beat that leads from one harsh, remarkable image to another. The song's title being withheld until the end, and then drawn out in a hissing, snaky line in Dylan's intense, bitingly enunciated voice, is genius.

Of all the songs on *Tempest*, "Scarlet Town" is, in its musical antecedents, closest to Shakespeare's day. The Scottish ballad "Barbara Allen" was not published until the late 1690s, but was being sung well before—as is so often the case with the oldest song-stories, we do not know exactly how long. Samuel Pepys, in 1666, called it "Barbary Allen"; though it is unlikely to have anything to do with North Africa, it might.[11] Dylan's lyrics, while echoing the "where I was born" and Sweet William on his deathbed, try almost militantly to be modern by the end, as if fighting their way out from under the weight of such a celebrated song and proving themselves. "Set 'em up, Joe," the singer challenges, sitting with his "flat-chested junkie whore." Yet in the end, the language falls back into the Elizabethan King James Bible, Ecclesiastes keeping company with Shakespeare's "Sonnet XIX" (1609) ("Devouring Time, blunt thou the lion's paws"[12]).

"Early Roman Kings" is a rhyming romp—lecherous and treacherous, peddlers and meddlers. It uses rhyme in a spell-casting way, as playwrights, by Shakespeare's day, had just begun to do. As previously noted, rhyming couplets, of which "Early Roman Kings" is entirely composed, serve to punch out an ending or render lines easy to recall. The Muddy Waters riff that drives "Mannish Boy" (1955), which Muddy in turn got from a hundred older bluesmen, pulls the words along in a river. The couplets turn it into sort of a voodoo song, with all the Roman kings dressed up like Baron Samedis. They're not in togas or on coins, but in their sharkskin suits, in their top hats and tails, nailed in their coffins (so they can't get out, presumably—though beware, they *do*). All the centuries are jumbled together like tossed cards—which, when you think about it, is pretty much the way human history goes down, and always will. When the singer starts cautioning you, near the end, that he's going to start acting like an early Roman king, stay on your toes. Or, better yet, head for the hills. That "Gonna shake 'em all down" sounds contemporary, or at least twentieth century; automatically, we associate shakedown with the Grateful Dead, yet, it too is Shakespeare's. Merriam-Webster lists its first use in 1859, but Shakespeare riffed it, with a double meaning, into *Coriolanus* before 1609.

"Tin Angel" is another ballad and an even darker one than "Scarlet Town"—though not as tragic as the title track. The setting is Scotland meets Mexico, a borderline Dylan loves: the bonnie bonnie banks of the Rio Grande. The plot of "Tin Angel" derives from traditional songs "The Raggle Taggle Gypsy" and "Gypsy Davy," with a dash of "Lord Darnell" thrown in. It is also rather *Romeo and Juliet*. Whenever a woman pulls out a knife and kills herself with it, between her two dead lovers both identified, variously, as her husbands, I have to think of poor Juliet. As in "Early Roman Kings," the diction is high and low, with antique and elegant words and phrases mixing with modernspeak in perfect chiasmus. And why not? We have such a rich language in English; use it all. Shakespeare did; he used old words, new words, words he'd just heard in the London streets, words he made up, nouns he verbed, and other parts of speech he switched and shifted. Words don't go away; we just keep making up more of them, and there is a wealth of ones in English alone that have fallen out of use. "Tin Angel" brings them back home. Here, people lower themselves on golden chains, and crumple at the waist like twisted pins; they feed their eyes and bow the heart, if not the knee. Recall Claudius, struggling to pray for the brother he's murdered in *Hamlet*: "Bow, stubborn knees; and heart, with strings of steel...."[13] It all feels fated, like a good ballad, and like any good tragedy. That the unnamed "murderous queen," her lover (or husband) "Old Henry Lee," and her pursuing husband all end up in a heap together, thrown in a hole, seems appropriate.

Dylan's song "Tempest" is a verbal and musical flood, less a matter of a particular ship sinking than the waters constantly rising and rising. From the setup for this nearly quarter-hour song (the scene of a woman in a saloon, getting ready to sing the song about the Great Ship), with its rolling, flowing 1–2–3 waltz ripple-beat, to the fade-out of its conclusion, "Tempest" is a mesmerizing ballad. It feels like someone is dangling a watch in front of your face, swinging it back and forth as what is going to happen inexorably comes to pass. You know the history of *Titanic*, you know the stories made of it from novels to recent movies (most notably the 1997 film *Titanic*, directed by James Cameron), and you can't stop it, you just have to sit there and respect it. As you listen, you bear witness. The ship's watchman is a perfect recurring figure to keep you company, watching along with you (he reminds me of the fez-wearing desk clerk in "Black Diamond Bay" [1976], also a cataclysmic Dylan ballad). The watchman's a fine character for a refrain, seen dozing while dancers circle; seen later as the ship begins to go down; and seen wanting, finally, to send a message to someone when it's far too late. The images are powerful: the dark cold sky full of stars; wealthy industrialist John Jacob Astor kissing his darling wife; even actor Leonardo DiCaprio (who starred in Cameron's film) and his sketchpad. Leonardo appears again, with Cleo this time, later in the song. He, and she, will make Dylanologists run amok linking DiCaprio and Cleopatra, I expect: two people famous for being in boats. After all, Cleo has that barge, in which she makes her triumphal entrance for Antony in *Antony and Cleopatra* (ca. 1607), one of the most famous, doomed, spectacular scenes in all of Shakespeare. What people won't concentrate on is what is simplest and happiest for a song: the fact that Leo and Cleo rhyme. The use of the film *Titanic* is good, and smart—it shows awareness, without judging the fact, that Cameron's film is what "Titanic" means to most people today. Like me, Dylan has remembered that stunning scene of the drowned woman in her long gown, floating in the risen waters above the elaborate staircase as if she's dancing; he refers to it powerfully. Certain lines, like the one about petals falling from the vases of fresh flowers in a first-class area, are particularly lyric. As I listened to this song, though, I thought about Noah and Hurricane Katrina in 2005 as much as I did about *Titanic*, possibly even more. To call it epic is not too strong.

How does Shakespeare's *The Tempest* figure in, if it does? There is no slow progression at its beginning, no stately ship steaming across a chilly sea. Shakespeare's *Tempest* begins in chaos, as the ship is splitting and the wet mariners (one of the few stage directions in Shakespeare) call goodbye to each other and their absent families. It takes some time before we come to know that it is all a dream; the ship did not really sink. The king is not lying five fathoms down in the water; the prince is not dead at sea. Dylan's song "Tempest," meanwhile, ends with the watchman lying and dreaming of the sinking of *Titanic*. If only a magic wand like Prospero's, a charm like the ones Ariel weaves, could be waved and woven over history; if only that iceberg could have been seen in time.

Unlike "Tempest," which eulogizes a number of people and events, "Roll On John" is an elegy. When you write an elegy paying tribute to one who has died, you use forms and models and all the elegies that have come before. When Milton wrote an elegy for his drowned friend Edward King, he used Greek models and translated lines from odes. When Shelley wrote "Adonais" (1821) for Keats, he used Milton; when Yeats elegized Robert Gregory, he used Shelley; when Auden elegized Yeats, he used Yeats. Shakespeare might, or might not, have written a funeral elegy for Mr. William Peter. He did write plenty of elegiac speeches in his plays, from the lengthy (Mark Antony's aforementioned praising of Caesar under the guise of burying him) to the searingly brief, as in *Hamlet*, speaking of his dead father: "He was a man, take him for all and all; I shall not look upon his like again."[14]

The title of this song is taken from an old folk tune Dylan sang fifty years ago, "Roll On, John," with his best-known performance of it coming on a radio show in March 1962. The old "Roll On, John" is a song of abandoned love and sunsets, travel and lonesomeness. The plaint of the refrain of that old tune is that John rolls on so slow. What breaks the heart, here, is the fact that John Lennon shone brightly for such a short time on this earth. Roughly the same age as Dylan, Lennon was just forty when he was killed, and his murder profoundly affected Dylan. The images in this song follow Lennon's musical life as a young man, from the Liverpool docks to the Hamburg streets, to the Quarrymen in the cellar, and on to New York. Yet there are also powerful images of silencing and captivity, things John never, ever put up with. A stanza about slave ships sailing the Atlantic, focusing on a man's mouth clamped shut, is stunning, and strangely reminiscent of the beginning of *The Tempest* and the "still-vexed Bermoothes" (*The Tempest*, Act 1 Scene 2 line 272) as well as of Ariel's longtime captivity. All the cast of the play, of course, are "cooped up on an island," as Dylan sings of Lennon. Whether Dylan means for the island to be what Lord Byron called "that tight little island" of England, or rock-ribbed, skyscraper-hemmed Manhattan, is unclear. The possibilities of life in a new world are fraught with old-style western ambush, Indian attack, being shot in the back: painful listening, as you remember that morning in December when most of us heard of Lennon's death. The final stanza is a gorgeous surprise; tying together the song's refrain of Lennon's having burned so bright in a perfect circle of the personal and the poetic "Tyger, tyger, burning bright ... Cover him over and let him sleep." You cannot but hear the echo, and the comfort, here, of "our little life is rounded with a sleep."

Dylan may be a modern Renaissance man, with possible kinships to Prospero, as many critics speculated upon with the release of *Tempest*. But this Prospero is not about to shuffle off into his study and leave things to Ferdinand and Miranda—any more than is the character in Shakespeare's play. Read your Shakespeare closely. At the end of *The Tempest*, Prospero is heading back to Milan to resume his position as head of one of Europe's richest dukedoms. He promises, early in Act V, to break his staff and drown his book, yet he has not done so yet. He just says that he will. That ringing epilogue to the play is spoken by him, and it does not give up a single thing. Instead, it draws us, the audience, into kinship—into cahoots—with him. We are all the spellbinders and spell-breakers together: master mage, and eager new followers.

If that's not entertainment, I don't know what is. Those who would like to find Dylan in this particular role as Prospero: go for it. You can still see him, most nights during the year, making his magic and then removing his hat, or raising his hands (one often holding a harmonica) in acknowledgment, freed by that applause to move on to the next town down the road, or over the sea.

NOTES

1. Mikal Gilmore, "Bob Dylan on His Dark New Album, Tempest," *Rolling Stone*, August 1, 2012. www.rollingstone.com/music/news/bob-dylan-unleashed-a-wild-ride-on-his-new-lp-and-striking-back-at-critics-20120927.
2. William Shakespeare, *Hamlet*, Act I, Scene 2, lines 87–88.
3. Ibid., Act I, Scene 5, lines 189–90.
4. William Shakespeare, *Henry V*, Prologue, lines 1–2.

5. Ian Bell, *Time Out of Mind: The Lives of Bob Dylan* (Pegasus, 2014), 520.
6. William Shakespeare, *The Merchant of Venice*, Act III, Scene 2, lines 48–53.
7. William Shakespeare, *Titus Andronicus*, Act III, Scene 1, lines 93–94.
8. Shakespeare, *Hamlet*, Act III, Scene 2, lines 184–85.
9. Shakespeare, *Hamlet*, Act I, Scene 2, line 79.
10. William Shakespeare, Sonnet 30, line 1.
11. Samuel Pepys, *Diary, Volume 41: January/February 1665-66* (January 2). www.gutenberg.org/ebooks/4163.mobile.
12. William Shakespeare, Sonnet 19, line 1.
13. Shakespeare, *Hamlet*, Act III, Scene 3, line 70.
14. *Hamlet*, Act I, Scene 2, lines 195–96.

CHAPTER FIVE

YOU CAN'T REPEAT THE PAST? BOB DYLAN'S *"LOVE AND THEFT"* AND THE EVENTS OF 9/11

Jesper Doolaard

On September 11, 2001, Bob Dylan's *"Love and Theft"* was released in the United States. Expectations were high, as it followed Dylan's most critically lauded and commercially successful album in decades, *Time Out of Mind*. *"Love and Theft"* managed to meet these expectations, and was received enthusiastically by both the general public and critics as a worthy successor to *Time Out of Mind*. After the comparatively lackluster output of the 1980s and early 1990s, the success of *"Love and Theft"* definitively confirmed Dylan's artistic renaissance in the new millennium.

That same day, the whole world watched as two airplanes crashed into the Twin Towers. The gruesome terrorist attacks on New York City, which are commonly referred to by their date "9/11," had far-reaching consequences on the global political landscape. In the United States, these events were widely interpreted as a sudden rupture, a definite turning point: a "world of certainty," which had existed since the end of the Cold War, was now "shaken to the core by the atrocities of 9/11."[1]

The fact that the release of *"Love and Theft"* coincided with the 9/11 terrorist attacks strongly affected the album's immediate reception. This association was particularly strong due to the lyrical and thematic content of the album, which somehow seemed to "fit" the events of 9/11—fit them so well, in fact, that it led some reviewers to ascribe Dylan a prophetic quality. For example, discussing *"Love and Theft"* in a review for *Village Voice*, Greg Tate asks: "What did Dylan know, and when did he know it?"[2] Tate's suggestion that Dylan was somehow in the know about the 9/11 attacks is a tongue-in-cheek reference to conspiracy plots, rather than a serious proposal. However, his question does offer an interesting starting point for an investigation into the unique relationship between *"Love and Theft"* and the events of 9/11.

The connection between art and 9/11 has been a subject of lively debate ever since the terrorist attacks. Much of this debate has centered around the question of how "post-9/11 art" can help reflect on, or help deal with, the trauma of the 9/11 events. Many critics have suggested delineating genres of post-9/11 art in order to study its effects properly. Specifically, the sub-genre of the literature of trauma, which is focused on one specific traumatic event, shows the kaleidoscopic response to the events of 9/11. Kristiaan Versluys, for instance, developed the genre of "9/11 fiction" to analyze the similarities between North American and European literature in dealing with 9/11. In his article "9/11 as a European Event: The Novels" (2007) and again in his full-length study *Out of the Blue* (2009), Versluys uses the literary responses to the events of 9/11 to underline the existence of a "continuing Western, transatlantic discursive community, sharing essential values and traditions."[3] Other constructions of genres of 9/11 art and literature show more challenging approaches to the nature of these traumatic experiences. Some critics question the traumatic effect of the 9/11 attacks. Richard Gray, for instance, developed the term "fiction after 9/11," which "encompasses a broader array of literature written in the time after the events of 9/11," challenging "the adage that 9/11 'changed everything.'"[4] Other critics are less optimistic about the role of art in relation to these events. With his genre of "literature of terror," for instance, Martin Randall aims to "challenge the ability of texts to adequately respond to the events of September 11."[5]

It is possible to read *"Love and Theft"* in relation to the events of 9/11. To do so raises interesting points about the events of 9/11; about their distorted temporality, about the nature of the "event," and about the way works of art can deal with trauma. What emerges is a reading of the album focused around the theme of the prophetic. Through the figure of the prophetic narrator in *"Love and Theft"* and his failed attempts at predicting future events, the album offers up a complicated message regarding the traumatic events of 9/11 and the way we can try to come to terms with them.

9/11: TRAUMATIC EVENTS AND TEMPORALITY

Most critics writing about 9/11 agree that the terrorist attacks that occurred on September 11 can be considered a "major event." They were an unprecedented and, in a certain way, incomprehensible occurrence that had traumatizing effects on a personal, but also on a national and international level. To understand their impact more precisely, we can turn to Sigmund Freud, who coined the term *Nachträglichkeit* ("afterward-ness") in order to describe the effects that lie at the heart of trauma. He understood the trauma experience as a distorting effect on the *temporal* experience of the subject. The "afterward-ness" points to a disconnect between the event occurring in time and the comprehension of the event itself. Our consciousness cannot absorb the shock of the event, because it "spans an individual's temporal continuum, constituting her past, present and future," "skewing temporal experience in general."[6]

Arguably the most comprehensible and elegant analysis of the nature of the traumatic experience of 9/11 is offered by French philosopher Jacques Derrida. In an extensive interview given in the months after September 11, Derrida discusses 9/11 and its relation to time and linear temporality. He notes that 9/11 "marks a date." The events of 9/11 have, or are *constructed* to have, "truly made its mark"; they have all the characteristics of a traumatic, "singular, and, as they say here [in America], 'unprecedented' event." The fact that we refer to the attacks as "9/11," Derrida argues, is already a sign of its traumatic nature, as it shows our inability to grasp its concept or meaning. The repetitive chant of the date 9/11 is an attempt to respond to the "powerlessness to name in an appropriate fashion";[7] the endless repetition stresses the uniqueness of the ungraspable events of September 11, 2001, the unimaginable and unprecedented qualities that we cannot otherwise express.

At the same time, Derrida notes, the practice of using a date to refer to these events is also a way to *neutralize* them, since every repetition is also numbing, a deadening; constantly using the term "9/11" is a strategy devised to "conjure away ... the 'thing itself,'" the unnamable that we cannot grasp, through repetition. As a result of this repetitive and paradoxical stressing of the temporality of 9/11, the unimaginable is pushed away into the past as well as into the future, blanked out and deferred. Here, the traumatic experience becomes notable, as the notion of a linear temporality starts to deteriorate. The term does not refer simply to a fixed date on the calendar, but expands well beyond its limits, "[taking] over our public space and our private lives." Saying "9/11" is an attempt to frame the traumatic within the calendar, but it fails to do so because it cannot really solve the inability to name the "unicity [of the 9/11 events] which has no generality on the horizon, or no horizon at all."[8] As a result, despite its name, the event of 9/11 starts "bleeding" into the past and the future.

In the context of trauma, art is often attributed a healing role. Works of art, it is argued, can offer strategies to repair this discrepancy between temporality and comprehension which lies at the heart of the traumatic experience. Works of post-9/11 art such as Art Spiegelman's graphic novel *In the Shadow of No Towers* (2004) and Jonathan Safran Foer's novel *Extremely Loud and Incredibly Close* (2005) are often read as attempts to explore "healing forms of temporal experience": using different (literary) techniques, they endeavor to mend "the rift between time and consciousness—developing a better way to incorporate time into the process of knowing."[9]

"Love and Theft" can be read in a somewhat similar way—although, unlike the works I have just mentioned, it does not refer directly to the historical events of 9/11. Of course, the interpretation of a work of art is up to its readers. To stay with an example from Dylan's back pages, the song "A Hard Rain's A-Gonna Fall" was written well before the Cuban Missile Crisis; nevertheless, it was interpreted as a powerful response to this particular situation. The relation between *"Love and Theft"* and 9/11, however, is based on a more particular kind of historical contingency. The fact that the album happened to be released on that date places the album in the eye of the storm: by happenstance it has come to incorporate the precise moment that, through the traumatic experience of those events, has become inaccessible to us. As such, *"Love and Theft"* is a work of "9/11 art" *par excellence*, as it bridges the rift between time and consciousness that constitutes those traumatic events in its very existence.

"LOVE AND THEFT" AND 9/11: DOOM SCENARIOS

Interestingly, it does not need a great effort on the part of the reader to read *"Love and Theft"* in relation to the events of 9/11. War, disaster, violence, and doom are prominent themes throughout the album. For example, the song "Mississippi" starts with the lines, "Every step of the way, we walk the line / Your days are numbered, so are mine." Throughout the album, we find Dylan painting a claustrophobic, dark, and fated world: in "Sugar Baby," we are warned that "every minute of the day / the bubble could burst"; in another song, "Moonlight," "the earth and sky melt with flesh and bone." The universe of *"Love and Theft"* is a violent, even apocalyptic one, something also evidenced by the fact that the first-person narrator often finds himself in life-threatening situations. In "Mississippi," he is shipwrecked: the sky is "full of fire, pain pourin' down"; his ship is "split to splinters" and "sinking fast." In "High Water (For Charley Patton)," he finds himself amidst a flood. Coffins are "droppin' in the street / like balloons made out of lead," and the narrator warns us: "it's bad out there—high water everywhere."

The apocalyptic background and specific reference to several catastrophic events invite an interpretation in the context of the 9/11 attacks. This reading is also supported by the textual structure of the lyrics themselves. The song texts on *"Love and Theft"* are collages, combining a myriad of characters, remarks, jokes, situations, and intertextual references from many different sources: Dylan takes lines from Junichi Saga's *Confessions of a Yakuza* (1991) and William Shakespeare, but also musical sources, like Dock Boggs's "Sugar Baby" (1927) and Billie Holiday's "Having Myself a Time" (1937) (a source for Dylan's "Bye and Bye"), to name just a few.

These borrowed (or, as some would have it, stolen) pieces of texts, however, are not put together to form clear, comprehensible, and uniform narratives. In a way reminiscent of William Burroughs's cut-up technique, Dylan's lyrics lean heavily on the accidental, and at times appear accidental and unmotivated. This collage technique forces the reader to take an active role; to make a coherent interpretation from the bits and pieces one finds on *"Love and Theft"* requires the use of a lens of some kind: if we want to invest these songs with meaning, we need a tool of coherence that can bring the meaning of the songs into focus. The event of 9/11 presents itself as such a lens. We can make sense of the chaotic assembly of musical and lyrical allusions, quotations, and samples through the construction of an "I" whose presence is a constant throughout the album. What is especially interesting in relation to the apocalyptic landscape of *"Love and Theft"* is that throughout the different songs, this "I" presents himself as a *prophet*.

The figure of the prophet has resonated throughout Dylan's career, in his music as well as in his public image. The earliest examples of this are his "protest songs" from the early 1960s, like "Blowin' in the Wind" (1962), "A Hard Rain's A-Gonna Fall," and "The Times They Are a-Changin'." Critics Clifton Spargo and Anne Ream argue that in these anthems of the folk revival movement, "Dylan's criticism of American society works in a prophetic vein."[10] The language in these songs is characterized by an authoritative quality: Dylan uses Biblical imagery to describe a rapidly changing, violent present, and "like a true prophet" criticizes the rigidity of institutions.[11] On consequent albums, he deliberately broke away from the stern and angry tone of his folk songs, instead adopting a much more individual style. But the prophetic aura stuck to him, and throughout the years, Dylan has oscillated between the role of "poet" and "prophet": after being a prophet of political change (as for the folk movement), he was a prophet of a broader cultural youth movement (in 1965–66); for a while, he even took on the role of the prophet in the more religious sense of the word, when he preached fire and brimstone from the stage in the late 1970s and early 1980s. What has remained a constant, however, is Dylan's effort to defuse his prophetic status as quickly as it appears: he has never been comfortable in such a role, shying away or flat-out denying the prophetic qualities he invokes in his songs.

Interestingly, in *"Love and Theft"* the prophetic is invoked exactly in this unstable manner. The "I" assures us that he knows and sees more than the people around him, thus presenting himself as a prophet of sorts. For instance, "Sugar Baby" starts with the lines: "I got my back to the sun 'cause the light is too intense / I can see what everybody in the world is up against." And in "Bye and Bye," the singer assures us that "Well the future for me / Is already a thing of the past."

Still, things have changed since "The Times They Are a-Changin'." If the first-person narrator in *"Love and Theft"* is a prophet—someone who can see what the world is up against, and knows the future as he knows the past—this prophet is not a regular one: he is an *unsuccessful* prophet. In fact, his relationship with time seems to have become confused to the extent where he can no longer predict accurately. This shows whenever he is concerned with the making of predictions. In "Lonesome Day Blues," for example, the narrator is trying to hear what is "blowin' in the wind," but fails: "Last night the wind was whisperin' somethin' / I was trying to make out what it was / I tell myself something's comin' / But it never does." The role of a prophet is usually to warn people something will happen in the future, but when the "I" in "Sugar Baby" warns us that "you always got to be prepared / but you never know for what," he is also talking about himself: he, too, suffers from the same unknowing condition. Despite his constant concern with different kinds of apocalyptic scenarios, and his search for foretelling signs, he seems unable to clearly see what is actually going to happen. We can relate the figure of the unsuccessful prophet to the temporality of trauma. Derrida remarks that "trauma is an event whose temporality proceeds neither from the now that is present nor from the present that is past, but from an *impresentable* to come (*à venir*)." Trauma is "terrifying because it comes from the to-come, from the future, a future so radically to come that it resists even the grammar of the future anterior."[12] This is how we should understand the prophet's dilemma: the fear of the future drives the urge to predict the terrifying events, but predicting them is impossible as it contradicts the nature of trauma itself.

This tension is displayed particularly well in the slower ballads on *"Love and Theft."* These songs describe quiet situations in which, it would seem, nothing much is happening: they exude a rustic quietude. In "Floater (Too Much to Ask)," for instance, the narrator tells us: "Honey bees are buzzin' / Leaves begin to stir . . ." Nonetheless, in these songs the narrator is constantly uneasy, as if a terrible event of some sort is waiting to happen. This results in a constant sense of paranoia. We get a hint of this in the next verse, when he remarks: "I keep listenin' for footsteps / But I ain't hearing any." Because throughout the album the narrator insists that he knows something that we do not know (namely, the future), his mentions of footsteps, of whispering winds, stirring leaves, and barking dogs take on a different meaning. Like the narrator himself, we start to read these peaceful scenes in terms of the absence of impending horror. His paranoia becomes ours: should the stirring of leaves concern us? And why is the narrator, at this particular moment, indulging in a love fantasy he knows is untenable?

These (musically and lyrically) more gentle songs stand in stark contrast to the apocalyptic scenarios on *"Love and Theft,"* most notably in "Mississippi" and "High Water (For Charley Patton)." There, the narrator finds himself in the middle of apocalyptic scenarios—events that he has apparently failed to foresee. It seems that the prophet in *"Love and Theft"* has lost his grip on temporality. Time, which has been "pilin' up," seems to have tumbled over: the skewed temporality caused by trauma makes it impossible for him to predict, as the lines between past, present, and future have been become distorted.

The unsuccessful or traumatized prophet struggles to make sense of the future. By making predictions—even when they are not successful—the prophet in *"Love and Theft"* challenges the traditional approach to the traumatic event.

FORESEEING THE UNPREDICTABLE: THE EVENTS OF 9/11

In the wake of the events of 9/11, some (mostly European) thinkers, among whom we can count Derrida himself, but also Jean Baudrillard and Slavoj Žižek, have challenged the general perception of these events as completely unprecedented, radically unique, and incomprehensibly unpredictable. They argue that it would be more accurate to see the 9/11 attacks as part of what Derrida calls an "autoimmunitary process," the "strange behavior where a living being, in a quasi-*suicidal* fashion, 'itself' works to destroy its own protection, to immunize itself *against* its 'own' immunity." This position has caused some controversy, as in a certain way, it traces the causes of the events back to the United States themselves: as Derrida puts it, the events of 9/11 "come from the inside, from forces that are apparently without any force of their own." He notes, for instance, that the attacks were committed by men trained in the United States, using "high-tech knowledge, [getting] hold of an American weapon in an American city on the ground of an American airport." In a broader sense, Derrida argues that the 9/11 attacks can best be understood in the context of the end the Cold War. The "victory" of the United States camp in the Cold War meant that the "balance of terror" between the United States and the Soviet Union ceased to exist. Emerging as the sovereign state, the United States has become the only global power. As such, what threatens the United States is "the 'total' threat [that] no longer comes from a state but from anonymous forces that are absolutely unforeseeable and incalculable." Thus, through the "*terrifying* autoimmunitary logic," what is put at risk is the "existence of the world, of the worldwide itself."[13]

In his essay "The Spirit of Terrorism," Baudrillard expands on this idea. Like Derrida, he argues that the system of a single world order "secreted its own counterapparatus, the agent of its own disappearance." This system can "face down any visible antagonism," yet gives rise to an invisible adversary "viral in structure," which constitutes a "form of almost automatic reversion of its own power [against which] the system can do nothing." Without downplaying the impact of the events themselves, Baudrillard argues that the 9/11 attacks should be understood not so much a "clash of civilizations or religions" as "triumphant globalization battling against itself." He argues that this also means, importantly, that the events of 9/11 were not necessarily unimaginable: "The fact that we have dreamt of this event that everyone without exception has dreamt of it—because no one can avoid dreaming of the destruction of any power that has become hegemonic to this degree—is unacceptable to the Western moral conscience. Yet it is a fact.... At a pinch, we can say that they *did it*, but we *wished for* it."[14]

If we follow Baudrillard in his assertions, we can see *"Love and Theft"* as part of this phantasmal space, a "predicting dream" of the events of 9/11. The (at times uncanny) relation between the songs on the album and the events that took place on the day it was released could be understood as such. By juxtaposing bits of texts from the past—an eclectic selection of fragments of blues songs, and other texts about wars, floods, and other memories that "can strangle a man" ("Honest with Me")—and combining them with music with origins in Western swing and rockabilly, Dylan's Burroughs-esque cut-ups seem to offer a glimpse into the subconscious Western fantasies of destruction that preceded (or coincided with) the events of 9/11. In this way, Greg Tate's question is very much to the point: in a way, the album shows us "what we did know."

But *"Love and Theft"* does more than display those fantasies. The album occupies an extraordinary position: it exists in what Slavoj Žižek describes as "the unique time between a traumatic event and its symbolic impact."[15] From this vantage point, it is *self-consciously* questioning the fantasies of the destruction it is a part of, and exploring different responses to the threat of violence. One possible response to traumatic events, the album suggests, is to try and look at the future to prevent threats. Yet the fact that the prophet's predictions are not very accurate makes us wonder whether trying to predict and control events of the future is really the best way to deal with the threats of the present. For the narrator, who spends all his time and energy searching for messages and worrying about the future, it does not seem to help much. In fact, his attempts might do more harm than good. As the narrator himself remarks, when you "try to make things better for someone, sometimes, you just end up making it a thousand times worse" ("Sugar Baby").

The potentially harmful side of predicting the future becomes apparent in the violent nature of the prophet's visions. Throughout the album, in songs that are seemingly peaceful (both musically and lyrically); the narrator shows sudden glimpses of a very violent personality. In "Floater (Too Much to Ask)," he warns us: "If you ever try to interfere with me or cross my path again / you do so at the peril of your own life." It seems that in these cases, the narrator is exploring the possibility of counteracting the apocalyptic events he anticipates with his own violence: in his own imagined future, he is violently counteracting violence. As he assures us in the last verse of "Bye and Bye": "I'm gonna baptize you in fire so you can sin no more / I'm gonna establish my rule through civil war."

This violence, he constantly assures us, aims to establish peace: "I'm preaching peace and harmony, the blessings of tranquility / yet I know when the time is right to strike" ("Moonlight"). The idea of responding to violence with violence is interesting, as we can compare it to the situation the United States faced in the wake of the events of 9/11. According to Žižek, in the aftermath of September 11 there was a strong need for the United States to "'go back to basics,' to reassert its basic ideological co-ordinates against the anti-globalists," which meant a "forceful reassertion of the exceptional role of the USA as a global policeman." It is telling that the prophet is (uncharacteristically) very confident in his predictions of violence. He becomes the voice of ideology, as in "Lonesome Day Blues," where he assures that after winning this war, (quoting Allen Mandelbaum's translation of Virgil's *Aeneid*) he is going to "spare the defeated" and "speak to the crowd / . . . teach peace to the conquered / . . . [and] tame the proud." It is the one case in which the threat of future events instills him with certainty: this future war is presented as a moment of clarification in which it is easy to pick sides, an ideologically justified "aggressivity towards the threatening Outside."[16]

The failing predictions of the prophet raise suspicion about his sudden certainty about his own imagined role in the future, and more alert to the ideological undertones in his discourse. In this context, it is also interesting to note that, throughout, his response to the threat of violence with violence is captured in the language of the Civil War. The argument in favor of a war to assure peace is further complicated by these references. It frames the conflict not as a clash between "us and them," but as an internal struggle, a "clash within civilizations." When we hear the prophet proclaims he wants to start a civil war to establish his rule and "teach peace to the conquered," it serves as a disquieting reminder that in the wake of a traumatic event, "precisely at the moment of apparent clarity of choice, mystification is total," and it is necessary to step back and reflect.[17]

■ ■ ■

In *"Love and Theft,"* prediction of the future is a complicated and highly unreliable business. One can wonder why the prophet cannot seem to stop trying to predict, and spends most of his time searching for messages. The constant anticipation of the paranoid prophet and his failure to predict future events could, perhaps, be read as an ironic commentary on this obsession of Western culture to constantly try to predict some sort of apocalyptic event. The need to prophesy—and the (failed) predictions that are made—can tell us more about ourselves than they can really tell us about the future. This is the most important lesson *"Love and Theft"* teaches us: making predictions about unexpected future events does not give us control of those events, but still enables a way to live in the present, to live with trauma as an event-to-come. After all, is it not his prophesying that helps the prophet rectify his own temporal problems, and "incorporate time into the process of knowing"?[18] For an individual to make sense of his situation in the midst of (impending) chaos, trying to predict the future can also be a way to shape a present. In his production of prophecies, we can recognize the two opposite effects of repetition Derrida notes: they emphasize the unimaginable "unicity" of the future, but at the same time they have a neutralizing potential. If it is possible to capture the present and the future in terms of the past, prophesying can act as a mechanism to keep the future at bay.

As we have seen, when describing his predicament and making his predictions, the narrator (Dylan) relies heavily on the past. Throughout, he is quoting from a highly eclectic and specific personal past (the American songbook, and a myriad of literary references). The music on *"Love and Theft"* only adds to this effect, as many, if not all, of the songs are based on popular American songs from the 1940s and 1950s. Through his process of repetition, shards of the past are reconfigured in a new framework, in an attempt to bridge the traumatic gap between time and consciousness. Living with trauma, in fear of events of the future, the prophet's predictions capture his uncertainty of the future in terms of a repetition of the past—a past of his own. If it is possible for him to repeat the past (and he assures us: "of course you can!"), he can create a form of stability in the present. Making predictions, flawed as they may be, offers reference points to make sense of his situation. As the narrator puts it: "I know who I can depend on, I know who to trust / I'm watchin' the roads, I'm studying the dust" ("Bye and Bye").

Ultimately, then, reading *"Love and Theft"* as a work of 9/11 is not only insightful but also leaves us with a hopeful message. While it criticizes our ability to predict or control future events, it shows how the urge to do so—uncontrollable and, it could be argued, justified—supports a strategy to make sense of this present. What emerges is an ironic and at times boisterously joyful attitude to life. This is reflected in deadpan humor and jokes, which parody the prophet's own paranoid concern with the threat of the future. The final verse of "Po' Boy" opens with a knock-knock joke with the punchline, "Freddy or not here I come!"

It seems that the prophet's concern with the future allows him to escape the dread of future threats, to anchor the present in an experience of the bliss of the now. Personal, emotional bonds offer a particular mode of knowledge that eclipses all his worries: "All I know is that I'm thrilled by your kiss / I don't know any more than this" ("Po' Boy"). This complete submersion in the present does not resolve the distortion of past, present, and future, but for once does not cause any confusion; if anything, it strengthens his personal relationships: ". . . the future for me is already a thing of the past / You were my first love, and you will be my last" ("Bye and Bye"). It should, then, not be read as a plea for a static *carpe diem* in the face of trauma; the prophet realizes that even though his temporal experience is skewed, time cannot be frozen, and we are heading at full speed toward an uncertain future. But as long as his baby sticks with him, he can face the threat of the future head on: "Stick with me baby, stick with me anyhow / Things should start to get interestin' right about now" ("Mississippi").

NOTES

1. Martin Halliwell and Catherine Morley, *American Thought and Culture in the 21st Century* (Edinburgh: Edinburgh University Press 2009), 1.
2. Greg Tate, "Intelligence Data," *Village Voice*, September 25, 2001. www.villagevoice.com/2001-09-25/music/intelligence-data/.
3. Kristiaan Versluys, "9/11 as a European Event: The Novels," *European Review* 15(1) (2007): 70.
4. Versluys, "9/11 as a European Event," 612.
5. Aaron DeRosa, "Analyzing Literature after 9/11," *MFS Modern Fiction Studies* 57 (2011): 615.
6. Mitchum Huels, "Foer, Spiegelman, and 9/11's Timely Traumas," in *Literature after 9/11*, Ann Keniston and Jeanne Follansbee Quinn, eds. (New York City: Routledge, 2008), 42.
7. Jacques Derrida, "Autoimmunity: Real and Symbolic Suicides—A Dialogue with Jacques Derrida," in *Philosophy in a Time of Terror: Dialogues with Jürgen Habermas and Jacques Derrida*, Giovanna Borradori, ed. (Chicago and London: University of Chicago Press, 2003), 86, 87.
8. Derrida, "Autoimmunity," 87, 85, 86.
9. Huels, "Foer, Spiegelman, and 9/11's Timely Traumas," 44.
10. R. Clifton Spargo and Anne K. Ream, "Bob Dylan and Religion," in *The Cambridge Companion to Bob Dylan*, Kevin J. H. Dettmar, ed. (Cambridge: Cambridge University Press, 2009), 88.
11. Spargo and Ream, "Bob Dylan and Religion," 89.
12. Derrida, "Autoimmunity," 97.
13. Derrida, "Autoimmunity," 94–99.
14. Jean Baudrillard, "The Spirit of Terrorism," in *The Spirit of Terrorism and Other Essays* (London and New York: Verso), 2002, 11, 5.
15. Slavoj Žižek, *Welcome to the Desert of the Real* (London and New York: Verso, 2002), 44.
16. Žižek, Welcome to the Desert of the Real, 49.
17. Žižek, Welcome to the Desert of the Real, 54.
18. Mitchum Huels, "Foer, Spiegelman, and 9/11's Timely Traumas" *Literature after 9/11*, Ann Keniston and Jeanne Follansbee Quinn, eds. New York City: Routledge, 2008. 42–59 (44).

CHAPTER SIX

A SUDDEN BLOW: THE STORY OF VIOLENCE IN *"LOVE AND THEFT"* AND *MODERN TIMES*

Nina Goss

> You would play upon me; you would seem to know my stops;
> you would pluck out the heart of my mystery; you would sound me
> from my lowest note to the top of my compass: and there is much music,
> excellent voice, in this little organ; yet cannot you make it speak.
> —**William Shakespeare,** *Hamlet*, III, ii, 394-99[1]

Bob Dylan's vast and discordant audience is better characterized by innumerable solitary quests for significance in his work than by a circle of people united by common enthusiasm. David Kinney's *The Dylanologists* (2004) is a good introduction to this discordance. In Kinney's patient and considerate book, you can meet a number of people for whom "Bob Dylan fan" is a constituent of their identity and who are yet incompatible with each other. Kinney's project is social culture; therefore he does not address the (I should say, hackneyed) question raised by reading *The Dylanologists*: whether value inheres in Dylan's, or any, art or is imputed to it by our attention. Is the intrinsic value of "Desolation Row" so certain and dynamic that sociopaths, discriminating intellectuals, outlanders, and rude mechanicals can all adore it? Or, have an eccentric variety of people discovered "Desolation Row" and chosen to inscribe their own visions onto its tortuous ambiguities and imagery?

One origin story for today's motley Dylanologists is the two audiences Dylan created in his early incarnations. Bob Dylan #1 of 1962–63 was the songwriter whose social and political purpose roused thousands to the moral high ground of witnessing and supporting the voice of truth against power.

85

The meaning of "Blowin' in the Wind" or "The Times They Are a-Changin'" seemed transparently anthemic and inclusive. Bob Dylan #2 of 1964–66 reinvented the song lyric into a cryptic personal language intoxicating additional thousands into the belief that Dylan's words are peculiarly encoded. The decoding itself became a more solitary political act; engaging the exhilaratingly strange and intimate language of "Gates of Eden" (1965) can feel like an escape from the obvious lies of power. Dylan's shift in style at this time famously cost him listeners who felt he had betrayed their collective righteous purpose, that they had lost the narrator of their here and now, a hero of their collective purpose whom they wished not to see exchanging their shared meaning for another. Above all, Dylan *means*, intransitively, and that he must *mean for me in my time*, is the story of his audience.

I chose violence as the topic of my exploration of *"Love and Theft"* and *Modern Times* because from cannonballs to shipwrecks, the destructive life of humankind has run through Dylan's work and seems a good laboratory for tests of relevance and significance. The "Dignity" piano demo (1989) started me off. "In the next room, a man fighting with his wife / Over dignity." There is always fighting in the next room and across the border. When does this next-door violence become our problem, our titillation, our suffering, our solution to a different problem, our inspiration, our art, our story?

Me in my time. While I type this, two images are fresh in my memory. In one, people in Ferguson, Missouri, walk in a carless street filled with smoke. In the other, a man with a shaved head and wearing a bright red oversized T-shirt kneels alongside a standing man with a long knife, this man all in black and his face covered too, but for his eyes. By the time you read this, the violent deaths of Michael Brown and James Foley will no longer be today's climaxes to centuries-long stories. And how many stories will have already been told for which the deaths of Foley and Brown could be employed as the climax? Their lives are done and violence has set these men into dramatis personae.

In Mark Danner's book *Stripping the Body Bare*, a collection of writings on the Congo, Bosnia, and the post-9/11 era of terrorism, he admits that as journalist and historian he composes narratives that entail aesthetic choices. Warfare, terrorism, and torture provide him a nearly irresistible palette for his work: "For the teller of stories, whether he assembles them from facts in the world, or ghosts in his imagination, violence offers, beyond the inherent emotional charge, the lure of resolution. To suspense, the engine of violence supplies climax and catharsis. From political conflict, the melding of thesis and antithesis that moves history, violence extracts synthesis."[2]

Violence is a bountiful device for several aesthetic satisfactions: frisson from descriptions of violent acts; psychological tension in the dramatic promise of violent conflict or its avoidance; the relief of a climactic narrative resolution; and the intellectual triumph of explicating the thesis, antithesis, synthesis that will become tomorrow's authoritative version of today's violence.

Danner's shrewd catalog applies to even a thin précis of the periods of Dylan's work in which violence is prominent. When Bob Dylan began to write songs, he "assemble[d] from facts in the world" his own blood-soaked folk ballads. By updating traditional folk themes of crime, corruption, revenge, and impulse with contemporary facts of racist brutality and Cold War terror, Dylan's early songs struck listeners as a populist cultural tradition in the service of contemporary events. From songs of poverty and alienation like "North Country Blues" (1964) and "The Ballad of Hollis Brown" to songs of murder or tyranny like "The Death of Emmett Till" (1962), "The Lonesome Death of Hattie Carroll" (1963), "Who Killed Davey Moore?", and "Masters of War" (1963), we meet a singer who articulates moral outrage with a combination of insight, ingenuousness, and felicity that can astound and inspire fifty years on. These compositions invite listeners to reflect, with satisfying humility, on our own implicit accountability in real acts and threats of violence. We use his artistry to recast our consciences, and we harmonize our consciences with each other and with the performer.

From 1966 to the early 1970s, violence in Dylan's work moved from "facts in the world" to "ghosts in his imagination." In *John Wesley Harding*, Old West gunfights and Old Testament lightning are refashioned to ambiguous modern allegories. In the seventies, violence is turned inward. The self-hatred, corkscrews, and mad winds in *Planet Waves* (1974) and *Blood on the Tracks* create an Ouroboros of passion. Yet through these violences both personal and figurative, Dylan continues to address us as companions; we think and feel with him through his anxious princes on the watchtower awaiting their inexorable siege, or through the personas of his self-lacerating lovers.

The content of Dylan's 1979–80 gospel work is "assemble[d] from the facts" of the supernatural world described by evangelical Christianity. In this world, violence is the defining feature of personal and universal "climax and catharsis." Throughout *Slow Train Coming* (1979), *Saved* (1980) and other songs uncollected on those records, Dylan sings of conversion as the destruction and remaking of the self, and of Judgment Day as the destruction and remaking of humankind. Dylan's faith is a bloody battlefield commanded by a crucified Lord. The singer enjoins us to conscript our bodies and souls to this war, or be lost forever to our unbelief. We have one choice if we wish to maintain a relation with the artist: undergo the psychic violence of conversion and accept the final destruction of Apocalypse.

In 2014, I hear in Dylan's millennial work the "inherent emotional charge" of violence. What does this language of violence sound like? Does Dylan use it to fashion a new relation with listeners, and a new vision of history?

"Love and Theft" begins with a theft—Dylan steals Lewis Carroll's contrary twins and looking-glass world and plays darkly with both. Our first encounter with Dylan's Tweedles cleverly recreates their appearance in *Through the Looking Glass* (1871): just as the pair materializes *ex nihilo* for Alice, so do they arrive abruptly in the song via a fast (and uncharacteristic) musical fade-in. Carroll's twins declare oxymoronically that they "agreed to have a battle"[3] and Dylan's Tweedles begin *"Love and Theft"* in a montage of puzzling, groundless violence. They throw knives into a tree as a game? For practice? The sudden two big bags of dead men's bones, one for each Tweedle, are the dreadful luggage of mass death. They have their noses to the grindstone in a cliché of grueling labor we link to their knife-throwing and sacks of remains. As Alice finds herself hilariously and also frustratingly involved in her Tweedles' causeless, urgent, and harmless battle, so do we find ourselves on uncertain ground in the first verse of the album's first song: are these protagonists cartoons or criminals?

Dylan creates a looking-glass world for his twins. His creatures live in a "happy harmony" that is contrarily defined by contradiction and volatility. A telling rhyme in the song is "going to the country, . . . going to retire / . . . taking a street car named Desire." Retire's passivity and desire's appetite are contradictory; in addition, the pair ride the streetcar named Desire only to be denied fulfillment. They gaze hungrily at a pie that is one of many things they can't have. Their bond is an affliction—"your presence is obnoxious to me"—and a compact—"what's good for you is good for me." There is something like honor here as "neither one's gonna turn and run," and they seem "determined to go all the way." However, we have no idea what they are confronting or what they are going all the way for. We hear echoes perhaps of "John Wesley Harding" wherein Dylan previously exploited tropes of action and heroism for a tale that finally tells nothing. The Tweedles are law-abiding citizens with a parade permit and a legitimate brick and tile company. Even better than legitimacy, they are VIPs with a police escort. And suddenly they fall to the ranks of criminals as fugitives "lying low." They're shamans fluent in nature's tongue; "they know the secrets of the breeze." Finally, Dylan offers his listeners fulfillment of "Blowin' in the Wind." Here are the oracles who do know the answer, my friend, and they turn out to be antic and implausible creatures.

Our narrator appears in two glimpses, both of which undermine any hope of a coherent vision of all this discordance. In verse 7, we meet him holed up against the rain and ruminating on futile love. The lyric's allusion to the blues classic "Love in Vain" lulls us to nostalgia. We easily see the lonesome bluesman in his leaky shack. But this folklorish bluesman is witchily cooking brains for lunch. This image suits the world of "Tweedle Dum and Tweedle Dee": gruesome, suggestive, realistic, and witty all at once. In verse 11, the singer interrupts his characters' tale to offer deceptive truisms. "A childish dream is a deathless need" suggests imprisonment in a Neverland where childhood fantasies will consequently overgrow into needs never satisfied. "A noble truth is a sacred dream" is a vacuous epigram and/or banal reference to Buddhist precepts. The image following these platitudes is a woman in an extravagant dress, "lookin' around." She is dressed for display and is restive; looking around in wonderland generally leads to trouble. Love, philosophy, the innocence of a child's dreams—all is undone in this world. "Tweedle Dum and Tweedle Dee" ends nearly as it begins, with stabbing, impetuous threats, and disharmony.

No moral or social order can hold sway for long in this world. We will not find politics in "Tweedle Dum and Tweedle Dee," and though there is the language of transcendent Power—hands of God, Master's voice—these certainties exist alongside caprice and menace. The song's physical violence suits the destabilized world. We meet mass death, reckless stabbings, childish taunts, and conflicts. Some once-living thing gave up its brains to the singer's meal. For all the allusions to death, all the belligerence, all the knives, this is also a cartoon world. The Tweedles are arbitrary and brutal but never come to harm and are never caught in an act of serious destruction.

> For, though I am not splenitive and rash,
> Yet have I something in me dangerous,
> Which let thy wiseness fear: hold off thy hand
> (*Hamlet*, V, i, 275–77)

The narrator who steps out of "Tweedle Dum and Tweedle Dee" to dominate the songs on *"Love and Theft"* is a looking-glass version of Hamlet, which is fitting in a record that includes two comical distortions of Shakespeare. Our man *is* "splenitive and rash" and repeatedly warns of something in him dangerous. He is a bully who threatens invisible enemies without motive or context and, unlike a tragic hero, remains indestructible. At the end of his series of battles he will surrender in exhaustion.

The hero of *"Love and Theft"* is a man fighting exhaustion with belligerent arbitrary outbursts. Our hero is alternately boastful, self-pitying, ruminative, clever, vigorous, seductive, depleted. In "Summer Days" he urges everyone to frolic with him although the season of frolic is done; he even warns his companions he will leave in wreckage the revels he started. What looks like hubris—he can turn the clock back: "what do you mean you can't [repeat the past]? Of course you can"; he can "break the roof in and set fire to the place as a parting gift"—is one man's desperate fury as time runs down. "Bye and Bye" is the weary aftermath to "Summer Days." After some torpid shuffling, weak puns, and admitting to having no better inspiration than clichés, the singer suddenly vaunts, "I'm gonna baptize you in fire so you can sin no more / . . . establish my rule through civil war." His intimidation sounds mighty but it is both licensed and ignoble. A ritual baptism by fire is torture serving as purification, and the governing that follows civil warfare must be on the back of a broken nation. The indolent crooner of "Bye and Bye" exploits power structures for his brutal impulses, whereas the last-gasp reveler of "Summer Days" is reckless and appeals to no legitimacy to back his threats. Neither song identifies antagonists.

Reigns of terror continue to interrupt torpor or self-absorption in "Lonesome Day Blues," "Honest with Me," and to a milder degree, "Floater (Too Much to Ask)." "Lonesome Day Blues" offers generic military backdrops with no named enemies. First the singer praises his captain for a pragmatic lack of compassion and then he assumes power and blusters in the nonsense of tyrants. He will "spare the defeated," "teach peace to the conquered," and "tame the proud." The defeated cannot be spared anything except their lives, now belonging in any case to the conqueror. The conquered are disarmed by force; they cannot learn peace, only obeisance. Taming the proud is the goal of all tyrants. An equivocating orator has grown from the victorious soldier, without a battle or a nation identified. This rhetorical outburst entailing brutal power over invisible subjects is brought on by nothing more potent than an old man's spasm of grief and nostalgia as he drives by a quaint mill and mourns his dead mother. In "Honest with Me," the singer complains of his isolation in an ominous city haunted by women who give him "the creeps." But his imagination is enough to destroy an inhospitable place and unwanted women. With the bloated redundancy of political rhetoric, he will create an "imperial empire" out of sheer loneliness. "Floater" takes us on a stream of thought in which there is no control over the "things [that] come alive or fall flat" in the acts of remembering. He remarks on impotent bullies, a peaceable marriage, ancestors' dreams lost to history, and once useful facts about building fires from timber. Against these desultory and enervating memories he asserts himself with a sudden threat: "I'm not as cool or forgiving as I seem," he reflects, Hamlet-like, as he gathers just enough strength to "kick somebody out."

"Moonlight" offers a portrait of the singer as a dangerous man disguised by rhyme, music, and a sensitive soul. Dylan's Gothic turn is irresistible: the nubilous, fecund world of dark seduction, the shiver of terror, and the glimpse of unexplained elusive evil. The delicious internal rhymes of "crimson" and "limbs an'" and the marvelous tongue-twisters of the opening couplets of verses 1, 2, 4, 5, and 6 are pearls he scatters carelessly—there are, his easy tongue implies, plenty more where these came from. The language easily seduces the singer's unidentified companion/victim and, in the same stupor, we listeners play right into the trap occurring in the bridge following the third verse: 'Well, I'm preachin' peace and harmony / The blessings of tranquility / Yet I know when the time is right to strike." This tricky character seems a cousin to the captain in "Lonesome Day Blues": only a tyrant is exempt from the hypocrisy of "preaching peace and harmony" and "knowing when the time is right to strike." Absolute power has no secrets or excuses. Our seducer craftily appeals to the high poetic canon of fate and mortality—Donne's bell tolls for all of us. This mask of lyrical solidarity rounds out the portrait of the elegant daemon-lover.

Like their progenitors the two Tweedles, the brutes who populate *"Love and Theft"* are indestructible. From the narrator of "Mississippi" who is impervious to apocalypse by either fire or water, to the Chaplinesque po' boy who survives his farcical gauntlet to end his day in peaceful domesticity, the central figures in *"Love and Theft"* steal their own lives from danger and death.

If you call up the Bob Dylan in the "Duquesne Whistle" video (2012) strutting over a dying boy, you may see the same creatures who stride through danger and wreckage in *"Love and Theft."* In "Mississippi," Dylan hints that one day's overstaying his welcome was either enough to set him on a hero's ordeal by fire and water, or that ordeals of fire and water were no match for the secret drama of that one day. Regardless, not even a sky full of fire or a tempest to split a ship to splinters can fell him. He will not buy into an apocalypse and when "pain's pouring down" he is free to bid farewell and leave town. Drowning in poison with nothing ahead or behind, he remains full of fellowship and emerges soaking wet but still fighting. We've already seen him in "Summer Days" promising destruction as a souvenir of his own bacchanal. We recall that it is not only a proud and sad solitude he suffers in "Lonesome Day Blues" as the only survivor of a family dead or scattered—our lonesome singer is also high and dry despite a washed-out road. The dawdler in "Floater" remarks that attempts to bully him have always had "the opposite effect." In "Honest with Me," he crashes a car "trunk first into the wall," and of course escapes unharmed.

"High Water" and "Po' Boy" are the record's poles of invulnerability. In "High Water," floods never cease to rise and people tread water in perpetual self-preservation. In a drowning world ransacked by theft and pelted by death, our unbreakable narrator drives through the flood in a muscle car and his girls can't get their clothes off fast enough. The paranoia unleashed by the flood is so severe that Charles Darwin must be a hunted fugitive where the natural order he explained is berserk. The singer endures by reassuming the character of the brute preacher: he will blind his followers in his fanatic certainty. He will stay dry, keep moving, and finally have the last brutal word as God's mouthpiece.

"Po' Boy" is our black comic relief. The jokes in the first and last verses depend on a knock at the door as in the great black-comic knockings of *Macbeth*: "Here's a knocking indeed! If a man were porter of hell-gate, he should have old turning the key" (Act II, scene iii). Dylan's song mocks the brutalities and desires of *"Love and Theft"* and the po' boy is a foil for the personas rampaging through the record. The song features an adulterous wife, a fugitive, and the scars of age and love, yet all is farcical and toothless. Our po' boy is the stock fool who steals his survival from his own stupidity.

In *"Love and Theft"* violence is personal, impetuous, and unaccountable. The frameworks of conquest, imperialism, religion, and warfare appear without context to serve the singer's impulses. Yet this pattern of flare-ups finally begins to wear itself out in "Cry a While," the record's penultimate song. In this song he claims to be done with the underworld, with the cheating Goldsmiths, and with the sacrifices for love. Instead of the hard-bitten isolations of the previous songs, in "Cry a While" the singer finally sets himself into an ordered world: the preacher rightfully in his pulpit, the baby safely in his crib. The singer has a conscience and piety. He cries to the Lord, tries to curb his impulsiveness, and is in his right mind trying to set us straight (e.g., the great winking wit of reassuring us he's a "union man"). Even though the song ends on a familiar threatening note—"could be your funeral, my trial"—for once he is accepting responsibility by standing justice. Finally, our hero is capable of weeping and of appraising justice and propriety. He has primed himself for his final submission.

Compare the musical intro to "Tweedle Dum and Tweedle Dee" with that of "Sugar Baby" and you may hear the emotions that frame *"Love and Theft."* We began with a rising, fervid riff, and we end with a melody so easeful that each note seems to stretch and yawn before it takes its place. The vocals match the weary pace, and thus the sound suits what begin with a retreat from all the sun in this record, from the dazzling sunlit rays, from the noise to the sun in "Tweedle Dum and Tweedle Dee" and the prolonged summer days. "I've got my back to the sun / Because the light is too intense." Hearing a reference to Plato's cave is irresistible; finally, the singer returns to all of us chained to the cave's shadows. To mix philosophies, he takes a Bodhisattva turn and apparently rejects the power of the philosopher-king able to stare into the sun in favor of universal compassion among the shadows. Now there is no turning back, no repeating the past. Sugar Baby is urged repeatedly to keep on going because her freedom will finally grant the singer his. In the refrain, our hero pleads for abdication from all the roles he has manipulated throughout the record: preacher, prophet, and lover. Long after a "master's voice" called inscrutably to Tweedle Dum, the singer turns to us with plausible altruism and exhorts us to "Seek your maker." *"Love and Theft"* seems to end in a redemptive reversal of the turbulence launched in "Tweedle Dum and Tweedle Dee." The music of "Sugar Baby" tolls and the vocals are grave as no other song on the record is. Violence seems to have burned itself out and the singer quietly concludes, "Love, see what you've done." We rest here briefly with our depleted and perhaps redeemed rascal, because when he gathers his strength for "Thunder on the Mountain," we will need energy to keep up with him.

The segue of "Sugar Baby" to "Thunder on the Mountain" offers a suggestive bridge linking the personas and motifs of the two albums. This bridge uncannily spans a deep rift in the collective history of the singer and his entire audience: *"Love and Theft"* was released on September 11, 2001. We left that album's protagonist appealing to all to turn attention to the higher world where the archangel of Judgment summons us. In *Modern Times*, the singer and his audience reconvene five years later, when—if we've been lucky and survived with whatever material and personal resources go into buying and enjoying a CD—our shared history has been marked forever as before and after September 11.

The Archangel and horn of "Sugar Baby" are reincarnated as the singer himself and his jazzy trombone in "Thunder on the Mountain" inherits the prophet. Energy revives and compassion is now a clear note. We met *"Love and Theft"*'s protagonist cooped up in a shack, brooding and hungry. We meet the protagonist of *Modern Times* in a mountaintop's clear air, where the sun is now welcome. Altruism inspires: "Gonna forget about myself for a while, gonna go out and see what others need." Other people make music he wants to lie down next to; he invites other people to come so close they may look into his heart. He sees everybody on the move and wants to be moving too. Truthfully, he is a contradictory fellow: his mission is quickly distracted by love; he can be lewd and admits he is no angel; he sometimes just wants to sleep where the music is. Although he is no stranger to warfare, his army of orphans has the ring of a crusade about it rather than *"Love and Theft"*'s flailings. The song even outdoes "Sugar Baby"'s redemptive spirit with this compassionate outburst: "For the love of God," he cries, "Have pity on yourself."

Compare the brutes on *"Love and Theft"* to the one boastful murderer on *Modern Times*: The silky, irreverent voice of "Spirit on the Water" admits he killed a man "back there" in paradise, so he can't go there "no more." He may be a threat, but unlike most of his predecessors in *"Love and Theft"* he is also accountable: he confesses his crime and accepts his exile. Each record offers a centerpiece song about a flood, although *Modern Times*'s "The Levee's Gonna Break" is no apocalypse; it is common disaster resulting from human error and heavy weather. "I worked on the levee Mama, both night and day." The singer helped build the levee; he knows how weak the structure is and conscientiously warns us it will breach. He touchingly promises a lover an eon of happiness after these few years of the hard work of mortal life. A recognizable world threatened by a fallible levee is a grounded moral plane unlike the universal doom of "High Water."

"Workingman's Blues #2" is crucial in recasting violence and warfare into the softer metals of *Modern Times*. The word *proletariat* once belonged to a vocabulary of utopian revolution, and our workingman uses it as a quaint, bitter commentary on his circumstances. In poverty and idleness and surrounded by indifference, he mourns a lost America, the "place I love best" now "a sweet memory," and endures his own sorry state with resignation, integrity, and defiance. He sees himself under siege, "ringed by countless foes," and repeatedly reminds his companion/lover/us that there are two choices: courage at the front lines or "hanging back" in cowardice or pacifism. He himself seems to want both options. He has laid his "cruel weapons ... on the shelf," and he threatens that he'll "drag 'em all down to hell and I'll stand 'em at the wall / I'll sell 'em to their enemies," but immediately sighs that this is a fantasy. He's only "tryin' to feed my soul with thought." *Modern Times*'s workingman cannot boast with the rashness of his predecessors. He is weary and poignant. The conflict on this record is generally marked by compromise and peacemaking.

So far I have told a character-driven story whose device is the "inherent emotional charge" of violence. Our *"Love and Theft"* protagonist uses the language of arbitrary violence to assert potency; our *Modern Times* protagonist uses the language of truce to appeal to sympathy and community. On both records, our protagonists sing to us from streetcars, rivers, mountains, nameless cities, levees, railroad tracks, cars, and nameless roads in a voice vigorous and ancient. His landscapes seem both archaic and bound to no time. Without context—more important, without clear currency—how can I answer the summons to make Bob Dylan matter, as I mentioned previously, for *us in our time*?

What about mundane topicality, material "assembled from facts," as so much of Dylan's early sixties material was ripped from headlines? As mentioned, *"Love and Theft"* was released on September 11, 2001, and *Modern Times* was plumbed for a response to that event. One moment in "Thunder on the Mountain" seemed at first hearing to radicalize topicality. "All the ladies of Washington scrambling to get out of town / Looks like something bad gonna happen, better roll your airplane down," is audible on the recording. The masters of war are now belittled to "ladies in Washington." We can picture Bush, Rumsfeld, and Cheney scrambling for safety, lifting their skirts, and looking up in terror at empty skies. Indeed, the reason the sky over Washington was without danger on 9/11/01 was because at least one man on Flight 93 said " . . . roll," and diverted the hijacked plane from its probable target of the Capitol. The implications of this reference are mortifying. For all of Dylan's complex dealings with conscience and morality, "roll your airplane down," seems in this context grotesquely impudent. The joke of course was on me and anyone else mishearing the line. It is not topical, not even penned by Bob Dylan, and his crafty vocals cause the mishearing. "*Lower* your airplane down" is lifted verbatim from Kokomo Arnold's beautiful 1937 song of peril, sorrow, and duty, "Mean Old Twister."[4] It's not the word *roll*: Dylan slurs two syllables into a ghastly false one.

In this case, our wicked old artificer cannot be blamed for playing blood-curdlingly fast and loose with history. Mistaken listeners may have inferred a factitious reference whose miscue remains, in the context of 9/11, factual. Our alertness to signs of our times could have been eager enough to force misprision. This is a provoking jumble, but we are nowhere near the timeless and relevant assembled-from-facts classics such as "Hattie Carroll" or "Who Killed Davey Moore?" Instead we are left in a liminal space neither past nor present, neither truth nor lie, neither our work nor Dylan's. Since liminal spaces where stable meaning cannot get purchase are home sweet home for contemporary critical theory, that is where we turn next.

Slavoj Žižek's book-length essay *Violence* (2008) offers a metaphysics of violence as a critique of the empirical tools mainstream journalism insists on using. Žižek implicitly assails writers like Mark Danner who describe terrorism, civil warfare, and metastatic government corruption in terms of identifiable agents acting within political and social contexts. Žižek argues that this vision cannot do justice to current conditions. We have to look beyond agents and contexts. "Particularity can indeed mask universality," he asserts in the context of his discussion of Hegel. *Violence* unmasks this universality. Žižek derides our habit of considering "obvious signals of violence [like] acts of crime and terror, civil unrest, international conflict" as "subjective violence." He argues: "[W]e should learn to step back, to disentangle ourselves from the fascinating lure of this directly visible 'subjective violence.' . . . A step back enables us to identify a violence that sustains our very effort to fight violence and to promote tolerance." For Žižek, "violence performed by a clearly identifiable agent" is only one third of a "triumvirate" that includes two forms of "objective violence." One is "'symbolic' violence embodied in language and its forms"; the second is "'systemic' violence, or the often catastrophic consequences of the smooth functioning of our economic and political systems." For Žižek, systemic violence is an emergent property of globalized culture. So convinced is Žižek that systemic violence is omnipresent and real that he carelessly compares it to the dark matter of physics: "It may be invisible, but it has to be taken into account if one is to make sense of what otherwise seem to be 'irrational' explosions of subjective violence."[5] From clashes in Syria to mass shootings in movie theaters to abusive clergy, violence cannot be explained away by concrete political history or individual pathology: it is part of the quantum nature of a world bound by ideologies dependent on fear and aggression.

Impetuous violence by a "clearly identifiable agent," yet without conclusively accountable antagonists or within a coherent political narrative, sounds like the world of *"Love and Theft."* There seems to be a dark matter of aggression swarming throughout the record and a subsequent effort to neutralize that dark matter in *Modern Times*. Perhaps the songs' metonymies of government, religion, and the military that promiscuously justify brutalities and tyrannies speak to Žižek's symbolic violence. Perhaps with these metonymies Dylan illustrates how meager and perfunctory is any appeal we now make to army or church in order to sponsor destruction. We might further support the dark matter argument by bringing in Bob Dylan's performance schedule and his recent collagist/magpie songwriting technique involving myriad embedded quotations. He tirelessly circles the globe; he glimpses shards of life and death in Pori, Athens, Cork, Brooklyn, and Osaka. He sees; he reads; he seizes; the text is now his; he disgorges it. The lord of song flies through land after land and becomes the occasion of (i.e., not the author of) songs peculiarly able to manifest the dark matter of objective violence.

This is starting to sound good to me. Bold, cool—I can get out there with this idea. When I start to feel this way I know I have been seduced by the high-class whore of critical theory and I need to stop and look. Arguments that cruelty swarms as dark matter, or that warfare and murder are two-thirds the work of a systemic intangible, quickly become antihistorical: there was a time when slaughter and torture were subjective and not systemic? The dark matter metaphor breaks down quickly; it is just another way of imputing specious supernaturalism to events and conditions of human actions. Since nothing that compels me to take the dark matter of physical science seriously compels me to take Žižekian dark matter ideologies seriously, I choose to continue my search for meaning.

A text Žižek would consider superannuated may help us. The title as well as the author photo of Teofilo F. Ruiz's 2011 book, *The Terror of History: On the Uncertainties of Life in Western Civilization*, let us know we are in good company for a humane intellectual journey. The title is a candid lament. The photo shows Ruiz appealing to the camera with an expression both grim and gentle: he's a dead ringer for Max von Sydow's Antonius Block, Bergman's seeker-knight in *The Seventh Seal* (1957).

Ruiz premises his book on a vision of history that may find sympathy from the dark-souled multitudes among Bob Dylan's audience. His project considers "ways in which certain individuals and groups hoped to flee from the death grip of history and, often, ahistorical lives. But this book also reflects on the meanings and usefulness of these diverse attempts to confront the weight of history and the uncertainty of the world."[6] Ruiz examines three kinds of escape from appalling disintegrations of value and meaning: religion; the sensuous life; and what he calls "knowledge and beauty," i.e., art, philosophy, and scholarship. Each mode offers an irresistible fantasy for transcending violence, suffering, and extinction that are the inescapably real conditions of every time and place humankind has ever occupied. Ruiz claims that people have battled pessimistic or fatalistic submission to these conditions through enthrallment to gods, to sensual pleasure, or to abstraction, imagination, exegesis, proposition, and speculation.

Ruiz ranges through history to illustrate his thesis. We visit medieval revelers using hedonism to flout the plague, and we visit contemporary suicidal evangelicals using fantasies of heaven to flout the chaos of twentieth/twenty-first-century life. Ruiz summarizes the third mode of escape as the humanist commonplace that "the art of writing, painting, composing, or making films about the dark events in mankind's history can offer redemption and catharsis."[7] Although his argument and examples sound like truisms, Ruiz's project uses peculiar choices and a rich, affecting mood of inquiry to play out E. O. Wilson's elegant statement, "The dominating influence that spawned the arts [in the context of cognitive evolution] was the need to impose order on the confusion caused by intelligence."[8] Ruiz invites his reader to explore the relentless creative impulse enacted by deeply conscious men and women who build imaginary and futile boats against their currents to bear themselves away from an intolerable reality.

Each fantasy mode is only effective because the labor and sacrifice required can produce results identical to reality. You may be called to the demanding rituals and ruthless introspection of the religious life; you may endure the addict's prison in the revels of hedonism; you may accept the expense and competition characterizing the creative/scholarly life. None of these escapes, however futile, is effortless and instantaneous. For each fantasy there is still the hard and constant work of rowing against inevitable suffering, cruelty, and decay. Ruiz sees himself rowing with everyone else. In addition to the book serving to explore questions raised by students in his UCLA course called "The Terror of History," it "is also an attempt to answer these questions for myself.... I have become even more confused than I have ever been, but also more keenly aware of our endless search as humans for meaning."[9]

Ruiz's book casts light on Dylan's millennial work. The songs' personas repeatedly face unseen enemies when the only real adversaries are time and age. The antique and ahistorical landscape of these records cannot be traveled outside the songs: shards of the Civil War are buried under mythic floods and nameless roads and allegorical rivers. Yet the presence of the voice singing these songs creates an insistent here-and-now. The rocks and gravel of Dylan's voice on *Love and Theft* and his honeyed crooning on *Modern Times* both command the listener's full sensuous attention with nimble phrasing and expressive tones. Dylan's voice forces our imagination into worlds shimmering among past, present, and no-time, and into actions that alarm or appease without justification. All the flailing and threatening and relenting on these records create the experience of thrashing about outside time and place while chained to inexorable mortal conditions and submitting to the sensual intoxication of music and rhyme. This is a passable summary of Ruiz's premise.

Ruiz ends his book discussing James Thomson's 1874 poem, *The City of Dreadful Night*.[10] In over 1,120 lines, Thomson allegorizes despair and isolation in a world without meaning. Thomson's Victorian vision certainly opposes Žižek's. Only subjectivity answers for Thomson's immiserated world because he sees human life through the eyes of an incurable melancholic. The poem is set in a labyrinthine city of dim streets and looming buildings that have never housed laughter or a roaring fire. The residents grieve endlessly for the dead, brood endlessly on past misery, and seek audiences for their miseries. In one scene, a minister addresses his bleak congregation who are still chained to the carcass of religion. With lurid excitement, the minister announces he can now offer them relief: explorers have returned from the farthest reaches of the universe with the proclamation that god does not exist. Therefore, hallelujah, suicide is no longer forbidden. Religion in the City of Dreadful Night authorizes its own nullity, and thereby achieves religion's purpose—the consolation of its followers.

Thomson's creative labor is a worthy adversary to his malignant vision. The extended allegory may be too redundant to inspire or impress new generations of readers, but Thomson's Dreadful Night is impressively visual and he does vivid justice to his own intimacy with harrowing despair. Ruiz does not argue for Thomson's greatness but asks the poem to serve as a companion in his project. "I felt," Ruiz writes, "as if I had discovered some kindred pessimistic soul."[11] An artist builds an imaginary boat with which to fight his own epoch's current of terror and uncertainty, and these boats may be strong enough to hold strangers from a future of new uncertainties. That of course is the dream of art's immortality.

In "Ain't Talkin'," where we will meet our final act of violence, Dylan shares Thomson's impulse to allegorize the loss of meaning and solace in an opaque and suffering invented world. However, for all the superficial pessimism and restiveness "Ain't Talkin'" shares with Thomson's vision, this song (to repeat Ruiz's words) "flee[s] from the death grip of history and . . . confront[s] the weight of history and the uncertainty of the world" with humanity, appetite, and luster that are Dylan's own.

There is at least one precedent in Dylan's work for the sudden blow that launches "Ain't Talkin'." In the 2003 song Dylan wrote for the soundtrack of the Civil War movie *Gods and Generals*, "'Cross the Green Mountain," a single voice describes the Civil War with both contingent and godlike vision.

The singer's preternatural scope can see that "the ravaged land lies for miles behind," and he can also ventriloquize individual characters including different soldiers and a soldier's mother. The song is delivered via epiphany: the singer sleeps by a stream on Green Mountain then suddenly, "heaven blazing in my head / I—I dreamt a monstrous dream." The singer receives the past in one blow that causes him to stagger; "I—I . . . ," he stutters with the force. In Yeats's "Leda and the Swan," the "sudden blow" is the character's curse and offers no vision. Leda is impregnated with the seed of calamity and no prescience that she will mother indelible history. Dylan's sudden blow is the inspired vision of past calamity; "Green Mountain" is the song born of this blow.

On the contrary, the blow to the head in "Ain't Talkin'" takes the singer *into real time*. The song begins in a morbid dream world unlike the Gothic and cocky setting of "Moonlight." In this "mystic garden / The wounded flowers were dangling from the vines." "Ain't Talkin'"s garden has fallen and is touched with dark arts. There is a "cool and crystal fountain," which seems to offer unhealthy charmed refreshment. The singer moves freely here. He "went out" of his own accord and takes his time to "[wander] by" the fountain. He's comfortable in the cover of night surrounded by dying things in a place unreal and suspicious. For the first time in this song cycle, the singer is attacked. "Someone hit me from behind."

This blow wakes him from his underworld into this world. Here things are "mysterious and vague," unlike the garden where myth and Romance allow a tired artist to tarry half-consciously. Now awakened, he is goaded and frustrated. There is no tarrying, just moving ever forward to endure what he meets despite his weariness and the world's obscurity. And he meets the grim and corrupted facts of love, virtue, faith, art, and hope. Desire torments his "miserable brain." Conscience shows him the evil dwelling in human hearts. Real cities are full of suffering. Only a few remaining companions share whatever unexplained "code" he can still follow honestly. He is empty of prayer for himself but appeals to his mother—or Mother—to intercede for him. He feels the "fire" that desires to create, even without the "light" that confers knowledge. And even so, it may not be too late for the "heavenly aid" of divine inspiration. But this song is not the product of the inspiration he wants: when he tells us he ain't talkin', we err in inferring he is just keeping his own counsel on the road and singing confidentially to us. The refrain may mean the singer has nothing to tell anyone and there are no secrets in these lyrics for a privileged audience.

Why leave a mystic garden for this hard and bitter work? He was even resting by a "cool" fountain; now his heart is miserably "burning." "Ain't Talkin'" is not surrender; it is the sheer effort of enduring doubt, unrequited desires, and pandemic suffering—and knowing no other form of endurance but song. Thematically, "Ain't Talkin'" may be a fine climax to this two-record song cycle characterized by the battle between vitality and lassitude. But "Ain't Talkin'" goes further to enact the mysterious imperative of creativity. The impulse that drives the persona of Dylan's song out of the half-life of his garden in order to describe the real "mysterious and vague" world cannot be identified or denied. To feel this impulse as a sneak attack from an unknown and cowardly assailant is to confess that life is a gratuitous, inexplicable, and binding contract.

On November 20, 2006, I stared down at the top of Bob Dylan's head from my high seat in New York's City Center, a classy venue on West 56th Street. This show was a one-off late addition to the fall 2006 tour. Seats were expensive and this was the only inarguably cool thing happening in New York the Monday before Thanksgiving. Therefore, the crowd was primarily smug and smartly dressed; the hardcore fans were in the minority. The theater was politely hushed at the opening of the first encore and then the miracle occurred that blasted my politeness to bits: Tony Garnier sat with a cello and sent forth the lovely lugubrious opening strain of "Ain't Talkin'"—the first public live performance of the song. On the bootleg recording of the show, you can hear my cry of welcome in the quiet space. I happened to be enduring at the time what Kingsley Amis calls a metaphysical hangover (it is exactly the same as a standard hangover, but what's left of one's dignity fights back in sorrow and pity) and this induced an excruciating sensitivity to anything mortal, beautiful, or redemptive. We also row against our own self-destructions. "Ain't Talkin'" is a masterpiece of mortality and beauty and redemption. So when the real Bob Dylan sang that blow to his head—right there below me—and went on singing of his brave odyssey through a wretched world, I felt as much Here and Now as I have ever been able to stand. If only Dylan would sing it again, and again. I dreamed of hearing it with a clear head.

If this sudden blow brought me relevance, it was self-centered relevance. The collective and the solitary have not sat together easily for the fifty years of Bob Dylan's audiences. In 1964 I would have shared with my seatmates a righteous and topical relevance hearing Bob Dylan sing of Hattie Carroll "killed by a blow." We would come together in complicity and in the urge to change and redeem the world. "Ain't Talkin'" and "The Lonesome Death of Hattie Carroll" bridge forty-two years of changing audiences and sensibilities, and at either end of the bridge are different definitions of *meaning for me in my time*. Did Bob Dylan engineer this bridge or did his listeners? Does the answer lie in how little we have in common, or how much?

The relation between acts of violence and moral understanding has been crucial to Dylan's work at different times, and continues to be crucial in ways that may not satisfy the generation who cut their teeth on "The Death of Emmett Till." Even today, this generation throws down gauntlets to newcomers. For example, David Dalton, in *Who Is That Man? In Search of the Real Bob Dylan* (2012), describes the audience at a post-2000 concert: "Sure there are all the old fogies, but they're in the minority. In their place are the too late born Bobcats, who missed the 60s but for whom that decade was the golden age, and Bob its avatar and masterpiece."[12] Dalton's nostalgia requires him to see the perspective of newcomers to Dylan's work through a narrow aperture: today's Dylan must be a false and idolized projection or a magnificently preserved fossil. Wresting Dylan out of the grip of that nostalgia can feel like a violent tug-of-war, so violence may be method and matter here.

NOTES

1. William Shakespeare, *The Tragedy of Hamlet, Prince of Denmark* (1603). http://shakespeare.mit.edu/hamlet/.
2. Mark Danner, *Stripping Bare the Body: Politics Violence War* (New York: Nation Books, 2009), xvii.
3. Lewis Carroll, *Alice's Adventures in Wonderland and Through the Looking-Glass* (New York: Barnes and Noble Classics, 2004), 188.
4. Kokomo Arnold, "Mean Old Twister" (1937). *MaxiLyrics*. www.maxilyrics.com/kokomo-arnold-mean-old-twister-lyrics-19a2.html.
5. Slavoj Žižek, *Violence* (New York: Picador, 2008), 155, 1, 2.
6. Teofilo F. Ruiz, *The Terror of History: On the Uncertainties of Life in Western Civilization* (Princeton and Oxford: Princeton University Press, 2011), 3.
7. Ruiz, *The Terror of History*, 135.
8. Edward O. Wilson, *Consilience* (New York: Vintage, 1999), 245.
9. Ruiz, *The Terror of History*, 2.
10. James Thomson, *The City of Dreadful Night* (1874). Project Gutenberg. www.gutenberg.org/files/1238/1238-h/1238-h.htm.
11. Ruiz, *The Terror of History*, 167.
12. David Dalton, *Who Is That Man?: In Search of the Real Bob Dylan* (New York: Hyperion, 2012), 332.

NARRATIVE IN "LOVE AND THEFT," MODERN TIMES, AND TEMPEST

Jonathan Hodgers

Bob Dylan is a storyteller. From his self-mythologizing days in Greenwich Village to his memoir, *Chronicles*, Dylan has shown a fondness for narrative both in his songwriting and his public persona. This article will center on how *"Love and Theft," Modern Times*, and *Tempest* continue to reflect Dylan's playful and experimental approach to the organizational framework of narrative, which in its broadest sense refers to the representation of a series of events.[1] Added to this one might include the idea of causality—that the events depicted are in some way related.[2] For Dylan, the most common outlet for this process is located in the songs' words and their delivery. With the emphasis on the linguistic and performative, how does Dylan approach narrative in these albums in a way that might reflect a change or an evolution from what has come before? Are there vestiges of linearity, or has he delved deeper into the break-up of time achieved for the first time on *Blood on the Tracks*?[3] This essay shows that Dylan may have moved further into this concept by divesting from his work the idea of an autonomous, self-sufficient text, and instead situated his work in a longitudinal spectrum of literary influences where narratives are suggested laterally throughout an album, as well as historically via the use of preexisting text.

To develop these ideas, the article will investigate how these albums fit into Dylan's established narrative norms, and the similarities and differences they share as storytelling pieces. Of particular interest are the effects of Dylan's copy-and-paste methodology, and the strategies Dylan employs to counterbalance these diffuse raw materials and suggest thematic unity. Whether the songs aspire to unity at all will also be explored by incorporating theories native to cinema studies—namely the principles of montage editing—which will be posited as a framework for understanding Dylan's recent output. An attempt will be made to bridge the gap between each record by teasing out their complementary lyrical/musical milieus, and by exploring to what extent the latter albums can be considered an evolution from *"Love and Theft."* The albums obviously do not exist in isolation, and where pertinent there will be an attempt to show how trends throughout these records extend backward and forward in his catalogue and throw light on earlier and later working practices. *Tempest* in particular can be seen as a further proponent of the methods found in *"Love and Theft"* and *Modern Times*, and will be explored as a spiritual sequel to those albums. To begin, the article will investigate the lyrical units by which Dylan constructs his songs: the couplets and the folk and blues floaters that comprise the narrative's building blocks.

The first step is to draw attention to Dylan's use of previously available literary and musical text as woven around his original text. Existing in various guises from his earliest recordings, this practice became dominant with *Time Out of Mind*.[4] On this album, Dylan once again became focused on exploring a particular set of concerns across the expanse of the album (namely lost love and aging) whose cumulative consideration influenced the album's mood and direction. Quotation and allusion in this case were put in the service of a unified narrative voice. This immersion in a particular phraseology was last heard on *Saved*. In that instance, Dylan foregrounded scriptural language at the expense of his own, original language.[5] As with *Time Out of Mind*, a stable narrator was implied with a consistency of tone and message, with allusion serving a single voice.

In *"Love and Theft,"* allusion is once again a key methodology, yet rather than employ allusion in the service of a theme, allusion and quotation are thematic material. The album's quilt or patchwork-like quality is implied by the often self-contained phrases or couplets that permeate the songs. Examples include: "Been workin' on the mainline—workin' like the devil / The game is the same—it's just on another level" from "Po' Boy" or "The ladies down in Darktown, they're doing the Darktown Strut / You always got to be prepared but you never know for what" from "Sugar Baby." Not only is the content resolved by the resolution of the sentence, but in formal terms the couplets' internal and end rhymes suggest completion. These "floaters"—single lines or couplets—often echo each other tonally and metrically yet freely traverse the album, undermining demarcations such as song titles and even distinctions between narrative speakers. Transferring lines from one song to another is not a new practice for Dylan,[6] yet their migratory potential in these latter-day albums is notable. Language as a context-sensitive construct emerges as a thematic concern.

Another feature of this style is the downplaying of narrative delineations. On many prior albums amid more symbolist lyrics, Dylan strikes a rich narrative vein, throwing the more stream-of-consciousness pieces into relief. None of the songs from *"Love and Theft"* chart a concrete sequence of events. Rather than the songs or album being taken to a narrative close à la *Blonde on Blonde* or *John Wesley Harding*, the final tracks and final lines instead form the last piece of a tapestry whose effect is strengthened by its proximity to other elements. Connective tissue like jokes and one-liners, Shakespearean references, references to family members, along with structurally similar tracks (twins such as "Cry a While" with "Honest with Me" and triplets like "Bye and Bye," "Floater," and "Po' Boy") contribute to the album's wholeness, with no one song functioning as a touchstone. Instead of the narrative resolution of a "Black Diamond Bay" or "Sara" (1976), the *"Love and Theft"* songs instead hint at an emotional resolution. Some of the tracks also gain momentum with a gradual, intuitive perception of or insight into the reality or essential meaning of something, usually initiated by a simple, homely, or commonplace occurrence or experience. An instance of this is the piquant close of "Floater (Too Much to Ask)": "It's not always easy kicking someone out / Gotta wait a while—it can be an unpleasant task . . ."

The use of traveling couplets and other supple phrases provides for the occasional juxtaposition of vaguely contrasting lines into one verse, unified by rhyme and meter but whose attitude is discordant. While in *"Love and Theft"* Dylan often ties the verses together using a consistent emotional tone (see "Summer Days" and especially "High Water") the practice throws up greater friction when he pursues it in *Modern Times*. In *"Love and Theft,"* for example, "Floater" contains the following verse: "If you ever try to interfere with me or cross my path again / You do so at the peril of your own life." The verse shifts the tone of the song, yet there is enough time spent accounting for the shift—the key line being "I've seen enough heartaches and strife"—that the transition does not jar. Conversely, in "Thunder on the Mountain" from *Modern Times* the listener hears: "Shame on your greed, shame on your wicked schemes / I'll say this, I don't give a damn about your dreams." This schism is furthered by Dylan vocally, who is percussive on the word "shame" both times around. This has the effect of sharpening the transition between the first and second couplet, and adding an off-kilter quality to the narrative voice.

Narrative blind spots frequently occur within the verses, almost as if conclusions are being drawn without the listener being guided through the thought process. An example can again be found in "Thunder on the Mountain": "I've been sitting down studying the art of love / I think it will fit me like a glove," which moves from tenderness, to chauvinism to rumination. While one can see this as overspill from Dylan's copy-and-paste process, he indulges its effect prolifically on *Modern Times*.[7]

DEFYING TIME

This leads to a facet of *Modern Times* that has its precedents in *"Love and Theft"* yet has become pronounced enough to be regarded as a singular quality of the later album. *Modern Times* fosters anonymity, vocally and musically, which unsettles listeners by denying us the moral/ethical position of the narrator. Concurrent with the delivery is the frequent use of erratic lyrics that resist basic categorizations such as time, space, and context. The effect of non sequiturs and the roaming couplets of *"Love and Theft"* are intensified. Having already looked at this effect from "Thunder on the Mountain," a further telling example is "Workingman's Blues #2."

The juxtaposing of verses in this song conveys a narrator expressing himself from several different perspectives—not necessarily different points in time as in *Blood on the Tracks* but from several variants of the narrator. Dylan places us in many locations throughout: "I'm listenin' to the steel rails hum," "Tossed by the winds and the seas," "Well, they burned my barn," and "All across the peaceful sacred fields." Such diffuseness is not altogether implausible in a balladic context, yet further fissions cast doubt on the sense of narrative consistency. An example can be found in the penultimate verse, where there is a gulf between the first and second ABAB unit. The initial four lines yield to a change in fortunes, as the narrator goes from destitute and alone to married and resigned: "Got a brand new suit and a brand new wife / I can live on rice and beans." These jump cuts undermine a criteria of narrative—that of connectivity between events. Dylan's songs are often not so traditionally story based, yet many do accrue tangible effects by the ordering of images. *Desire* co-lyricist Jacques Levy perceptively highlighted this feature of Dylan's writing: "It's not easy for him to stick with a narrative. He's much stronger with ... a series of images that are sometimes quite abstract, but little by little open up the idea that you're after. There may be many narratives in it for one or two verses, but the whole thing usually is not part of one long narrative."[8] "Workingman's Blues #2," like "Thunder on the Mountain," ventures further than this, with frequent discord in the song's spatiotemporal orientation. "The

Levee's Gonna Break" is likewise bustling with discord, while the fixity of impending disaster forms an ironic counterpoint. The result is a song whose narrative is prismatic. There is an implication of multiple presents as part of an expansive Venn diagram of dialogic voices.

To borrow a term from cinematic discourse, this method of songwriting could be considered analogous to the Kuleshov effect, where raw materials (not necessarily original) are juxtaposed by the artist to create meaning. With this method, it is not the content of the images in a film that is important, but their combination. Identified most strongly with Sergei Eisenstein—director of *Strike* (1925), *Battleship Potemkin* (1925), and *October* (1928)—the theory of montage as adapted from the original theorist Lev Kuleshov is that collision or conflict must be inherent to all visual signs. An example provided by Eisenstein himself is a set of shots depicting a poor woman with her starving child sitting at a table where an empty bowl sits, then a cut to a second group of shots depicting an overweight man covered in jewelry and seated at a table laden with food. The rapid juxtaposition of these two sets of images causes a third set to emerge in the spectator's mind of the inequality existing between the proletariat and the bourgeoisie.[9] Dylan seemed to attest to the strength of such stark juxtaposition, especially in relation to class. In his (in)famous interview with *Time*'s Horace Judson featured in *Dont Look Back*, when pressed on what he considered the "truth," Dylan responds: "A plain picture of, let's say, a tramp vomiting, man, into the sewer, and next door, Mr. Rockefeller, or Mr. C. W. Jones, on the subway going to work."[10] A similar process is at work in *Modern Times*. In "The Levee's Gonna Break," Dylan sings: "Some people got barely enough skin to cover their bones," neighboring the line with a verse that begins: "Put on your cat clothes, Mama, put on your evening dress," showing a gulf between rich and poor not only with his choice of imagery, but also in the narrative gap between the end of the chorus and the beginning of the next verse.

With this assemblage style, the listener is responsible for creatively interpreting what he or she hears. Comments made by Dylan suggest that he facilitates this listener-centric approach. In a 2001 interview he bristles at the idea that he is responsible for the songs' meanings on *Time Out of Mind*: "People say the record deals with mortality—*my* mortality for some reason.... It maybe just deals with mortality in general.... But I didn't see any one critic say: 'It deals with *my* mortality'—you know, his *own*."[11] In 2004, when confronted by Robert Hilburn with the lyrics to "Just Like a Woman" (1966), Dylan responds: "I'm not too good at defining things. It's up to the listener to figure out what it means to him."[12]

"HISTORY, TRUE OR FEIGNED"

Up to this point, analysis has concentrated on juxtaposition between the songs' verses and choruses. I would like to turn now to the actual language Dylan uses in both these albums, and how it relates to his previous and later work. In contrast with the magnanimousness of *"Love and Theft,"* *Modern Times* is increasingly circumspect. *"Love and Theft"* often features disarming verses where the narrator shares with his audience unguarded family history such as "mother was a daughter of a wealthy farmer" in "Po' Boy" or "my pa he died and left me" in "Lonesome Day Blues." *Modern Times* presents itself in a more stately fashion, and is carefully checked by the singing and the music (see "Workingman's Blues #2" with its precisely fashioned "My cruel weapons have been put on the shelf / Come sit down on my knee..."). Dylan's vocals and his production duties as Jack Frost contribute to this tone. Developing from its predecessor, *Modern Times* hones the non sequiturs and sudden detours into a construct that approaches abstraction. The terseness in the language does not allow for careful explanation as to who is talking or when and where. As seen already in "Workingman's Blues #2," many different versions of the working man jostle together, sometimes blended and other times set apart, but without the lyrical addenda suggestive of a consistent first-person narrator, or one that might individualize the songs' characters. A sense of communal solidarity pervades, with all voices and feelings united under the roof of Dylan's vocals.

Dylan has shorn his narrative of all sense of context, using a type of imagery and language that downplays the importance or even relevance of boxing-in devices like chronology, location, or identity. His use of this durable, elemental imagery—such as the train, the farmer, the river, and other generationally neutral signifiers—in a given combination of couplets and phrases creates the third images in Kuleshov's model. Regarding the actual lexicon from which he draws these archetypes, Dylan has been clear: "My terminology all comes from folk music. It doesn't come from the radio or TV or computers or any of that stuff. It's embedded in the folk music of the English language."[13] This use of imagery is addressed by Dylan in a conversation with Bill Flanagan on painting in 2009:

> DYLAN: Images are taken at face value and it kind of freed me up.
> FLANAGAN: In what way?
> DYLAN: Well for instance, if there are shadows and flowers and swampy ledges in a composition, that's what they are in their essence. There's no mystification. That's one way I can explain it.

FLANAGAN: Like a locomotive, a pair of boots, a kiss or the rain?

DYLAN: Right. All those things are what they are. Or pieces of what they are. It's the way you move them around that makes it work.[14]

How transferable and adaptable these elements are—"the way you move them around"—appears key to Dylan's construction of meaning in his recent material.

Dylan's lyrical preoccupations, be they "a locomotive, a pair of boots, a kiss or the rain," are all seemingly used for their instant aesthetic resonance, or their "face value." This leads to the imagery becoming rarefied, and taking on an archetypical significance that overrules the importance of contextual detail. This use of archetypical language fosters "applicability" over more reductive, specific language. To borrow a quote from J. R. R. Tolkien: "I cordially dislike allegory in all its manifestations. . . . I much prefer history, true or feigned, with its varied applicability to the thought and experience of readers. I think that many confuse 'applicability' with 'allegory'; but the one resides in the freedom of the reader, and the other in the purposed domination of the author."[15] This reader-centric approach employed by Tolkien finds a parallel with Dylan's listener-centric direction, where the listener is encouraged to respond from his or her experience and not that of the author's. "Workingman's Blues #2" in particular uses a rustic, historic vocabulary but the sentiments expressed can be transposed onto many analogous situations in the present. There is a gathering sense that names and locations are transient and that mood, sentiment, and symbolic value are the consistencies that deserve the most attention. This is writ large in *Modern Times*, where there is a stripping away of too-defined contexts and parameters that could narrow the applicability of the song. The language therefore is detached from its time of recording, and the old-time milieu is prefigured as a group of archetypes and imagery that transcends national boundaries and overrides any of the alienating effects of specificity. This stands in contrast to the specificity of certain eighties-era songs ("Union Sundown," "Neighborhood Bully" [both 1983]) and marks a return of sorts to the lyrical openness of "Blowin' in the Wind" or "Masters of War", yet with a highly stylized lexicon of archetypical figures and imagery.

THE PERFECT STORM?

To close, a few observations on Dylan's recent narrative journey are necessary, if only to attempt a snapshot of Dylan's latest writing mode *in media* res. Since *Modern Times*, Dylan has released two studio albums of original material, allowing us to see how narrative construction in *"Love and Theft"* and *Modern Times* has been advanced or jettisoned, as well as Dylan's continued exploration of the montage-based writing first hit upon in *"Love and Theft."* Of particular interest is *Tempest*, due to its confluence of Dylan's montage-based writing style and older balladic traditions.[16]

Tempest, like *"Love and Theft,"* establishes motifs that are revisited throughout the album. In the case of the latter, references to family, Shakespeare, and minstrelsy pervade numerous songs. With *"Love and Theft"* they are integrated into the thematic fabric of the song, and clearly signposted with proper nouns connected to the topic ("I wish my mother was still alive," "Othello told Desdemona" and others). Slavery is a recurring motif of *Tempest*, yet is integrated in a more shadowy fashion with Dylan's linguistic "applicability" in full force. In some cases this is suggested by words and images that reverberate with thematic connectivity, such as this example from "Narrow Way": "This is hard country to stay alive in / Blades are everywhere and they're breaking my skin." The threat of a violent death, the play on "country" as both nation and geographic area, the weary protraction of the term "struggling hard," and the proximity of "skin" and "scarred" all accrue resonance with the phraseology of slavery. If we focus for a moment on "Pay in Blood," a look at one verse in particular highlights some of the nuance that can emerge from this writing strategy, this time via the added layer of quotation. lines hint at the theme of slavery, yet as one registers Dylan's source material, the effect becomes reinforced and enriched. From the second verse of "Pay in Blood": "I got something in my pocket make your eyeballs swim / I got dogs could tear you limb from limb." While already open to a reading that suggests slavery, Dylan accentuates this with a reference to abolitionist poet John Greenleaf Whittier in the line: "I'm circling around the southern zone."[17] While Whittier's original phrase is couched in the idiom of weather, Dylan implies a wry double meaning in the term "southern" by implying the American South, with all its attendant resonances throughout the music and writing of *Tempest* and beyond. Given the inference of Whittier, who carries with him the evocation of an era and the subject matter of slavery, both that topic and its Civil War milieu emerge from the passage more strongly and contribute to an album-wide trend. There is also an irony at play here in the use of the abolitionist Whittier's phrase in such proximity to the line: "I got dogs could tear you limb from limb." While the line by itself evokes no particular time frame, the subsequent line evoking Whittier places the listener in the slavery-era American South, where the dread of trained dogs loomed large for the runaway slave.[18] The dichotomous push and pull between an abolitionist's phraseology and the repressive sentiment also has a dark irony, and seems to play into Dylan's oft-returned to concern with how original meanings and contexts are open to inversion and corruption. The antebellum insinuation has a knock-on effect on the refrain of "I pay in blood but not my own," which, in this context, suggests the suffering of the slaves for the profit of their masters. Whittier's presence enhances the richness of the passage by coloring the surrounding lines with the context of the South's era of de jure slavery. It also allows Dylan-as-narrator to signpost his intentions and make more explicit his thematic concerns, giving the line "I'm circling around the southern zone" a multifaceted importance.

While the existing verse already hints at the topic, a deeper reading discloses further shades of meaning that add complexity to the material. Along with the judicious use of applicability that bolsters the slavery motif, Dylan also continues to explore the effects of the floating couplets looked at previously. This too shows further development in *Tempest*, with Dylan trading off the familiarity of certain phrases to subvert expectations, in particular exploiting the couplet's two-line format to create interesting poetic effects. While Whittier enhances the slavery theme in "Pay in Blood," the implications suggested by the words of others is arguably most salient in "Roll On John," where phrases associated with the late Beatle are more overt to the casual listener than a Whittier or Ovid. While Dylan uses some of Lennon's phrases to fresh and poignant effect—such as the use of the opening line from a "A Day in the Life" (1967): "I heard the news today, oh boy" to evoke the news of John Lennon's death—Dylan interestingly defers to William Blake's "The Tyger" (1794) for the final verse, and interposes a line from an eighteenth-century children's prayer: "Tyger, tyger burning bright / I pray the lord my soul to keep." Blake's "The Tyger" carries an abundance of associative ideas and themes. Not least among these is the manufacturedness of the eponymous tiger, and the incredulity of the narrator at the boundless scope of its creator ("Did he who made the Lamb make thee?"). In associating Lennon with Blake's tiger, Dylan makes Blake's wonder his own in the light of contemplating Lennon. Dylan's use of Blake here is also a subtly personal touch, and a witty one in the light of Lennon's closeted reading of the poet, according to Marianne Faithfull's recounting of the meeting between Dylan, Allen Ginsberg, and the Beatles in August 1964. (A defensive Lennon, having been quizzed by Ginsberg, reportedly said he had never heard of William Blake, to which Cynthia Lennon balked, "Oh, John, stop lying."[19]) Dylan's granting of Blake's words to the standoffish

Lennon therefore works as a subtle olive branch offered to the more interior and personal space kept guarded by the singer.

Aside from the resonances brought about by evoking Blake, Dylan is using these borrowed lines in a way that trades off their familiarity. These lines, unlike the Whittier reference in "Pay in Blood," are likely to be noticed by most listeners. The strange bifurcation of one of poetry's most famous couplets with yet another famous line has the effect of delaying the expected in a blatant fashion. It is easy to jump ahead of Dylan's languorous phrasing after the initial "Tyger, Tyger burning bright" to the familiar "In the forest of the night," yet Dylan inserts "I pray the lord my soul to keep," the second line of another famous couplet, "Now I lay me down to sleep / I pray the Lord my soul to keep." The expectations that emerge from the two famous couplets are deferred, each missing a line that would naturally be heard next to the other. Only with the third line of the verse does Dylan deliver on the expectation of Blake's famous opening line. We could be excused for expecting some variant of the missing line from the eighteenth-century prayer, and Dylan duly delivers it with a twist: "Cover him over and let him sleep," which owes something to the missing line: "Now I lay me down to sleep." The transpositions produce interesting effects on a conceptual level. The delivering on expectations is playfully withheld, and just as a pattern is suggested, Dylan subverts it by rewriting the expected line. The arch playfulness seems reflective of Lennon, and works as a knowing subtext underneath Dylan's sincere delivery.

Dylan adds yet another interesting aspect to this final line, in the use of the Dylanesque broken grammar of the phrase "Cover him over." This deliberately slippery construction (one thinks back to "all *along* the watchtower") is such a consistent feature of Dylan's writing that it elicits in the avid listener a spark of recognition. This is the voice of a historic Dylan persona, as opposed to Blake, or *The New England Primer* (1687–90).[20] After the previous three lines, quoted verbatim from other sources and eminently public domain in status, a familiar "Dylan" effect is dropped in by the writer, evoking himself in a way as obvious to his long-term listeners as "The Tyger" and the children's prayer would be to the general public. In this verse, Dylan has withheld his own lexical stamp—the three previously lines were emphatically not his own—so that when the familiar Dylan returns, the poignancy is increased by our awareness that the sentiment is resoundingly "his."

Tempest is also notable for retaining the process of montage writing and applying it to balladic material told in a more conventionally narrative fashion. At least two songs seem to marshal the strengths of the montage style and integrate them into a more disciplined narrative structure. Compositionally, "Tin Angel" and the title track are the most redolent as they mark a definite revisit to the balladic narrative tradition in contrast to *"Love and Theft"* and *Modern Times*. Yet Dylan has not necessarily sacrificed the strengths of one writing method in returning to an older form. The ballad "Tempest" in particular seems to adapt the montage-writing predilection for gathering multifarious references from disparate time frames and sources and applying them to the disciplined telling of a prolonged story. Source material for the song includes the Carter Family template, including the conceit of the watchman figure dreaming of the ship's fate. Edgar Allan Poe's "The Raven" (1845) provides "Nameless here forever more" in the thirty-seventh verse. Juvenal's *Satires* (ca.1st–2nd century CE) gave Dylan "Davey the brothel-keeper" who "Came out dismissed his girls," as well as the brandy-pouring host who "stayed right till the end, he was the last to go."[21] The reference to "Leo" in particular is an effective conflating of fact, fiction, genre, and chronology, suggestive of an oceanic no-time in which the *Titanic* tragedy occurs.[22] The song also manages to strike a balancing act between ambiguity (such as the "watchman") and concrete sensual detail. "Tin Angel," the other pointedly narrative song, shows Dylan embracing the archetypes hinted at in *"Love and Theft"* and *Modern Times* in particular (the song is clearly modelled on the itself-archetypical "Gypsy Davey" [trad.]), and indulges in their associated character arcs, lingering to regard the ritualistic nature of the format in savory detail. Similar to *Modern Times*, Dylan's narrator is omniscient, reporting back from the gods in the upper balcony with a detachment that precludes judgment or a moral/ethical standpoint.

One final point to make here is that the curious amalgam of writing styles and the tone struck by Dylan's narrators in *Tempest* do not conclude its connections to *Modern Times*. *Tempest* seems in some instances to have revisited the framework of certain of that 2004 album's songs, "Narrow Way" being redolent of "The Levee's Gonna Break," while "Scarlet Town" strikes a similar chord to "Ain't Talkin'." The tight musicality of *Modern Times* also has more in common with *Tempest*, as does the diversity of the songs contained therein. *Together Through Life*, with its brevity and amiable tone and musicianship, seems slightly set apart canonically in terms of construction. With the renewed interest shown by Dylan in the heavily montage-based assemblages derived from the *Modern Times* mold, a continuance of the writing strategies of *Modern Times/Tempest* in the future is not inconceivable. Yet as Dylan is not immune to sequencing prescient final tracks on his earlier albums, the concluding tracks of the *Tempest* album may be an indication of an increasing interest in long-form narratives with a clear chronology, bolstered by the montage philosophy.

"UP THE ROAD, AROUND THE BEND . . ."

In broad terms, we can discern a way of seeing Dylan's later work as having a unique internal logic whose codes and stratagems favor a listener-centric approach, a playful eschewal of a reliable narrator, and a folk derived wordscape upon which perpetually relevant concerns can be projected.

What might be construed as a change in Dylan's narrative style between the two albums could be the shift in the positioning of the listener from participant in *"Love and Theft"* to spectator in *Modern Times*. Several incremental factors in the earlier record accrue to a conviviality that places the listener in a meta-dialogue with the narrator. Elements contributing to this effect are the confessional tone of the lyrics. One example is the sudden poignant transition into longing on "Lonesome Day Blues" where Dylan sings "I wish my mother was still alive." For a contrasting treatment of the same archetypical figure on *Modern Times*, "Ain't Talkin'" features considered language and delivery that keeps both the narrator's addressee and the listener at arm's length: "They say prayer has the power to help / So pray for me mother" and "I'm trying to love my neighbor and do good unto others / But oh, mother, things ain't going well." To further its personable tone, *"Love and Theft"* is littered with mini-narratives about the narrator's family and lifetime. *Modern Times* keeps many of its songs in the present, and is speculative as to the future. The aloof quality extends to the more ostensibly romantic songs. Where "Moonlight" hinges on an imploring question that hangs in the air, the comparable "Spirit on the Water" maintains a declarative tone, extended even to the question the narrator puts to his partner, whereupon he answers himself: "You ever seen a ghost? No / But you have heard of them." The song also courts a wryly ominous tone when the narrator tells her: "I wanna be with you in paradise / And it seems so unfair. . . ." It is this flexible narration that Dylan draws on most with the advent of *Tempest*, when he again picks up the montage-like format from *Modern Times*.

This brings us to our last point. Narrative in this mode of songwriting (compiling?) extends longitudinally rather than laterally throughout the song. In using preexisting sources, connections to other contexts outside of the song are the prerogative of the listener, aping a particularly modern concept of hyperlinking to connected texts. There is a sense that as of *Time Out of Mind* Dylan is pioneering a lexicon layered with subtextual mini-narratives. The adaptation and tacit acknowledgment of existing texts (verbal and musical) is as old as Dylan's career, yet only with the release of *"Love and Theft"* has the practice become formalized as a songwriting tool, and apparently an integral part of all new output.[23] While the present analysis has been concerned with the effect of surface forms and how juxtaposition and contrasts create meaning, these meanings can however be subverted or enhanced depending on the listener's attunement to Dylan's sources. As attested to by *Tempest*, Dylan is continuing to advance his thematic concerns with the breadcrumbs of quotations and allusions, and in the process, deepening and adding complexity to his own material in a manner that engages the listener in a pan-textual dialogue. As the literary excavation of his writings continues to flourish, Dylan's art will likely continue to reveal greater and greater depths.

NOTES

1. H. Porter Abbott, *The Cambridge Introduction to Narrative* (New York: Cambridge University Press, 2002), 12.
2. Abbott, *The Cambridge Introduction to Narrative*, 12.
3. Bob Dylan's terminology, taken from his interview with Matt Damsker on September 15, 1978, quoted in Bert Cartwright, "The Mysterious Norman Raeben," in *Wanted Man: In Search of Bob Dylan*, John Bauldie, ed. (London: Penguin, 1992), 96.
4. Michael Gray, *Song and Dance Man III: The Art of Bob Dylan* (London: Continuum, 2004), 16.
5. Heylin, *Still on the Road: The Songs of Bob Dylan*, 193–220.
6. Damien Love, "Bob Dylan: *Tell Tale Signs* Special—Mark Howard," *Uncut*. www.uncut.co.uk/bob-dylan/bob-dylan-tell-tale-signs-special-mark-howard-interview.
7. See also "Someday Baby," "Rollin' and Tumblin'," and "Spirit on the Water."
8. Derek Barker, "Apathy for the Devil: Jacques Levy, Desire, Joseph Conrad, and 'Black Diamond Bay,'" in *ISIS: A Bob Dylan Anthology*, ed. Derek Barker (London: Helter Skelter, 2004), 174–87 (182).
9. Susan Hayward, *Cinema Studies: The Key Concepts*, 2nd ed. (London: Routledge, 2004), 96.
10. D. A. Pennebaker, *Dont Look Back* (New York: New Video Group, 2006), 125.
11. Mikal Gilmore, "Interview with Mikal Gilmore, Rolling Stone, December 22, 2001," in *Bob Dylan: The Essential Interviews*, Jonathan Cott, ed. (New York: Wenner Books, 2006), 415 (italics in original).
12. Robert Hilburn, "Interview with Robert Hilburn, *Los Angeles Times*, April 4, 2004," in *Bob Dylan: The Essential Interviews*, 432. Hilburn observes in this interview that "most critics say Dylan's sometimes competing images are his greatest strength."
13. Jann S. Wenner, "Bob Dylan Hits the Big Themes, From Religion to the Atomic Age," rollingstone.com, www.rollingstone.com/music/news/bob-dylan-hits-the-big-themes-from-religion-to-the-atomic-age-20110511.
14. Bill Flanagan, "Interview with Bob Dylan," bobdylan.com, accessed March 17, 2009, http://www.bobdylan.com [URL n/a].

15. J. R. R. Tolkien, foreword to the 2nd ed., *The Lord of the Rings* (London: Harper Collins, 2007), xxiv.

16. *Together Through Life* by no means abandons the format established in the previous two albums, but I have chosen to focus on *Tempest* in order to highlight its relationship to *Modern Times*, and possibly its role as a culmination or apex of the montage style.

17. Whittier's "Snow-Bound: A Winter Idyl" (1866) provided the original formulation:

> *All day the gusty north-wind bore*
> *The loosening drift its breath before;*
> *Low circling round its southern zone,*
> *The sun through dazzling snow-mist shone.*

See John Greenleaf Whittier, "Snow-Bound: A Winter Idyl," The Poetry Foundation, www.poetryfoundation.org/poem/174758.

18. Chris Pearson, "Slavery and Dogs in the Antebellum South," *Sniffing the Past: Dogs and History*, http://sniffingthepast.wordpress.com/2012/02/23/slavery-and-dogs-in-the-antebellum-south/.

19. Marianne Faithfull, *Faithfull: An Autobiography* (New York: Cooper Square Press, 2000), 55. Faithfull continues in the same anecdote: "Dylan didn't pay much attention to the Beatles at all actually, except for John. John he adored."

20. The initial source of the precise words "I pray the Lord my soul to keep" based on Joseph Addison's original "When I lay me down to Sleep, / I recommend myself to his care," and titled "Prayer at lying down" therein. See *The New England Primer: A Primary Source*, http://cdlrsandbox.org/neprimer/versiononepages/page19.html.

21. *Satires* references spotted thanks to Scott Warmuth and Robin Clemens.

22. Dylan confirmed to Mikal Gilmore that he was in fact referencing Leonardo DiCaprio in James Cameron's *Titanic* (1997): "I don't think the song would be the same without him. Or the movie." See Mikal Gilmore, "Bob Dylan on His Dark New Album, *Tempest*," rollingstone.com, www.rollingstone.com/music/news/bob-dylan-on-his-dark-new-album-tempest-20120801. Dylan notably does not refer to "Jack," the fictional character played by DiCaprio, instead referencing the actor.

23. Analogous qualities can be found in his numerous other projects. Much terrain of *Chronicles* has been sourced to pre-existing text, while numerous examples of his painted output—such as compositions in "The Asia Series" in 2011—can be sourced to older photographs. The deference to the words of others can also be seen in the recent collaborations with Robert Hunter, *The Lost Notebooks of Hank Williams* (2011) project, and the all-covers *Christmas in the Heart*, *Shadows in the Night*, *Fallen Angels*, and *Triplicate*, while the music and lyrics of *Together Through Life* and *Tempest* have many antecedents in the folk/blues lexicography and other artists' back catalogues. Scott Warmuth's contributions in this area have been revelatory. Embracing the internet's multifarious formats, his detailing of Dylan's sources can be found across four websites: Pinterest: https://www.pinterest.com/scottwarmuth/boards/. Blogspot: http://swarmuth.blogspot.ie/. Youtube: https://www.youtube.com/channel/UCmjLqe2G5pxgkYOhlNooLZg. He also uploads Dylan connections on twitter: https://twitter.com/scottwarmuth1.

DYLAN'S DIRECTION HOME THROUGH THE WORLD'S MIGHTY OPPOSITES

Jamie Lorentzen

The searing destruction of September 11, 2001, ensuing wars in Iraq and Afghanistan, Hurricane Katrina, and other formidable fires and floods constitute a sort of paralyzing Mississippi River fog upon the currents of this dawning century. Amid it all, Bob Dylan produced the album *"Love and Theft"*; the film *Masked and Anonymous*; the first volume of his autobiography *Chronicles*; his interview in Martin Scorsese's film documentary *No Direction Home*; and the album *Modern Times*. In addition, Dylan navigates ever more bracingly between the world's mighty opposites—opposites that constitute a sort of lateral buoy system to mark safe river passage. The cargo yields an increasingly abiding and deepened respect on Dylan's part for the powerful reality of dialectical tensions between those port and starboard opposites. Tensions, for instance, between romantic love and divine love, violence and frivolity, black despair with softly-beating hope and faith, and homelessness and homecoming become more seamlessly joined together even as their contrary parts—when treated in isolation—conspire to put asunder. This essay surveys Dylan's lyrical mapping of these tensions from *"Love and Theft"* through *Modern Times*—maps that also help chart Dylan's own direction home through the fog.

TUNING UP

Played in stereo with another lyricist of mighty opposites—nineteenth-century Danish author Søren Kierkegaard (1813–1855)—Dylan's dual sense of human existence becomes more salient. With an equally prodigious penchant for paradox, Kierkegaard's lyrical and philosophical explorations venture out in contrary directions to chart and distinguish between extreme poles of worlds inhabited by heart and mind. The mapping allows Kierkegaard himself to find some direction home, especially with the discovery that individual poles cannot be denied and that only by the poles' dual existence is rotation and orbit possible. Kierkegaard, in other words, accepts all dualities and strives to discriminate between the unruly elements before fusing them together, rendering them integrated and dynamic wholes—"to separate what is inseparably joined," Kierkegaard writes, "in order to put it together again."[1] This double shuffle resembles how Dylan recognizes that visual artist Red Grooms "incorporated every living thing into something and made it scream—everything side by side created equal—old tennis shoes, vending machines, alligators that crawled through sewers, dueling pistols, the Staten Island Ferry and Trinity Church. . . . Everything [Grooms] did crushed itself into some fragile world, the rickety clusters of parts all packed together and then, standing back, you could see the complex whole of it all." Dylan, then, also expertly straddles the poles of human existence without tipping the ever-unsettled balance. His lyrics resemble his description of blues guitarist Robert Johnson's lyrics: "so elemental in meaning and feeling and gave you so much of the inside picture. It's not that you could sort out every moment carefully, because you can't. There are too many missing terms and too much dual existence."[2]

The missing terms and dual existence may be found in the clipped voices and furtive side-glances of hundreds of characters that populate Dylan's imaginative world from the genesis of his career. Included in the menagerie between 2001 and 2006 is a Tweedle Dee twin on the verge of fratricide; a penitent convinced he can't come back while a worn-out star is convinced that he can; a thief of love who knows when the time is right to strike while some joker wants to be with his beloved in paradise but for the murder he committed back there; Siamese twins coming to town; and a man who's nobody's well-trained maid while another man is a willing servant both night and day.

Amid so much dual existence, the minions nevertheless yearn for and are inclined toward some kind of self-interested love, whether erotic, romantic, platonic, or conjugal. Some even hint at the need to share in more selfless forms of love. Without exception, all have difficulty ethically relating to themselves and to others. Some wonder what it means to be or to become human. Others try to imagine themselves and their dreams along certain esthetic, ethical, and religious trajectories. Others attempt, usually in vain, to make sense of contrary, oppositional aspects of their souls from which sorrows stem and forlorn hopes grow of being led off by another in a cheerful dance. Amid the general chaos of modern times, conscience surfaces like a bloated carcass after a flood. As Dylan's narrator in "Honest with Me" sings, "lots of things get in the way when you're tryin' to do what's right."

True to Dylan's bloodshot vision, they all wear the same thorny crown.

SOUND CHECK: DYLAN AND KIERKEGAARD IN STEREO

In a letter to a close friend, twenty-five-year-old Kierkegaard describes the kind of polyphonic and harmonic yearnings that his literary-poetic voice would eventually command: "I need a voice as piercing as the glance of Lynceus, as terrifying as the groan of the giants, as sustained as a sound of nature, extending in range from the deepest bass to the most melting high notes, and modulated from the most solemn-silent whisper to the fire-spouting energy of rage. That is what I need in order to breathe, to give voice to what is on my mind, to make the viscera of both anger and sympathy tremble."[3]

In *Chronicles*, Dylan describes musical voices he respects and (in his own inimitable way) eventually appropriates, which are comparable to voices young Kierkegaard respected and appropriated. Of Woody Guthrie: "His voice was like a stiletto [and he] tore everything in his path to pieces.... [He was] the poet of hard crust and gumbo mud.... Each [of his songs] seemed like a towering building with a variety of scenarios all appropriate for different situations." Of Roy Orbison: "His stuff mixed all the styles and some that hadn't even been invented yet. He could sound mean and nasty on one line and then sing in a falsetto voice like Frankie Valli in the next. With Roy, you didn't know if you were listening to mariachi or opera.... He sounded like he was singing from an Olympian mountaintop.... He made you want to drive your car over a cliff.... His voice would jar a corpse." Of Robert Johnson: "He could have sprung from the head of Zeus in full armor.... [His songs] felt like a ghost had come into the room, a fearsome apparition.... [Compositions were] big-ass truths wrapped in the hard shell of nonsensical abstraction—themes that flew through the air with the greatest of ease.... 'The stuff I got'll bust your brains out,' he sings. Johnson is serious, like the scorched earth.... I wanted to be like that, too."[4]

Austrian poet Rainer Maria Rilke (1875–1926) perhaps best sums up the kind of polyphonic and harmonic aspirations of poets like Kierkegaard and Dylan:

> We must accept our reality as *vastly* as we possibly can; everything, even the unprecedented, must be possible within it. This is in the end the only kind of courage that is required of us: the courage to face the strangest, most unusual, most inexplicable experiences that can meet us. The fact that people have in this sense been cowardly has done infinite harm to life; the experiences that are called "apparitions," the whole so-called "spirit-world," death, all these Things that are so closely related to us, have through our daily defensiveness been so entirely pushed out of life that the senses with which we might have been able to grasp them have atrophied. To say nothing of God.[5]

As for "'apparitions,' the whole so-called 'spirit world,'" Dylan's narrator in "Spirit on the Water" offers at least an invitation to consider the possibility of something beyond our ken: "You ever seen a ghost? No / But you have heard of them."

To say nothing of God.

KEY SIGNATURE: C MAJOR

Dylan's need to offer some Christian conception of God in his lyrics confirms Kierkegaard's ethical call to poets who would prefer to ignore religious issues: "If poetry becomes aware of the religious and of the inwardness of individuality, it will acquire far more meaningful tasks than those with which it busies itself now."[6]

Born Jewish in a predominantly Christian community, Robert Zimmerman was heavily influenced by American folk and gospel music, and their Christian themes. The songs' messages likely lay the groundwork for his late-1970s conversion to Christianity. "Here's the thing with me and the religious thing," Dylan says in a 1997 *Newsweek* interview: "I find the religiosity and philosophy in the music. I don't find it anywhere else. Songs like 'Let Me Rest on a Peaceful Mountain' or 'I Saw the Light'—that's my religion. I don't adhere to rabbis, preachers, evangelists, all of that. I've learned more from the songs than I've learned from any of this kind of entity. The songs are my lexicon. I believe the songs."[7]

Dylan's religiosity and philosophy throughout his canon are also informed by texts like Woody Guthrie's *Bound for Glory* (1943), the poetry of William Blake (1757–1827), and the works of Herman Melville (1819–1891). He reveres such texts in part because they evoke the imagistic and thematic force of metaphor that traffics upon language stretched to the mightiest opposites of mortality and immortality, time and eternity, and necessity and freedom. Such language best exposes what Kierkegaard calls "the fundamental derangement at the root of modern times," namely, the obliteration of "the deep qualitative chasm in the difference between God and man"[8]—what Dylan similarly identifies in our own modern times as the "breaking down [of] the distance between right and wrong" ("Ring Them Bells" [1989]).

Such language also gains momentum by its simple, nimble movements between metaphorical meanings. Its implicit dualistic construct allows for as many interpretations of meaning as there are ideas generated by readers. That said, "the spiritual person and the sensate-psychical [read: secular] person say the same thing," Kierkegaard writes, "yet there is an infinite difference, since the latter has no intimation of the secret of the metaphorical words although he is using the same words."[9]

The first stanza to "Thunder on the Mountain" exemplifies the dual snake-like, swan-like ease by which Dylan traffics between secular and religious language. His words evoke imagery that shine light on both late-night bar crowds bound for after-hours parties and sinners standing before another bar at the dawn of Judgment Day when the last trumpet blows: "Today's the day, gonna grab my trombone and blow / Well, there's hot stuff here and it's everywhere I go."

Wherever there is a poet whose imagistic powers are unflinchingly unsentimental *and* who also cannot seem to get the eternal out of his head, there's hot stuff there. Even Dylan's eschatology both separates the Epicurean mantra *carpe diem* from the ethical-religious mantra *This Very Day* . . . and fuses them. Especially these days, it's everywhere he goes, even to his album *Tempest*. And as he continues to sing with his tongue on fire, he also continues to build a head of steam. If audience members do not have ears to hear that Duquesne whistle blowing ("like she's on a final run," "like she ain't gonna blow no more," "like the sky's gonna blow apart"), then they are not hearing Dylan's slow train comin' at the world's end.

FIRST SET: ROMANTIC LOVE AND DIVINE LOVE

Dylan has spent most of his career writing love songs that attempt to say something durable about love. When the narrator in "Sugar Baby" speaks to the limitless "amount of trouble women bring," he also says "Love is pleasing, love is teasing, love's not an evil thing." There are, in other words, many forms of love. In *"Love and Theft"* and *Modern Times*, love is vain, sexual, neighborly, cocky, incestuous, and familial. It is skin-deep, unhappy, obsessive, unsympathetic, religious, selfish, selfless, and foolish. It is begging, easy, grateful, sacrificial, burning, and yearning. It is loyal, vindictive, transient, regrettable, and forgotten.

Kierkegaard, too, addresses the many forms of love. Kierkegaard translators Howard V. and Edna H. Hong note that Kierkegaard's book, *Works of Love* (1847), "aims to find a reader where he is, in the ambiguities of his understanding of the nature of love," ultimately to show that "love in its works (because it is a deed, not a volatile, lovely feeling) is the highest good of ethical vision." *Works of Love* is also "Kierkegaard's climactic consideration of erotic love and Christian love against the background of the multifarious characterizations of love."[10] These varied characterizations of love may be divided between forms of *preferential* love (forms that a person may naturally prefer based upon shared likenesses, such as narcissistic love, erotic-romantic love, friendship, and conjugal love) and *non-preferential* love (namely, ethical and ethical-religious self-love, neighbor-love, and love of God).

Given their gifted powers of discrimination, Kierkegaard and Dylan fast become capable guides for finding readers and listeners *where they are* along love's spectrum. Their ethical-literary goal is ultimately to help readers and listeners discriminate between (to use Dylan's terms) the kinds of love as *stuff that ain't real* and love that's *really real*. Kierkegaard's terms frame it this way: "[Preferential] erotic love and friendship ... contain no moral task.... Erotic love is defined by the object; friendship is defined by the object; only [non-preferential] love for the neighbor is defined by love.... Love is a matter of conscience and thus is not a matter of [erotic] drives and inclination or ... feeling."[11]

At least as far back as "It Ain't Me, Babe," Dylan (like Kierkegaard) subordinates preferential romantic love and friendship to non-preferential neighbor-love. Even in his most touchingly romantic-erotic love songs, narrators generally remain wary of friendship or romantic-erotic love's limited and ephemeral qualities, or they simply see their beloved as consenting adults instead of vulnerable prey. For instance, as much as the enmeshed, overly dependent "babe" in "It Ain't Me, Babe" wants the narrator to "die for [her] *and more*" [emphasis added], the narrator knows that such love is not real, hence his answer: "It ain't me, babe." Or when the beloved in Dylan's "Don't Think Twice, It's Alright" wants the lover's soul, Dylan's lover-narrator knows to give the beloved no more than his heart. By offering only his temporal romantic love and not his eternal being, Dylan's poet-narrator instinctively knows what Kierkegaard knows, namely, that "lovers no doubt think that in erotic love they have the highest."[12] By knowing this, Dylan's poet-narrators, on the whole, shed selfish masks of romantic-erotic love and don the ethical mask of neighbor-love. Subsequently, narrators speak not to curry romantic-erotic favor but to help others understand and see through the world's deceptions and individuals' self-deceptions, to help them become more inward, human, rounded, and less artificial, over-dependent, flat.

Dylan, in other words, learned early that humans regularly fall short of and are in need of voices with messages that run deeper than yearnings for requited romantic love or oaths of friendship in which most pop songs find their themes—voices with messages of neighbor-love and love of God that chime in civil rights, protest, and gospel songs of Woody Guthrie and other folk artist greats. Relationships that could blossom into time-bound erotic love or friendship are instead "abandoned" for expressions of love that are less time-bound and thereby more durable, especially because they are expressions that do not beg for something in return. As Dylan's narrator in "Thunder on the Mountain" sings: "Gonna forget about myself for a while, gonna go out and see what others need."

Then there are songs that only a poet of mighty opposites can pen—songs that pit romantic love against divine love while fusing secular and religious aspects of such distinct forms of love in ways that pay homage to both forms of love. A representative example of this romantic-divine love song, and perhaps his most perfect love song, is Dylan's "When the Deal Goes Down." Its perfection consists in the impenetrable ambiguity that renders it impossible to determine if the love relationship is between a living lover romantically addressing a living beloved; a living lover religiously addressing a beloved who is dead; one who is dead religiously addressing in romantic terms a beloved still living; or one who is alive religiously anticipating meeting his Maker. Without dint of anxiety or fear, the song speaks to timely romantic love and timeless divine love with tender equanimity. Death is not the end of love, nor is romance love's ultimate expression. Despite everything the finite can throw at a person (struggling wisdom amid strife, bewilderments, toils, darkness, living, dying, eating, drinking, thinking, straying haunted regrets, frail precious hours, deafening noise, transient joys, disappointment, and pain), the beloved comes to the narrator's eyes "like a vision from the skies." He owes his heart to this vision. He will be with the beloved and will greet the beloved at the end of time.

Another song from *Modern Times* attempts to fuse the finite and the infinite, the romantic and the divine. In "Beyond the Horizon," the narrator anticipates timelessness beyond time where it is easy to love, even for a wretched heart still pounding. He builds his world around the beloved (whether that beloved is worldly-romantic or divine) and 'round about midnight (either death or closing time), divides are crossed and love that waits forever waits no more. It does not have to, for it is requited.

Not all Dylan songs that attempt to fuse the romantic and the divine are composed as seamlessly as these two songs. Nonetheless, many of them aspire to such fusion in ways that inspire (as Kierkegaard notes) "to separate what is inseparably joined in order to put it together again."[13] In "Mississippi," the narrator admits romantic love's mood shifts: "Last night I knew ya, tonight I don't." The narrator does not deny, however, the ethical need to maintain the commitment: "I need somethin' strong to distract my mind / I'm gonna look at you 'til my eyes go blind."

Like the narrator in "Mississippi," the narrator in "Nettie Moore" knows that he has painted himself into a corner: he's "got a pile of sins to pay for and [he] ain't got time to hide." Then, blending romantic and divine language of love so as to render the romantic almost divine and the divine almost romantic, he croons: "I'd walk through a blazing fire, baby, if I knew you was on the other side"—an image Dylan no doubt saw in Dante's romantic-divine tight connection to Beatrice's heart and soul near the end of *Purgatorio*. Yet even as Dylan eyes the gates of earthly paradise and is prepared to walk through love's true fire, he still cannot ignore nor deny the existence of so many fires of so-called "divine love" to which he glances askance with deepest distrust, namely, religious fanaticism's false fires. And so he returns again to antipodal hells of humanity.

SECOND SET: VIOLENCE AND FRIVOLITY

From east to west, ever since the world began, violence seldom gets more savage than when it is linked to religious fanaticism. How a delirious dervish of any creed is so willing to hate and kill for the love of and respect for the creed's paternity is no sublime paradox, but rather a massive contradiction, a moral atrophy. Often ending with bomb and suicide, the carnage does little more than mock the very deity the fanatic presumably glorifies.

In "High Water (For Charley Patton)," a black man says to three (presumably non–African American) guys, "You can't open your mind, boys / To every conceivable point of view." Which is true? Humans are not omniscient;

but that is not to say that such a line should give a myopic religious fanatic carte blanche to assassinate Darwin in the name of creationism's creed—but try telling that to the judge who strings up the black man's advice and turns it on its head: "I want him dead or alive / Either one, I don't care." There's high water everywhere because of such fanaticism, rendering the song's next lines of betrayal and self-betrayal a tragic dénouement: "I'm preachin' the Word of God / I'm puttin' out your eyes."

With Dylan, unreflective frivolity is never far from violence. Like Michelangelo's *Last Judgment* (ca. 1425–31), Dylan's vast fresco in which he portrays humanity is obliged to disclose the dirt of inhumanity that the world regularly sweeps under the rug. What begins as a joke (Did you hear the one about the Englishman, the Italian, and the Jew?) ends with violence and another corpse dragged through the mud. Other scenarios with similar contradictions include the following lines from "Thunder on the Mountain": "I've been sitting down studying the art of love / I think it will fit me like a glove." What *is* the matter with this cruel world today? When paired with savage violence, it is Jokerman-like frivolity that ushers abject meaninglessness into the world. In one of Kierkegaard's most famous parables, penned under the pseudonym of a despairing young esthete speaking of frivolity amid end-of-world violence, a clown tries to warn an audience of a fire offstage: "The clown came out to tell the audience. They thought it was a joke and applauded. He told them again, and they became still more hilarious. This is the way, I suppose, that the world will be destroyed—amid the universal hilarity of wits and wags who think it is all a joke."[14] Meanwhile, lines in the final monologue of Jack Fate (played by Dylan) in *Masked and Anonymous* speak to how this world is ruled by violence, whether or not it's shrugged off with a joke and a laugh: "Things fall apart. Especially all the neat order of rules and laws. The way we look at the world is the way we really are. See it from a fair garden and everything looks cheerful. Climb to a higher plateau and you'll see plunder and murder."[15] To say nothing of despair.

THIRD SET: BLACK DESPAIR AND SOFTLY BEATING HOPE AND FAITH

Especially in the latter half of his career, Dylan's images of despair are prevalent, piercing, penetrating, and remarkably relentless. Lines from *"Love and Theft"* to *Modern Times* offer more than enough fuel to feed these smoldering coals that warm not:

I tell myself something's comin'
But it never does ("Lonesome Day Blues")

The world has gone black before my eyes ("Nettie Moore")

Well, the emptiness is endless, cold as the clay ("Mississippi")

The suffering is unending
Every nook and cranny has its tears ("Ain't Talkin'")

Equally remarkable, however, is how the singer keeps standing despite *and* because of how despair keeps on floating along the surface of his oceanic oeuvre like so much flotsam and jetsam. This relentless striving amid and against darknesses made visible is what animates hope in Dylan's literary corpus.

There are, in other words, abysses, like the universe in Dylan's "Cold Irons Bound" (1997), that have the look and feel of a black hole of despair swallowing the whole of one's existence. Walls of those abysses that grow up in strife, however, form equally prodigious peaks of wisdom on which a Job or a Solomon could perch. They are powerful, therapeutic mounts of self-examination, clarity, illumination, and possibility. They are peaks that transcend the abysses even as their existences frame with rock and wall the abysses themselves. They are peaks like invisible prayers that hang like clouds in the air.

Meanwhile, far below, a sailor sings: "Well, my ship's been split to splinters and it's sinking fast / I'm drownin' in the poison, got no future, got no past." An authentic sense of what Viktor Frankl calls tragic optimism[16] thereby comes to exist in Dylan's lines amid utter tragedy and failure—an optimism where gratitude is founded upon total loss, hope upon endless emptiness. Ethically considered, relinquishing a claim to a future and a past establishes a powerful present for one who apparently may have no direction home but who also knows it's not dark yet. It informs hope that Kierkegaard calls "infinite humiliation and grace, and then a striving born of gratitude."[17] Shortly before his death, Kierkegaard writes: "God help the one who had no predecessor and no successor. For him life truly becomes what it . . . is supposed to be: an examination in which there can be no cheating."[18]

Even in the suffering of such striving against all odds amid an indifferent universe, if that striving is genuine, then it is not cheating because it does not have to cheat—for, at that moment (as Dylan's thief says to the joker), there is no need to talk falsely now: the hour is getting late. Such striving is the honest, humble striving of the human relating itself to itself and with some other, human or divine.[19] Such striving imitates the apostle Paul's striving to live in the world without being of it, which requires knowledge of the world's vast corruptions and sadnesses. Such striving knowledge and faith maintains a certain radical goodness and joy. Such striving is also the ethical demand placed upon each human being. For Kierkegaard, the alternative is disintegration and despair's deathlike disconnect. As for Dylan, his narrator in "Every Grain of Sand" (1981) speaks of "the morals of despair," and he's right to describe despair as a moral issue; whereas clinical depression is now regarded as not a moral but a chemical and biological issue, despair as a spiritual category has morals—this, despite the despairer presumably not caring about anything.

In his more ornery later years, Kierkegaard goes so far as to forcefully assert with uncharacteristic directness that Christianity had come to lack a compass as well, claiming that Christianity no longer exists in an overaccommodating and tepid Danish Lutheran Church.[20] The narrator in Dylan's "Ain't Talkin'" talks similarly of "practic[ing] a faith that's been long abandoned." In this particularly hopeless context, Kierkegaard and Dylan know despair at its most elemental level. Continuing to practice such faith despite massive institutional failure is representative of a philosophy of hope built upon a bedrock of despair. It is a philosophy that may best be summarized by Howard Hong as one "that has to do with human nature, with anxiety and despair, which we don't like, but nevertheless are signs of the potential greatness of every human being. This is what it is to be human in the context of a philosophy of the future that redeems the past, a philosophy of possibility where there is no human possibility, a philosophy of hope in the midst of despair."[21]

Kierkegaard and Dylan's like-minded philosophies balance extremes of utter despair (universe-as-meaningless jest) and expectant hope (universe-as-meaningful gesture). This balancing act and the fulcrum upon which the balance is exacted reflect their shared genius. What Dylan essentially understands about the nature of human beings is what Kierkegaard essentially understood. And what Kierkegaard understood, according to Hong, was "human beings in their possibilities of depths and heights. In the face of humankind's common disease, despair, [Kierkegaard] would agree with Pascal that 'the greatness of man is great in that he knows himself to be miserable. A tree does not know itself to be miserable. It is then being miserable to know oneself to be miserable; but it is also being great to know that one is miserable.' [Such] despair... is a negative mark of being a creature of possibility, intended to become genuinely human."[22] In "Series of Dreams" (1989), Dylan says it this way: "And the cards are no good that you're holding / Unless they're from another world."

If (as Kierkegaard asserts) despair is the essential presupposition to earnest faith, then the continued protraction of radical doubt will always be both penalty and gift, rendering faith an endlessly "restless thing."[23] For all that, faith becomes ever meaningful, complementing Kierkegaard's famous notion that life must be lived forward but understood backward.[24] Such a notion does not deny regret's despair over the past, nor does it allow regret's despair to bankrupt hope for the future. "Faith simply means," Kierkegaard writes, "... what I am seeking is not here, and for that very reason I believe it. Faith expressly signifies the deep, strong, blessed restlessness that drives the believer so that he cannot settle down at rest in this world, and therefore the person who has settled down completely at rest has also ceased to be a believer, because a believer cannot sit still as one sits with a pilgrim's staff in one hand—a believer travels forward."[25]

In Martin Scorsese's *No Direction Home*, a sixty-five-year-old Dylan—reflecting on his early years—says it like this: "An artist has got to be careful never really to arrive at a place where he thinks he's *at* somewhere. He always has to realize that you're constantly in a state of becoming. And as long as you can stay in that realm, you're [going to] be all right."[26]

FINALE: HOMELESSNESS AND HOMECOMING

"I had ambitions to set out and find like an odyssey of going home somewhere," Dylan notes at the outset of *No Direction Home*: "I set out to find this home that I left a while back, and I couldn't remember exactly where it was, but I was on my way there. And encountering what I encountered on the way was how I envisioned it all.... I was born very far from where I'm supposed to be and so, I'm on my way home."[27] The documentary's second scene shows a 1960s performance by Dylan of "Like a Rolling Stone," in which the narrator accuses "babe" of having no direction home. This is the line in which Scorsese finds the theme for his movie of Dylan's early years.

The mighty Homeric opposite that is homelessness and homecoming thus reaches crescendo early in Dylan's professional career. Remarkably, the crescendo never fades away throughout the half-century that follows. Instead, it is continually renewed and remains both audibly deafening and emotionally visceral whenever Dylan sings "Like a Rolling Stone" in concert—and for good reason. Hearts and minds that yearn to be forever young are arguably right to champion the good feeling that having no direction home affords, for the feeling asserts the emotional independence and sensation of a road trip with no destination but the road.

Although fifty years of concertgoers have ecstatically affirmed that the feeling of no direction home is good, the intent of the song, as suggested by Dylan in his opening monologue in Scorsese's documentary, is that homelessness is not necessarily supposed to feel good. Similarly, in "Like Rolling Stone," "babe" may suffer from no direction home, but Dylan's narrator does not share her position.

Just as homelessness implies a concept of home, no direction home implies a concept of direction. Dylan has a home—he says as much—and he also says he is on his way home, which argues for direction. That said, Dylan not only claims that he was born very far from where he is supposed to be, but he also claims that as an artist he "has got to be careful never really to arrive at a place where he thinks he's *at* somewhere," and that he "always has to realize that [he's] constantly in a state of becoming."

So . . . where *is* home for Dylan? What is the direction to it? How does he know he is even on his way there? What is clear from Dylan's fifty-plus-year homeward-bound lyrical odyssey is that he has crisscrossed the South, especially Louisiana and Mississippi, more than any place in the world. "Highway 61, the main thoroughfare of the country blues," Dylan writes in *Chronicles*, ". . . begins about where I came from. . . . I always felt like I'd started on it, even down into the deep Delta country. It was the same road, full of the same contradictions, the same one-horse towns, the same spiritual ancestors. The Mississippi River, the bloodstream of the blues, also starts up from my neck of the woods. I was never too far away from any of it. It was my place in the universe, always felt like it was in my blood."[28]

Highway 61 runs east of Hibbing, Minnesota, and south through Duluth. At Minneapolis it begins following the Mississippi River down to the Gulf of Mexico: through Hannibal, St. Louis, Memphis, then along the western border of the state of Mississippi—through Clarksdale (west of Oxford), Vicksburg, Natchez—before draining into Louisiana and New Orleans. In "Tangled Up in Blue," the narrator had a job in the great north woods before drifting down to Delacroix. In "Not Dark Yet," the narrator has been to London and to gay Paree before following the river right down to the sea; another narrator has spent time in Oxford Town; another has traveled through East Texas, where martyrs fell, just across the Louisiana line ("Blind

Willie McTell"); another witnesses water pouring into Vicksburg and hears thunder rolling over the birthplace of the blues.

Between antipodes as extreme and oppositional as North and South (Duluth to New Orleans) and West and East (New Orleans to Jerusalem), the nexus that is the backyard of the blues seems as close as Dylan gets to home, whether that home is actual, esthetic, philosophical, or spiritual. In *Chronicles'* largest chapter, the pivotal and transformative moment that ushers in his mature years seems to be borne of his New Orleans–based experience of recording *Oh Mercy*, with songs that speak poignantly of a world rife with political corruption and bereft of love, where everything is broken, where teardrops fall, where warning bells ring, where all conceit is disease, and where most of the time one wonders if one is doing any good to anyone at all. Talk about the Blues.

The South in general and Mississippi in particular is also where the narrator of "Mississippi" stayed a day too long, and the delay is the narrator's only mistake, his only regret, the only thing he did wrong. He never says why he believes it is the only thing he did wrong—but, then, the particular trespass is not the point.

What *is* the point is this: The narrator, by virtue of his confession of some guilt, is capable of regret amid love and theft in modern times. The narrator is willingly prepared to suffer, a painful emotional act that is unfashionable these days—days in which individuals can make themselves over with Botox and Facebook's virtual reality and thereby repress or ignore even the sigh of a regret. Why is he prepared to suffer? He knows (or has faith that) regret remains one of the few psychological concepts that recognize and assert an individual's conscience and self-honesty and free will, human capacities that Dylan always has championed. Owning wrongdoing by expressing regret is not only the strongest self-assertion of conscience and self-honesty and free will but also, according to Kierkegaard, is "the strongest self-assertion of existence."[29] Regret, in other words, is a rover or rambler's most genuine homecoming, with the self bringing all of itself back home to its most authentic self, its dearest home, its better angel.

Regret also acknowledges that some choices not only may have been wrong but also may remain wrong without remedy, as the "Mississippi" narrator sings: "So many things that we never will undo / I know you're sorry, I'm sorry too." Regret's great value is thereby in its assertion that, without the possibility of wrong choices, right choices would hold no intrinsic or enduring value. In a world without regret (in these modern times, in these

"New Dark Ages" in which history is bunk and the esthetic virtual world supplants the actual ethical world[30]), the obvious but ignored question becomes whether or not any choice a human being makes is worth anything at all. Despite how anyone tries to live at such virtual distances from actual face-to-face contact without regret, however, *real* regret nevertheless has powerful future-oriented therapeutic value toward the development of a contrite and open heart. Acknowledging paradise lost with contrition may be the only hope to regain it. If faith that has been long abandoned is still practiced, grace is still in the cards—especially when, as Dylan asserts in *Bringing It All Back Home,* "there are no truths outside the Gates of Eden."

ENCORE: DYLAN KEEPING TIME

For lyrical rovers and ramblers like Kierkegaard and Dylan, journeying far and wide to explore mighty opposites in a world gone wrong ultimately directs them home to the realization that humans are on the whole in the wrong,[31] that the cards are no good that they're holding. For Kierkegaard, such ego-stripping means that he is obliged to exist in this prison cell of a world as a penitent.[32] For Dylan, it means "Ain't No Man Righteous, No Not One" (1981), the title of one of his performed but unrecorded Christian-era songs. Given these intimately related revelations, suffering penance spawned by regret for being in the wrong has less to do with inflicting external self-whipping and internal self-loathing and more to do with igniting one's ethical or ethical-religious imagination. Regret's exhale prepares the penitent to inhale clean air. Penitence means to serve time for what Kierkegaard calls "the possibility of the good"[33] and what Dylan calls being forever young. To serve time for the good—to be forever young—means that the sooner one can be good and do good in wicked worlds, the sooner one may get out of whatever penitentiary one is in. Or as the narrator of "Nettie Moore" sings: "If I don't do anybody any harm, I might make it back home alive."

As for Bob Dylan: If there is some truth to the fact that the only thing he did wrong was, figuratively speaking, stay in Mississippi a day too long, then perhaps there is more truth to the notion that staying in Mississippi a day too long was the essential thing Dylan did right. He never cut and ran from this Palace of Gloom, this Mississippi-world of lapse and sorrow, this place of dual existence and mighty opposites where everything is broken. And without him being entirely of the world—without, in other words, him becoming swallowed whole by the world—he endures and prevails as a poet of mighty opposites ... and a penitent. In that dark and dreary place, and despite being weakened and weary, he was born there and he'll die there.

In the interim, may his home be in his heart, and may he sing along with the "Highlands" narrator that "I'm already there in my mind / And that's good enough for now." Let us all hope the Mississippi fog eventually rolls out as the century's dawn breaks to day. As for Bob: May he continue to roll on and sing to the cheap seats that fill up into the night.

NOTES

1. Søren Kierkegaard, *Eighteen Upbuilding Discourses* (KW 5), 160. Note: Kierkegaard citations are from either the twenty-six-volume *Kierkegaard's Writings* (KW) series (Princeton: Princeton University Press, 1978–98) or the seven-volume *Journals and Papers* (JP) series (Bloomington: Indiana University Press, 1967–78). Citations from KW will include book title followed by KW volume and page number. Citations from JP will include volume number followed by journal entry number.

2. Dylan, *Chronicles*, 269, 284.

3. Søren Kierkegaard, *Letters and Documents* (KW 25), 54.

4. Dylan, *Chronicles*, 33, 244, 245, 247, 282, 283, 285.

5. Rainer Maria Rilke, *Letters to a Young Poet*, Stephen Mitchell, trans. (New York: Modern Library, 2001), 88–89.

6. Søren Kierkegaard, *Fear and Trembling* (KW 6), 91n.

7. David Gates, "Dylan Revisited," *Newsweek*, October 7, 1997.

8. Søren Kierkegaard, *Journals and Papers* 5:6075.

9. Søren Kierkegaard, *Works of Love* (KW 16), 209.

10. Kierkegaard, *Works of Love* (KW 16), xi.

11. Kierkegaard, *Works of Love* (KW 16), 50–51, 66, 143.

12. Kierkegaard, *Works of Love* (KW 16), 61.

13. Kierkegaard, *Eighteen Upbuilding Discourses* (KW 5), 160.

14. Søren Kierkegaard, *Either/Or I* (KW 3), 30.

15. Larry Charles, dir., *Masked and Anonymous* (Culver City, CA: Sony Picture Classics, 2003).

16. Viktor Frankl, *Man's Search for Meaning* (Boston: Beacon Press, 1991), 139–40.

17. Kierkegaard, *Journals and Papers* 1:993.

18. Søren Kierkegaard, *Late Writings* (KW 23), 354.

19. Søren Kierkegaard, *The Sickness Unto Death* (KW 19), 13.

20. See Kierkegaard, *Late Writings* (KW 23).

21. Ben Alex, *Søren Kierkegaard: An Authentic Life* (Kelowna, BC: Northstone Publishing, 1997), 52.

22. Howard V. Hong, "Trying to Do the Right Thing," *Reece Report* (Northfield, MN: Richard Reece) 7, no. 1 (January 1992), 9, 18. Pascal passage quoted from his *Pensées*, no. 397 (New York: Dutton, 1931), 187.

23. Søren Kierkegaard, *For Self-Examination* (KW 21), 17.
24. See Søren Kierkegaard, *Early Writings* (KW 1), 255 (Notes).
25. Søren Kierkegaard, *Upbuilding Discourses in Various Spirits* (KW 15), 218.
26. Martin Scorsese, dir., *No Direction Home: Bob Dylan* (Hollywood: Paramount Pictures, 2005).
27. Scorsese, dir., *No Direction Home*.
28. Dylan, *Chronicles*, 240–41.
29. Søren Kierkegaard, *Concluding Unscientific Postscript* (KW 12.1), 528.
30. Bob Dylan, liner notes to *World Gone Wrong* (1993).
31. See, e.g., Søren Kierkegaard, *Either/Or 2* (KW 4), 339.
32. Kierkegaard, *Journals and Papers*, 6:6317.
33. Kierkegaard, *Work of Love* (KW 16), 251.

CHAPTER NINE

PERFORMATIVE LYRIC VOICE AND THE REFRAIN AS AN ARCHITECTONIC ELEMENT IN BOB DYLAN

Fahri Öz

"I wrote the songs to perform the songs."[1]

"Have I ever played any song twice exactly the same?"
"No, Bob, no."
"See? I don't do that."[2]

Author's Note: The writing of this essay dates back to 2012 and 2013. Bob Dylan was then among the nominees for the Nobel Prize in Literature, giving rise to unending discussions as to whether he deserves it. The year 2016 turned out to be Dylan's annus mirabilis when he was awarded the prize "for having created new poetic expressions within the great American song tradition."[3] As a Nobel laureate, Dylan has secured his place among the poetic giants even though this apparently was not something he aspired to.

As a musician and songwriter Bob Dylan derives inspiration from a wide range of musical and poetic genres. Awarded the Nobel Prize in Literature in 2016, Dylan's work continues to occupy music critics, scholars, and fans; though deemed a poetic genius, he elicits differing opinions. Reservations about his poetic and literary standing range from the contention that it is difficult to place Dylan within the poetic pantheon since he is merely a performer to the allegation that his lyrics depend on the recycling of, and borrowing from, previous poets and texts.[4] Such reservations seem to overlook the fact that Dylan is a performing poet, that poetry in its infancy was a performative art, and that the lyric was originally a spectacle delivered by a bard or rhapsode performing in front of an audience. Such performativity also harbored the image of a poet playing or singing or improvising to the accompaniment of a musical instrument. A closer look at Dylan's songs shows that he is a mixture of Homeric performer and a modern poet well-read in the Western literary canon.

Dylan is a highly productive composer and singer, and the changes in his style and manner of singing his own songs attest to his performative nature. As Betsy Bowden elucidates in *Performed Literature: Words and Music by Bob Dylan*, Dylan's songs cannot be treated as rigid forms or texts in print because they are not intended as poems but songs to be performed, "words and music combined for oral performance."[5] Paul Williams, too, approaches Dylan "as first and foremost a performing artist, as opposed to a composer or songwriter... [whose] songwriting is best understood as an activity directed by and in service to the needs of the performer."[6] Though such performative accounts of Dylan's work are valid, I hold that his lyrics deserve a poetic analysis, and that it is possible to treat his studio recordings as performative acts too. In other words, this essay hopes to reconcile the treatment of Dylan the poet with Dylan the singer.

Though it is difficult to arrive at a universally accepted definition, performance can be described as "an action that is carried out, judged, and appreciated according to a set of commonly shared aesthetic, literary, or social codes."[7] Critic Richard Schechner emphasizes the idea of audience in his definition: "a performance is an activity done by an individual or group in the presence of and for another individual or group."[8] He further observes that performance is some sort of role-play or make-believe in which some of the performers can play the role of the audience in the absence of real audience, or, as stated by John Cage, simply framing an activity as performance can turn it into one.[9] During the 1980s, Dylan himself was not happy with the studio atmosphere in which musicians were isolated among electronic equipment; he saw it as "an austere, clinical, and dead environment," and "had often complained that his songs lost their vitality and character when recorded in this way or when performed in too many times in this environment. Of performing live he later remarked, 'Going onstage, seeing different people every night in a combustible way, that's a thrill.'"[10]

This essay will analyze the performative role of the refrain in a selection of Dylan's work including "Mississippi" from *"Love and Theft"* and "Ain't Talkin'" from *Modern Times*. With their vatic and sibylline aspects, these albums exemplify the performative and improvisatory nature of his music, which finds its expression in the use of the refrain. I intend to lay bare the way the refrain functions within the architectonics of Dylan's highly allusive lyrics, some of which are not coherent or "well-made poems."

Basically a technique that goes back to oral poetry, the refrain involves issues of communality, dialogue, rhythm, melody, mnemonics, and architectonics. And a live concert is ideal to observe the function of the refrain. For example, I had the opportunity to see Bob Dylan perform in Istanbul on May 31, 2010. The show, which took place in a magical venue, the Harbiye Cemil Topuzlu Amphitheatre overlooking the Bosphorus, was alleged to be the most expensive Dylan concert in the world by a Turkish daily.[11] Tickets being rather pricey, I and my colleague Devrim Kılıçer, who had enticed me into attending the show, bought the cheapest seats in the upper circle. We had driven all the way from Ankara, a six-hour bus ride, for this concert, and it was the first time I had seen Dylan live. Though I knew very well what Dylan looked like from the album and book covers, TV shows, newspaper articles, and music magazines, at the concert I felt I might as well be watching his double or lookalike because Dylan was hardly discernible: from such a distance he was almost the size of a needle, a lean figure switching between guitar and keyboards in a sea of shifting spotlights with a dazzling spectrum of colors. Though the concert set list included only two songs from his latest album, and most of the songs were very well-known pieces, it was difficult to identify which song he was singing; to figure out which song was being performed sometimes you needed to listen halfway through to where the refrain began.[12] Without the refrains or choruses, the live versions of some songs would have remained nearly inscrutable, lacking the familiarity a concert audience expects despite the impeccable sound system. This illustrates how crucial a role the refrain has in establishing communication between the performer and the audience, and giving the audience a sense of familiarity and identification.

REFRAIN, BURDEN, REPETITION

The refrain may easily be confused with other poetic devices such as repetition, and the boundaries between these devices prove to be cumbersome. Therefore, a brief explanation of the term is necessary. According to *The New Princeton Encyclopedia of Poetry and Poetics*, the refrain is "A line, lines, or part of a line repeated verbatim at intervals throughout a poem, usually at regular intervals, and most often at the end of a stanza—a burden, chorus, or repetend."[13] The burden refers to the repetition of a whole stanza, the chorus to the repetition of a stanza by a group of people, and the incremental repetition or the repetend to the repetition of words in an irregular fashion. Here the terms chorus and refrain will be used interchangeably, with the awareness that the former foregrounds the musical and the latter the textual/verbal aspect of the lines repeated.

Though the refrain is very common in, and arose out of, oral poetic forms, it also appears in written poetry. Edgar Allan Poe acknowledged the poetic and architectonic import of the refrain in written poetry. In his essay "The Philosophy of Composition" (1846), Poe defiantly reveals the secrets of his craft, explicating the steps he followed while composing his narrative poem "The Raven" (1845). Having decided on the "the length, the province, and the tone,"[14] Poe searches for a keystone upon which the whole structure of the poem should depend, and concludes that architectonically the refrain is the most valuable and popular tool: "As commonly used, the *refrain*, or burden, not only is limited to lyric verse, but depends for its impression upon the force of the monotone—both in sound and thought. The pleasure is deduced solely from the sense of identity—of repetition."[15] Because it is short and easy to memorize, the refrain helps the reader to easily identify the text/song he or she is reading or listening to. The refrain, then, is one of the elements that facilitate both the process of cognition (identification) and that of pleasure (repetition) in the reception of a poem. In musical terms, it is like a percussive instrument that highlights the main theme, and, in textual terms, it is a significant item in the construction a poem. In "The Raven," however, Poe does not stick to monotony; instead, he attempts to create diversity in unity by limiting the refrain to one single word or sound and introducing variety within the repeated line. In *Modern Times* Dylan uses a similar technique in the refrain stanza of "The Levee's Gonna Break," in which he alternates the third line in each occurrence: "Everybody saying this is a day only the Lord could make . . . / Some of these people gonna strip you of all they can take." The refrain, like the rest of the lyrics, is based on rhyming tercets (a-a-a), with the first two lines being identical, and the third line introducing a new and longer line. Though Dylan's refrain does not contribute to a narrative unity, it serves to introduce a sense of urgency, warning, or even threat, depending on the preceding lines.

While Poe focuses on the function of the refrain in the structure of a narrative poem, Jonathan Culler emphasizes its lyrical aspect. In his lecture "Why Lyric?" Culler states that, through ample use of the refrain, the ballad tries to remain lyrical while relying on narrative structure.[16] While the ballad has a narrative quality, it also gains a lyric quality by means of the refrain. The word "refrain" derives from the Latin "frenulum," which translates to bridle or restraint. While the narrative quality urges the poet to continue telling a story, adding details to his or her account, the refrain reins in the galloping story, giving both the poet and the reader a break from this linearity and narrative push. The refrain acts as a means of control, checking the poet from being carried away with his or her narrative. In other words, it functions as a pause during which the poet gives the audience a chance to digest the words. By dissecting the narrative into manageable chunks, the refrain renders easier the job of the bard as well as that of the audience. For the bard, it means getting rid of the narrative pressure to continue the story, and thus having the chance to design or remember the following lines. On the other hand, it provides the audience with the opportunity to take part in the song and to absorb what has so far been transmitted.

The refrains in Dylan's lyrics play an important role, functioning as cement between the lines. In some cases, as in "Blowin' in the Wind," the refrain gives the answer to a set of seemingly prophetically inspired questions.[17] Nonetheless, Dylan has an inconsistent relationship with the refrain, especially the burden, or repetition of a whole stanza. While he employs lengthier choruses in his earlier albums, his latest albums contain shorter refrains.[18] One of his earliest compositions, "Mr. Tambourine Man" from *Bringing It All Back Home,* for instance, exhibits the paramount use of the burden with a four-line stanza, each couplet beginning "Hey Mr. Tambourine Man" followed by "I'm not sleepy and there is no place I'm going to," then "In the jingle jangle morning I'll come followin' you." What is interesting about this song is that the lyrics open with the burden itself, which is repeated five times, highlighting the poet's search for support or inspiration. In "One More Cup of Coffee (Valley Below)," the gypsy blues from *Desire,* the three-line burden provides the brokenhearted speaker with a kind of recess from his long complaint about the end of an affair: "One more cup of coffee for the road / One more cup of coffee 'fore I go / To the valley below."

Similarly, the familiar six-line chorus in "Like a Rolling Stone," "How does it feel … / Like a rolling stone," has a crucial role within the architecture of the song. The country singer Rodney Crowell, who plays Dylan's famous hit almost every night, observes the importance of the refrain in this song: "I did it as a lark, to show off to some of the guys in my band that I knew all the words. But I was immediately struck by the audience response to the song. From six-year-olds to seventy-year-olds—they all know the chorus to that song. I couldn't put it away; every night, it's a unifying thing."[19] While Christopher Ricks stresses the double-edged quality of the question in the refrain,[20] Keith Negus highlights its dialogic function: "In concert, the phrase 'How does it feel?' is no longer addressed to a character embedded in a lyrical narrative. Instead, it is transformed, becoming 'how does it feel?' in the here and now of the concert. The refrain becomes a multivocal celebration of how it feels to be part of the moment and the history of Dylan singing this song."[21] As these examples show, some of Dylan's previous songs establish a complementary, dialogic, or cooperative relationship with the audience.

In his recent albums, however, Dylan does not attempt to build such an overtly dialogic relationship with his audience, and his lyrics focus instead on the implied listener. Dylan's use of the refrain naturally increases in albums where he interprets traditional ballads, blues, and gospel songs (for instance, *World Gone Wrong*). Yet it might be misleading to assume that Dylan's use of the refrain has dwindled in time as his ninth album *John Wesley Harding* depends least on the use of repetition or refrain of any kind. Except for "Down Along the Cove" and the closing track, "I'll Be Your Baby Tonight," both of which repeat only the eponymous line, this album interestingly does not take recourse to the refrain.

This wavering affair with the refrain continues in "*Love and Theft*" and *Modern Times*, where the refrain appears in different forms. The use of the burden (repetition of a whole stanza) is limited. In "*Love and Theft*" only "Sugar Baby" has a four-line burden; in *Modern Times* "Workingman's Blues #2" has a four-line burden and "Nettie Moore" has a six-line burden. In some cases, a single line ("When the Deal Goes Down," "Cry a While"), a couplet ("Mississippi," "Honest with Me"), or a stanza ("Nettie Moore," "Sugar Baby") is repeated, while in others the refrain appears with slight alterations ("Rollin' and Tumblin'," "Ain't Talkin'"). Not all the songs contain a refrain; for example, in "Bye and Bye" the refrain function is delegated to two rhyming couplets as opposed to the other quatrains with envelope rhyme scheme a-b-b-a; in "Lonesome Day Blues" the first two lines of each stanza are repeated, and in "Spirit on the Water" the refrain function seems to be distributed among the frequently used pronouns "I" and "you." Instead of songs with long refrains (burdens), a song with a two-line refrain ("Mississippi") and another with a refrain containing alternating lines in each occurrence ("Ain't Talkin'") will be analyzed in order to pay closer attention to Dylan's wavering affair with the refrain.

"MISSISSIPPI"

"Mississippi" promises to tell a story, yet abstains from fulfilling that promise. The refrain plays a significant role in the song, underlining the speaker's hopelessness. Written in rhyming couplets, "Mississippi" gives voice to a man who realizes that he is nearing the end of his life ("Your days are numbered, so are mine"; "Walking through the leaves, falling from the trees"; "Well my ship's been split to splinters and it's sinkin' fast / I'm drowning in the poison, got no future, got no past"). The setting of the song, based on images of shipwreck, drowning, and wet clothes, is Mississippi. It is remarkable that Dylan chose Mississippi, which has inspired countless authors from Mark Twain to Langston Hughes, and played a significant role in the formation and proliferation of the blues. Dylan himself drew on blues music, and—as the song ("High Water"), dedicated to the Mississippi-born blues singer Charley Patton implies—*"Love and Theft"* has a bluesy feel. As Negus succinctly observes for *"Love and Theft"* and *Modern Times*, Dylan's songs are pervaded with blues imagery drawn from the landscape of the Mississippi Delta—the river, the floods, the levees, the lowlands—as well as various stock phrases from the blues ("woke up this morning," "jump and shout," "rollin' and tumblin'").[22] Speaking of Highway 61, Dylan himself mentions the Mississippi River as "my place in the universe,"[23] which illustrates his wish to express his indebtedness to the blues. Yet the speaker in the song is too vexed to talk about the merits of the river and the city; instead he refers to the problems and drawbacks of getting stuck in Mississippi.

There is an addressee in the lyrics, and in every stanza he or she is directly spoken to. The addressee is old like the speaker, and both find themselves imprisoned in a modern waste land: "Every step of the way we walk the line / Your days are numbered, so are mine." The speaker finds himself almost in a Dantesque Hell where the dictum is "Abandon hope all ye who enter here." The setting for this city is full of chaos, and replete with distraction; trying to escape is futile. Allegorically, Mississippi is the modern City of Destruction or Vanity Fair, and the speaker is an aged Everyman or Christian, who comes to realize that the urban setting he has been living in is doomed to perish and he must run away from it. The speaker gives clues about his background in the second stanza: "City's just a jungle; more games to play / Trapped in the heart of it, tryin' to get away." These lines are interwoven with parallel structures, and despite the lack of a conjunction in the third line, it is not difficult to provide one: "I was raised in the country, [but] I been workin' in the town."

The way Dylan introduces the speaker's confessions at the beginning raises the expectation that this is the biographical account of an individual, a verse *bildungsroman*. As Matt Shedd states, "It's the typical American coming of age story, it's older than America; it's the prodigal son. But Dylan tells the story in a specifically rural American vernacular. He's talking about America in America's own tongue."[24] The lyrics in a sense promise to tell the story of a man with a rural background who is driven to live in an urban setting and who has failed to find the happiness he seeks. From this point onward, however, these expectations are not met. This may have something to do with the fact that Mississippi has deprived the speaker of his expressive or artistic faculties: "All my powers of expression and thoughts so sublime / Could never do you justice in reason or rhyme." The refrain of the song is introduced here, in the fourth stanza, and the expectation for a narrative is further heightened: "Only one thing I did wrong / Stayed in Mississippi a day too long." However, no reliable narrative ensues. The speaker was probably a travelling youth seeking fortune in the land of hope, and he has somehow become trapped here, changing his life irreversibly. He has become a ghost, a nonentity that can leave no imprint on anything or anybody except the addressee who accompanies him: "Walkin' through the leaves, falling from the trees / Feelin' like a stranger nobody sees." The speaker seems to find good company in the listener as they both have their regrets and feelings of remorse: "So many things that we never will undo / I know you're sorry, I'm sorry too." The speaker later declares that he has crossed the river to be with the addressee, yet this seems to contradict with what he states in the refrain that appears three times in the song.

In the penultimate stanza, the addressee turns out to be the long-awaited sweetheart ("So give me your hand and say you'll be mine") that will lighten the inescapable bitter end, yet the narrative incongruities remain unresolved. The final stanza again resorts to a bleak state of mind: "Only one thing I did wrong / Stayed in Mississippi a day too long." "Mississippi" fails as a narrative, as it is impossible to get a clear and detailed storyline out of the lyrics. However, the above refrain foregrounds the speaker's account of his life and feelings about Mississippi. The refrain persistently repeats the speaker's feelings of remorse through the sonorous vowels: "only," "wrong," "long." What matters most is the decision the speaker has made by staying in Mississippi, rather than what has happened since he came there ("I been in trouble ever since I set my suitcase down"). The whole matter seems to issue from making a choice or failing to make one, as in Robert Frost's "The Road Not Taken" (1916), in which the speaker repeats over and over again the irreversible consequences of his decision:

> I shall be telling this with a sigh
> Somewhere ages and ages hence:
> Two roads diverged in a wood, and I—
> I took the one less traveled by,
> And that has made all the difference.[25]

The refrain, in short, acts as a key element highlighting the speaker's desolation and regrets. Thus, it becomes the reader's/listener's duty to fill the gaps within the narrative by using the emotive clues in the refrain.

"AIN'T TALKIN'"

While "Mississippi" focuses on a specific place, the setting in "Ain't Talkin'," the final song of the album *Modern Times*, is a Biblical one; and it is rife with ambiguities and aporias like "Mississippi." The song similarly begins with a line promising to reveal a story: "As I walked out tonight in the mystic garden." Greil Marcus observes the virtues of the song's first line, stating: "It is a great opening line for anything: a song, a tale, a fable, a novel, a soliloquy. The world opens at the feet of that line. How one gets there—to the point where those words can take on their true authority, raise suspense like a curtain, and make anyone want to know what happens next—is what I want to look for."[26] The lyrics vibrate with narrative fecundity and anticipation; thus, the audience find themselves in the position of the sultan in the *Arabian Nights* who is captivated by what Scheherazade has to say next.

The orchestration of the song also contributes to the foregrounding of the lyrics. The haunting and melancholy-sounding first three measures of the song are made up of a minimal concoction of guitar and cello. As in "Love Sick" from *Time Out of Mind*, the rhythm is almost onomatopoeic, recreating the slow, pensive steps of a man taking a walk, setting the scene for a linear narrative. With each step, the audience hopes to be provided with how the story evolves. "The mystic garden" implies a setting and heightens the expectations for a sequential story. This garden, however, is devastated or defiled, where "The wounded flowers were dangling from the vines." The first stanza ends with the unexpected line "Someone hit me from behind." The speaker is hit in an ambiguous way since there is no further reference to this assault, its agent, or outcome. He is hit but he survives this blow, the details of which remain a mystery. Kees de Graaf puts forward that this line refers to the scene in the Garden of Eden after the eating of the Tree of Knowledge.[27] If one follows de Graaf, who interprets the song as a text about the Fall of Man, the anonymous person who hits the speaker is nobody other than Satan. After all, the narrative frame is there only to provide the speaker with a set of loosely organized clues which serves to foreground his isolation and estrangement. Though a Biblical analysis would not be irrelevant for many songs by Dylan, it does not apply to this song as a whole. Therefore,

I suggest that the speaker is rather an allegorical figure who stands for the Western individual of our age: wavering between the need to stick to a grand narrative (religion, politics, art) and the realization that this narrative has become outdated and in some way superfluous.

The refrains in "Ain't Talkin'" enact, in a different permutation, what Poe preaches in "The Raven." The first and third lines in Dylan's song remain the same while the second and fourth change in each case; for example: "Ain't talkin', just walkin' / Through this weary world of woe." The first refrain resembles the confessions of a man who has experienced the slings and arrows of time, and apparent in his words is the sense of defeat and fatigue resulting from having said too much so far with no avail. Since words fail to make a difference, the speaker opts for walking in the highly alliterative and consonantal "weary world of woe." Not only himself, but also the world he inhabits is old and desolate. The speaker is like that of the poem "I Look into My Glass" (1898) by Thomas Hardy, who complains about time, which "shakes this fragile frame at eve / With throbbing of noontide."[28] Though old, Dylan's speaker is still beaming with energy and passion inside ("Heart burnin', still yearnin'"). He also announces his views on Christianity, which he believes has failed to address people's needs: "I practice a faith that's been long abandoned." Despite this confession, he does not seem to have given up all hope: "They say prayer has the power to help / So pray from the mother [sic]."

The religious allusions are augmented with phrases that have a biblical sound, such as "the mystic garden," which stands for the speaker's modernized version of Garden of Eden, "cities of the plague" (alluding to Sodom and Gomorrah), "no altars on this long and lonesome road," the unending suffering, and the symbolic gardener who tends his garden no more. The refrain's equally important acts of talking and walking boil down to the same thing, enabling the speaker to explore and express his thoughts. Since he is not concerned with presenting a coherent picture of himself or telling a complete story, the lyrics digress from religious issues to political and personal ones. In terms of politics, the speaker adopts the discourse of an aggressive global power: "If I catch my opponents ever sleepin' / I'll just slaughter them where they lie." His attitude is not groundless, since animosity is pervasive: "The whole world is filled with speculation / The whole wide world which people say is round."

In addition to the religious and political problems, the speaker suffers from personal problems too ("Now I'm all worn down by weepin' / My eyes are filled with tears," "I'll avenge my father's death then I'll step back"); yet the causes of his personal suffering remain unknown.

As in "Mississippi," there are indications of the presence of an addressee in the song: "I'll burn that bridge before you can cross," "They'll be no mercy for you once you've lost." However, it is not always clear whether the pronoun "you" is an indefinite, impersonal "you," or a personal pronoun. "Ain't talkin', just walkin' / Eatin' hog-eyed grease in hog-eyed town." In some cases (as in "They will crush you with wealth and power / Every waking moment you could crack") the addressee is an anonymous "you," the receiver of the prophetic declarations, while in other cases it is a specific person, whom the speaker asks to give him his walking cane, or an implied listener whom he needs to get "out of [his] miserable brain."

Further ambiguities concern the identity of the speaker, who introduces himself as a lonely farmer in destitution ("My mule is sick, my horse is blind / ... Thinkin' 'bout the gal I left behind"). The speaker is worried not only about himself but also about the ways of the world; this makes him feel as he is "Walkin' with a toothache in my heel," an allusion to Genesis 3:15: "And I will put enmity between thee and the woman, and between thy seed and her seed; it shall bruise thy head, and thou shalt bruise his heel." This biblical and Hamlet-like speaker produces a deluge of statements about a number of issues both personal and universal.

Both "Mississippi" and "Ain't Talkin'" lack a coherent story. Furthermore, the lyrics of these songs do not provide us with a clear picture of the speaker, his motives, and sometimes even his whereabouts. In this sense they are far from being called unified texts. The refrains appear as the mechanisms that connect these desultory observations. Thanks to these refrains, the audiences have a more solid idea about the effect the songs are trying to create.

PERFORMATIVITY AND INTERTEXTUALITY

Dylan is famous for the length of some of his songs. He writes in his *Chronicles* about the issue of length after mentioning the dwindling attention span among people in postwar American society: "With the three minute song, the listener does not have to remember anything as far back as twenty or even ten minutes ago. There is nothing you have to be able to connect. Nothing to remember. A lot of the songs I was singing were indeed long, maybe not as long as an opera or a symphony, but still long ... at least lyrically. 'Tom Joad' had at least sixteen verses, 'Barbara Allen' about twenty. 'Fair Ellender,' 'Lord Lovell,' 'Little Mattie Groves' and others had numerous verses and I did not find it troubling at all to remember or sing the story lines."[29] Though he talks of the ease with which he can memorize long verses, processing such long lyrics can be problematic for the listener and requires certain techniques. With long songs the refrain is usually a lifesaver. With a very short (probably his shortest) song, Dylan used it as a lifesaver too. His album *Self Portrait*, which did not get friendly reviews, contained (along with traditional and cover songs like "Blue Moon") a song that sounded like a nursery rhyme: "All the Tired Horses," which to my mind is an indication of writer's block. Dylan, like many artists, had fallen prey to infertility. And the solution was to turn this impasse into a playful song: "All the tired horses in the sun / How'm I supposed to get any ridin' done?" This song is unique in Dylan's discography in that it does not feature his own voice. The incantation-like lyrics are sung by female vocalists. Christopher Ricks, who has studied Dylan's lyrics in terms of the seven deadly sins, puts forward that the song deals with sloth.[30] Without a doubt, the song has a languid feel, it is slow, these two lines are hummed many times in a lethargic tone; in short, it is suggestive of sloth. I believe, however, that the song has more to do with coming to terms with authorial barrenness. Dylan, therefore, steps aside in a gesture signaling his own helplessness arising from a writer's block and allows his backup vocalists (who in a sense stand for his worn muse or muses) to take the stage. The subject is redolent of the Shelleyan speaker in "Ode to the West Wind," who implores the wind to bring him inspiration: "Oh, lift me as a wave, a leaf, a cloud."[31] Shelley's ode does not have refrains, but the speaker repeats his yearning throughout the poem by means of subjunctives and apostrophes. In fact, Dylan's lullaby-like song conjures up the idea of "writing" through its close homophone "riding." Dylan's song, however, is pure refrain, pure subjunctive denoting a desire, a fulfillment, an expectation, stammering the speaker's wish throughout the song.

This desire is evident in the musical and lyrical structure of "All the Tired Horses." The whole song is made up of these two lines, a couplet repeated over and over again followed by humming, alternating with the yearning violins. Here is a songwriter/poet who cannot find any inspiration, which he wittingly turns into a powerful creative act. The horses (the winged horse, Pegasus), the harbingers of divine/artistic inspiration, are in the sun, as if let out thoughtlessly in the open to the devastating, parching effects of the elements. They are not located in the shade, or better, moonlight, which is more conducive to poetry. And this is what the poet ends up with: a confessional statement, an outcry acknowledging one's lack of creative powers. Because the speaker cannot produce poetry and establish a dialogue with the audience, he makes do with these two lines.

Luckily, Dylan has not suffered from the long creativity crises that he sings of in "All the Tired Horses," and has continued to produce songs. The antipode of this artistic aridity is highly allusive and intertextual lyrics where the central position and hegemonic power, and, hence, the responsibility to concoct a linear, consistent narrative vanishes. Richard F. Thomas lays bare the intertextual quality of Dylan's songwriting process in explicating the allusions to classical authors such as Virgil, Ovid, Homer, and Dante as well as the nineteenth-century Mark Twain and the twentieth-century Junichi Saga in "*Love and Theft*" and *Modern Times*. Treating Dylan's borrowings as intertexts rather than plagiarism, Thomas rightly states that "Intertextuality allows internal narratives and connections to suggest themselves."[32] Thus the poet is redeemed of the obligation to act as the sole author of his own verses, and becomes a mere intermediary, a sibylline character voicing the voiceless, disclosing what has been hidden for centuries, even millennia. Dylan's predominantly intertextual lyrics bring him closer to the rhapsode whose sole function is to perform rather than compose. Hence maybe his mask-erade tactics!

However, though Dylan is similar to a Homeric rhapsode, he is not simply a songster producing replicas of previous lyrics. He alters and reinterprets them. In an article published in May 1972, Frank Kermode and Stephen Spender succinctly summarize Dylan's habit of recycling: "Some of Dylan's work is avowedly based on traditional models, but he always reinvents them; a poem that starts 'As I went out one morning' soon loses its resemblance to its predecessors, and even in straight imitations of ballads about folk heroes he tends to shed the regularities of rhyme and metre which, in the old days, were an unconscious tribute by the poet to high-class culture."[33] Dylan's almost defiant attitude toward others' work suggests that he acts as if he were an artist before copyright laws were introduced, when music and lyrics floated freely in the pool of anonymity, in the collective memory of the public. This is also reminiscent of ancient poets borrowing from others at will and making such borrowings unmistakably their own by means of their rendering. In ancient Greece such appropriations were not considered a crime because everything belonged to the collective memory of the audiences. The Russian critic Bakhtin reminds us that the audiences of Homer were familiar with the epic cycles; therefore, where Homer started or ended his story was of no great import.[34] Dylan's oeuvre, too, in a way resembles the Homeric performance: Dylan concocts his songs from fragments of the world's literary (oral and written) and musical heritage. If one looks with a discerning eye, his songs constitute the cultural unconscious of our times.

One does not need to depend on a complete story; a few key words or images will suffice to provide the audiences with necessary cues.

Dylan's prophetic function is also supported by his recycling of old songs (both his own and others') by introducing modifications in lyrics and music. Focusing on the idea of "performative variation," Richard F. Thomas establishes the dual character of Dylan's artistic process: "Seen from the perspective of Homeric poetics, Dylan works like a blend of rhapsode (performance artist) and a poet on the cusp of oral and literary cultures.... Like Homer, he is the original creator and original performer of his narratives and lyrics, the seeds of which may be found in a whole range of texts from the Bible to the blues.... But Dylan himself is also a rhapsode who has performed his enormous corpus with powers of memory that seem Homeric in scope over the last 45 years."[35] Dylan's performative quality is clearly visible in the number of concerts he has given (over three thousand)[36] and different versions of his own songs[37] within a span of almost half a century. Linking Dylan's art with the social and communal practices of music making, Negus stresses the fact that Dylan is a performer in his own right, not simply a poet whose lyrics are to be perused on the page; he is, in other words, a descendant of a long oral tradition of "folk and blues, street-sung broadsides and work songs, the melodic observations of medieval troubadours, and the sacred rhythms of Christianity and Judaism."[38]

Marcus's observation about "folk-lyric song" "The Coo Coo Bird" applies also to Bob Dylan's songwriting: "That meant it was made up of fragments that had no direct or logical relationship to each other, but were drawn from a floating pool of thousands of disconnected verses, couplets, one-liners, pieces of eight."[39] Depending on and drawing from such diverse traditional and oral resources, Dylan builds a bridge between himself and his audiences by means of the refrain that facilitates a dialogic and performative relationship: "When audiences sing along at concerts, the performer can recognize and discern the very tangible way that the melodies of the songs have connected with the public. This connection can be heard on the performance of 'It Ain't Me Babe' on the album *Real Live*, recorded live in England and Ireland during the summer of 1984, when Dylan stands back from the microphone and allows the crow to sing the 'no, no, no' refrain."[40]

Rainer Vesely, commenting on the narrative loopholes and confusion about the characters in "Tangled Up in Blue," rightly remarks, "Perhaps we should go further and establish that Dylan does not tell a story, but sketches particular situations, model miniatures of multifaceted relationships between men and women which have a 'thematic' but no 'narrative' link."[41] But in fact this seemingly patchy, fragmented song gains its total effect by means of the refrain carrying the whole load of the song. Though singing along is one of the main manifestations of the communal link between the singer and audience, Dylan in many cases consciously subverts it. I agree with Negus on the oral and communicative function of the refrain, which does not necessarily have to harbor a narrative consistency or unity: "Singing along, symbolically and quite tangibly affirms the relationship between artist and audience. When the audience participates in singing the song, artists often stop singing and let the audience take over. Singing along with choruses is also one of the clearest examples of how the words of pop songs become detached from their semantic significance within the song's lyrical narrative or argument."[42] Whether the singer allows his audience to take part or not, the refrain plays a vital performative role in music, especially in the comparatively long lyrics of Dylan, who likes bending his melodies out of shape and derailing the expectations of his audiences. When confronted with the metamorphosed songs in live performances, the audience, if not endowed with exceptionally fine ears, has to wait for the refrain so as to identify and take part in the song.

The refrain or chorus in Dylan's songs functions as the thread that brings together the loose filaments of impressions, anecdotes, images, and the like that do not always add up to a consistent, linear totality. It acts, however, as the signpost for the mood the speaker finds himself in; while the rest of the lyrics may allude to a plethora of different incidents and seemingly disparate images, the refrain is the organizing principle, the magnet attracting all the pieces. Dylan's recent albums tend to be more contemplative: he seems to be less interested in establishing a communion with his audience than with his implied addressee. Though *"Love and Theft"* and *Modern Times* depend less on the use of the refrain, they still manage to establish a closer affinity with the audiences as Dylan talks about issues of which they are aware.

NOTES

1. Martin Scorsese, dir., *No Direction Home*.
2. Mark Howard, engineer and producer, relating the dialogue between Bob Dylan and Tony Garnier, his regular bass player. Chris Shaw, "Life with Bob Dylan, 1989–2006" *Uncut*, www.uncut.co.uk/bob-dylan/life-with-bob-dylan-1989-2006-feature (accessed September 3, 2012).
3. "The Nobel Prize in Literature 2016." Nobelprize.org. Nobel Media AB 2014. Web. 6 December 2016. www.nobelprize.org/nobel_prizes/literature/laureates/2016/.
4. See, for example, Kermode and Spender, who suggest that Dylan's lyrics do not fall strictly within the confines of poetry: "It is difficult to judge the lyrics as 'poems' because they

don't really have to be poetry. They just have to produce their effects of feeling, colour and mild wit, which show in the voice and are not outrhythmed by the guitar.... They don't have to be poetry, nor do any ballads, but some, like those in various anthologies, have succeeded in being it." "The Metaphor at the End of the Funnel," in *The Dylan Companion*, Elizabeth Thomson and David Gutman, ed. (New York: Da Capo, 2001), 161.

5. Bowden, *Performed Literature*, 1.

6. Paul Williams, *Performing Artist: Bob Dylan, Performing Artist, 1974–1986: The Middle Years* (London: Omnibus, 1992), xiii.

7. Haruo Shirane, "Performance, Visuality, and Textuality: The Case of Japanese Poetry," in *Oral Tradition* 20(2) (October 2005): 217–32.

8. Richard Schechner, *Performance Theory* (New York: Routledge, 1988), 30.

9. Schechner, *Performance Theory*, 30.

10. Keith Negus, *Bob Dylan* (Bloomington: Indiana University Press, 2008), 63.

11. Nilay Örnek, "En pahalı Bob Dylan konserini Türkler izledi," *Haber Türk*, www.haberturk.com/kultur-sanat/haber/519935-en-pahali-bob-dylan-konserini-turkler-izledi (accessed on August 22, 2012).

12. "Andrew Muir has suggested that Dylan's live arrangement and willful disruption of familiar melodies are an attempt to subvert and undermine the audience's attempt to sing along." Keith Negus, "Living, Breathing Songs: Singing Along with Bob Dylan," in *Oral Tradition* 22(1) (March 2007): 71–83. Negus later on introduces his reservation, saying that this is not always the case. A very recent example of such versions is a highly contorted rendering of "Blowin' in the Wind" in Dresden in 2012. The song is available online on Youtube: http://www.youtube.com/watch?hl=en&v=vVLlN6hoLXQ&gl=US.

13. Alex Preminger and Terry V. F. Brogan, eds., *The New Princeton Encyclopedia of Poetry and Poetics* (Princeton, NJ: Princeton University Press, 1994), 1018.

14. Edgar Allan Poe, "The Philosophy of Composition," *Poe's Poems and Essays* (London: Everyman's Library, 1969), 168.

15. Poe, "The Philosophy of Composition," 168.

16. Jonathan Culler, "Why Lyric?" Cornell Cast, www.cornell.edu/video/index.cfm?VideoID=619.

17. Kermode and Spender, 157.

18. This is the case with some of the tracks on his latest three albums. For instance, "Lonesome Day Blues" (*"Love and Theft"*), "Spirit on the Water" (*Modern Times*), and "Tempest" (*Tempest*) do not have refrains.

19. Greil Marcus, *Like a Rolling Stone: Bob Dylan at the Crossroads* (New York: Public Affairs, 2006), 87.

20. Christopher Ricks, *Dylan's Visions of Sin* (New York: Ecco, 2005), 203.

21. Negus, "Living, Breathing Songs: Singing Along with Bob Dylan," 79.

22. Negus, *Bob Dylan*, 81.

23. Dylan, *Chronicles*, 241.

24. Matt Shedd, "Bob Dylan's Folk Poetics in the Later Albums: Telling the Story of America in Ruins in Simple Poetic Language," *Rupkatha Journal on Interdisciplinary Studies in Humanities* 3(2) (2011), http://rupkatha.com/V3/n2/07_Bob_Dylan_Folk_Poetics.pdf (accessed August 14, 2012).

25. Robert Frost, *The Complete Poems of Robert Frost* (New York: Holt, Rinehart and Winston, 1964), 131.

26. Greil Marcus, *Bob Dylan: Writings 1968–2010* (London: Faber, 2010), 354.

27. Kees de Graaf, "Bob Dylan's 'Ain't Talking'—The Old Testament revisited—an analysis by Kees de Graaf—Part 1." www.keesdegraaf.com/media/Misc/3293p16bfeaap41ckroqq1hs dqmn19441.pdf.

28. Thomas Hardy, *The Complete Poems*, James Gibson, ed. (Houndmills, UK: Palgrave, 2001), 81.

29. Dylan, *Chronicles*, 56.

30. Ricks, Dylan's Visions of Sin, 120–24.

31. P. B. Shelley, "Ode to the West Wind," *The Norton Anthology of Poetry* (New York: Norton, 1983), 622.

32. Richard F. Thomas, "The Streets of Rome: The Classical Dylan," *Oral Tradition* 22(1) (March 2007): 45.

33. Kermode and Spender, "The Metaphor at the End of the Funnel," 155.

34. Mikhail Bakhtin, *The Dialogic Imagination: Four Essays*, ed. Michael Holquist, trans. Carly Emerson and Michael Holquist (Austin: Texas University Press, 2000), 32.

35. Thomas, "The Streets of Rome," 48–49.

36. Expecting Rain. Discussions. "Dylan Is a Touring Machine." www.expectingrain.com/discussions/viewtopic.php?f=2&p=1250514&sid=5aedde2bf43eb91209f964474939b778.

37. Chris Shaw: "His songs continuously evolve. For him, it's all about getting the track to fit the words, not the other way round. That's why there are so many bootlegs, six versions of 'Like Rolling Stone,' four 'Visions of Johanna.'" "Life with Bob Dylan, 1989–2006," *Uncut*, www.uncut.co.uk/bob-dylan/life-with-bob-dylan-1989-2006-feature (accessed September 3, 2012). See also Alan Light, who remarks that Dylan is eager to show "his songs aren't permanently fixed museum pieces"; "Dylan as Performer," in *The Cambridge Companion to Bob Dylan*, 57.

38. Negus, "Living, Breathing Songs: Singing Along with Bob Dylan," 71.

39. Marcus, *Invisible Republic*, 116.

40. Negus, "Living, Breathing Songs: Singing Along with Bob Dylan," 78.

41. Rainer Vesely, "Tangled Up in Blue." *Bob Dylan: Five Songs: Lectures Accompanying the Exhibition Bob Dylan. The Drawn Blank Series at the Kunstsammlungen Chemnitz*, ed. Ingrid Mössinger and Wilfram Ette. Berlin: Kerber Art, 2008. 66–78, 72.

42. Negus, "Living, Breathing Songs: Singing Along with Bob Dylan," 78–79.

THE LAST BOB DYLAN RECORD

Nick Smart

Bob Dylan's last record will have his whole career on its back; it has always been that way. A review[1] of his third record, *The Times They Are a-Changin'* (1964), complains that it is not a marked step forward from *The Freewheelin' Bob Dylan* (1963). Given what Dylan becomes capable of, maybe that reaction is legitimate. We could not wait for his promise to be elaborated, and kept. That Dylan could answer our impatience then is how his ability to renew became both legend and burden.

The Keatsian burst of creativity that yielded 1965's electrifying *Bringing It All Back Home* and *Highway 61 Revisited*, and another surge the next year, with what is for many an aesthetic zenith, the "wild mercury sound" of *Blonde on Blonde*, assured that Dylan would no longer be compared to any as-yet-unreached potential, but only judged in relation to the standard he had set.

By living and writing and playing (so much), Dylan burdens himself with the obligation not just to meet but to elevate the standard of his greatness. If it is ever really concluded that Dylan is done being Dylan, as was thought during the time of the Christian records, and the seemingly unremarkable stretches between *Infidels* (1983) and *Oh Mercy*, and *Time Out of Mind*, a devaluation of the entire career will occur. Every new record will be the measure of existing potency. And now, six decades into this career, the new record might really be the *last* record, the thing he did for us lately. So the pressure becomes more intense.

The desire to defend felt in the heart when a friend dismisses Dylan on the grounds that he was dreadful in Denver last night are tiny aftershocks of the eloquent earthquake of resentment directed at his critics as Dylan accepted the MusiCares Person of the Year Award for 2015: "Critics have always been on my tail since day one. Seems like they've always given me special treatment.... Times always change. They really do. And you have to always be ready for something that's coming along and you never expected it." The "special treatment" to which we subject Dylan is a love test: Tell him to write us thirteen new songs, really brand new and just like before. These are the conditions of reception under which Dylan and his listeners cannot help but operate. They make it an intense project to figure out how good the last Bob Dylan record really is.

And as soon as we get started, there is trouble. The most recent release (at the time of this writing), *Shadows in the Night*, is a Frank Sinatra covers album. In anticipation of *Shadows*' arrival, Dylan doubters coughed and scoffed while the loyalists—the perennial concertgoers, Bob-loving bloggers, and the Dylan teachers too—mustered considerable enthusiasm. Tribesmen and -women knew just how to fit Bob's desire to uncover Sinatra's song and story into our own avidity. Certain signs had prepared us. Tracks like "*Love and Theft*"'s crooning "Moonlight" were just the sound Sean Wilentz locked into when connecting Dylan's work in the nineties and aughts to a "minstrel voice" in the sonic texture of which Sinatra and Bing Crosby are distinguishable elements.[2] So Dylan's installation in October 2014 of "Stay with Me" (1965) as the show closer (an honored position the 1965 number from the cannily titled Sinatra release, *The Singer Today*, held through April 2015), we knew that *Shadows* would be, like the Christmas album and Dylan's satellite radio show, and maybe even the Chrysler commercial ("Is there anything more American than America?"), a visit to a prefiguring monument of Dylan's own ethos. As *the* indispensable figure in American music for six decades, Dylan has acquired a steward's role in the keeping—and telling—of the tradition.

The student of literature reading along here might accept the analogy that Dylan's interest in our interest in Americana is something like T. S. Eliot behind the microphone at the BBC lecturing on the metaphysical poets.[3] But Eliot's radio days are not why we teach him in surveys of English and American literature, and it does not make much sense to discuss *Shadows in the Night* in the context of the surprising resurgence of Dylan's talent and reach to which Wilentz refers. Better we should talk about *Tempest* when we attempt to look beyond the late and great streak of records—*Time Out of Mind*, "*Love and Theft*," and *Modern Times*—that proved Dylan to still be in possession of the canon-making capacity associated with achievements like *Highway 61 Revisited*, *Blonde on Blonde*, or *Blood on the Tracks*.

Is *Tempest* speaking directly to these records when it says, in "Narrow Way," "if I can't work up to you / you'll surely have to work down to me someday"? That's an admission of the weight of precedent, but it does not mute the tone of imperial agency that sounds so boldly four tracks later: "I ain't dead yet / my bell still rings / I keep my fingers crossed / like the early Roman kings." It has been several years since *Tempest*'s release and its songs are still making up the backbone of his concert set list. For those who like to let Dylan be the first authority on Dylan, this inclusion gives the record's songs—their sound and their words—a reflexive property, a capacity to comment on their own place in the oeuvre.

Yes, it seems we are discussing with each other something Dylan discusses with himself. What do the old and new say to each other when they meet? How is the curation of legacy affected by their conversation? Another analogy from the captain's tower hints at how significant these questions are and helps us begin to answer them.

T. S. Eliot's "Tradition and the Individual Talent" (1919) lays out the poet-as-critic's conviction that essential greatness puts all master works in relation to one another. In the essay's later portions Eliot explains how poets come by the capacity to make great poems, but his foregrounding critical assumption insists that artistic merit is its own critical and categorizing imperative: "I mean this as a principle of aesthetic, not merely historical, criticism. . . . what happens when a new work of art is created is something that happens simultaneously to all the works of art which preceded it. The existing monuments form an ideal order among themselves, which is modified by the introduction of the new (the really new) work of art among them."[4] So, "Narrow Way" was right. The songs of *Tempest* will pull *Blood*, *Blonde*, and *Bringing* in their direction even as they move up to the ethereal heights the tracks of those albums occupy.

Scrutinizing the last Bob Dylan record in terms of Eliot's formula would seem to settle questions of value rather quickly. Say that it is 1985, *Empire Burlesque* has just come out, sounding, as a student of mine observed recently, "just like the eighties." Very possibly the synthesized backing and unsettling mixture of pitch, tempo, and nasality in Dylan's singing will not compare favorably to the near perfect sonic union of Mark Knopfler's crystalline echoes and Dylan's open intonations on *Slow Train Coming*. And then a year later *Knocked Out Loaded*'s seemingly unfocused songwriting compared to the incisions of *Infidels* might lead to the conclusion that Dylan's edge is permanently blunted and the order of his great works becoming static.

But in 1989 *Oh Mercy* will demand a little room, and though the climate of its release is a little different from *Tempest*'s, there is a paradigmatic lesson—a lesson of paradigmatic change—to be noted. Critics were relieved—grateful—that *Oh Mercy* rose to a standard that suggested Dylan's concern for his art and his talent still existed, a proposition that most of the decade had left in doubt. In satisfaction of Eliot's formula for the reception of great works, the new record contained the old Dylan. Yet, as we learn from *Chronicles*, the relationship between *Oh Mercy* and the past was not an easy one; Daniel Lanois, *Oh Mercy*'s producer, wanted to couple old words with the new sound he was engineering, as Dylan relates here: "Off and on during the time we were cutting 'Series of Dreams,' he'd say to me something like, 'We need songs like "Masters of War," "Girl from the North Country," or "With God on Our Side."' He began nagging at me, just about every other day, that we sure could use some songs like those. I nodded. I knew we could, but I felt like growling. I didn't have anything like those songs."[5]

The songs Lanois wishes for come from *Freewheelin'* and *The Times They Are A-Changin'*, from 1963 and 1964, respectively. They are the evolved folk of Dylan's first original voice, the very mode from which he departs in 1965–66, when the electric and the surreal become his next, and for many most compelling, signature. It is probably those songs—"Like a Rolling Stone," "Ballad of a Thin Man," "Visions of Johanna"—that Dylan refers to during the endless round of interviews that accompanied the *Chronicles* release when he confesses that he can no longer summon the "penetrating magic" of his earlier writing.

How is it that songs not conjured by the old magic come to form a respectable album like *Oh Mercy*, or a stunning one like *Time Out of Mind*? The answer is that *magic is never old*. This is not the way the formula of Tradition and Talent works. The new does not resemble the old by copying it; the new comes to resemble the old by sharing a comparison to the understanding of greatness that both old and new, in connection, create. Two notes on this process, one from the artist and one from the critic, will put us in the position to give *Tempest* a fair hearing.

In an interview coinciding with *Tempest*'s release, Dylan describes the most recent modality of his writing, and marks the beginning of its era: "The songs on *Time Out of Mind* weren't meant for somebody to listen to at home. Most of the songs work, whereas before, there might have been better records, but the songs don't work. So I'll stick with what I was doing after *Time Out of Mind*, rather than what I was doing in the Seventies and Eighties, where the songs just don't work."[6] Knowing that he now writes strictly in anticipation of the way the songs will fit into the hundred or so sets he plays each year helps structure our understanding of where the artist is at any moment. It seems that Dylan has settled for himself the question of whether to think in terms of poetry or performance well before the critical imagination attempts to resolve the opposition.

In his essay "Dylan and the Academy" for *The Cambridge Companion to Bob Dylan* (2009), Lee Marshall faults critical opinion on Dylan for treating him as either a poet or a musician, and thereby failing to adequately address the category of performance in which the songs under consideration should be thought to reside. This interpretive rubric is crucial, even for the consideration of songs written before Dylan announced live performance as his imperative. As Marshall observes: "When we read a poem, we read it in our own voice, at our own speed. With a song, we have no such control; the singer controls the pace at which we hear a song and the voice in which we hear it ... This is particularly important for a singer like Dylan who has such a distinctive voice. When you hear that sound, you know who is singing, and what we know about Dylan affects how we respond to the song."[7] Marshall's discussion hopes to push academic writing about Dylan toward a dynamic of consideration better suited to music and this musician than are critical paradigms imported from literary studies. And by arguing that the way in which we listen to Dylan can govern the way we write about Dylan, Marshall gives the problem of the last Bob Dylan record a discourse-defining capacity. When the last record throws its listeners into the Eliotic arena, making Dylan harmonize or clash with Dylan, the conditions for quality reception are already present.

By merely taking *Tempest* on its own terms, as an example of a more recent paradigm of Dylan production, we honor Marshall's wisdom and Dylan's declared intention by activating a mode of response that treats the songs emerging from the albums as phenomenological events. What does each track do to us and through us in the moment we hear it? This is the first consideration, and as we engage it, the relationship between this moment and all the Dylan moments before it adjusts and is announced.

So, let *Tempest* play. Listen to the first offering, "Duquesne Whistle," which, like a poem's epigram or a novel's frame, will condition us though semantics and sound to receive the last record as a comment on its own place in the discography. Relax, suggests the first forty-five seconds of sweet nostalgia, a tooting aural eponym put in place by a bending lap steel and a six-string's comfortable bounce. When drum and bass join the mix to convert the sonic icon to a musical mode, a western swing, the journey becomes no less pleasant. We are to feel no anxiety of Bob-on-Bob influence; as Eliot knows, that will all sort itself out. Let the song's freewheelin' momentum, its twang of Nashville skyline—not sung but certainly suggested—and the American-roots journey implied by the song's place names and allusions gather your interest in its sweep.

This is the nature of Dylan's songs written for the stage. They are all movement, collection, then letting go. "I'm gonna stop in Carbondale and keep on going," says the rasping voice that is so often now made the sign of either decline or persistence. This is to be read as acknowledgment of the last-Bob-Dylan-record paradox. What here is signified, more or no more?

The lyrics of "Duquesne" deliberately preserve the listener's dilemma. Using Robert Johnson's tropology of train lights, or at least using it the way Jagger and Richards did, the Duquesne train appears with "blue light blinking red light glowing." So the lesson is taught. For this song, this record, and this career, the stops and starts are not functions of receptive temperament or artistic merit; they are the nature of the offering. The declaration "You're the only thing alive that keeps me going" forces the question of what momentum dead things have, and should temper demands that Dylan always come out sounding just like, and at the same time a little better than, some ancient Dylan.

This is the phenomenon of Eliot's order of great works again, now described with full awareness that the old's authorization of the new has no canonical priority over the new's reanimation of the old. In pursuit of that logic, *Tempest*'s second track, "Soon After Midnight," looks directly back at "*Love and Theft*"'s "Moonlight." Like its predecessor, "Midnight" proceeds at a much sweeter and slower tempo than the tracks that surround it. Moreover, it is sung with as little rasp as Dylan can manage. Like the lovers in "Moonlight," Midnight's listener is at peace in its sway and lull, a respite that will be enjoyed again in the Sinatra covers that now cannot be shelved as pure novelty because it is clear that Dylan places great stock in their mid-twentieth-century sound.

But first, having fit itself into history, *Tempest* delivers its emblematic tracks. "Narrow Way," "Long and Wasted Years," "Pay in Blood," and "Early Roman Kings" make us revel in their badness. Their sound is almost classic blues, and so our heads nod, our shoulders roll, our feet rise and fall. But there is something here more urgent than the blues. The rhythm is not meant to cajole and contain us. Rather, we are ejected, sent out on the road with the songs' warrior-speaker whose tragic origin ("there's a bleeding wound / at the heart of town") determines the nature of his victories for us and over us ("I can strip you of life / strip you of breath"). Those lines, lifted whole from Robert Fagles's translation of the *Odyssey*, put us in the compositional terrain of "Thunder on the Mountain," and "High Water (For Charley Patton)," which are both gems from the recent burst. Linking to those songs reveals connections to *Street-Legal*'s "New Pony" ("She broke her leg and needed shooting / I swear it hurt me more than it ever could have hurted her"), and

"Idiot Wind" from *Blood on the Tracks* ("One day you'll be in the ditch, flies buzzin' around your eyes / Blood on your saddle").

These are all songs of onslaught. In each the listener is addressed deadeyed with raw tone and images. Each song blares, its instrumentation full but not lush, and Dylan's voice nearly hectoring, a sound emitted way after cautionary tales have failed. This kind of performance deserves the title *Tempest*. It has been occurring all along, and now we know what to call it: the invocation of devastation. "Long and Wasted Years," helps determine the purpose of *Tempest* songs. It is a scaling sermon, mean and tender at the same time, offering the lesson that painful defeat can be celebrated as the occasion for empathy ("my enemy crashed into the dust / stopped dead in his tracks and he lost his lust"). In deference to the poetics of set lists, let us note that Dylan shows from the period discussed earlier featured "Long and Wasted Years" as the last number before the encore, which was always "Blowin' in the Wind" and Sinatra's "Stay with Me." "So much for tears / So much for these long and wasted years" were the last new words Dylan offered each night.

Yes, exactly. The last Bob Dylan record will always reckon with its listener's anticipation of the end of a career. But *Tempest* leaves the career as alive as are the great poets when a new voice stirs them. The idea that Dylan reinvents himself should not be understood merely in terms of those shifts from acoustic to electric or pagan to Christian that dominate the telling of his history. What it means is that Dylan kind of sounds like Dylan, and Dylan, all rolled into one.

NOTES

1. Steven Thomas Erlwine, review of *The Times They Are a-Changin'*. www.allmusic.com/album/the-times-they-are-a-changin-mw0000202344.
2. Wilentz, *Bob Dylan in America*, 263–76.
3. Todd Avery, *Radio Modernism* (Hampshire, UK: Ashgate, 2006), 111.
4. T. S. Eliot, *Selected Prose of T. S. Eliot* (New York: Farrar, Straus and Giroux, 1975), 38.
5. Dylan, *Chronicles*, 195.
6. Mikal Gilmore, "Bob Dylan Unleashed: A Wild Ride on His New LP and Striking Back at Critics," *Rolling Stone*, September 27, 2012, n.p.
7. Lee Marshall, "Bob Dylan and the Academy," in *The Cambridge Companion to Bob Dylan*, Keven J. H. Dettmar, ed. (Cambridge: Cambridge University Press, 2009), 103.

CHAPTER ELEVEN

"EVERYBODY GOT TO WONDER WHAT'S THE MATTER WITH THIS CRUEL WORLD TODAY": SOCIAL CONSCIOUSNESS AND POLITICAL COMMENTARY IN *LOVE AND THEFT* AND *MODERN TIMES*

Thad Williamson

Bob Dylan has spent much of the past fifty years trying to escape the label of "protest singer." Over the past decade, there have been plenty of serious topics for the topically minded songwriter to address: the Iraq War, threats to civil liberties, rising economic inequality, the financial collapse of 2008 and "Great Recession" that followed. Unlike his musical peers Neil Young (*Living with War* [2006]) and Bruce Springsteen (*Wrecking Ball* [2012]), Dylan to date has not addressed those events in any direct way, through new topical songs, in the last stage of his career.

Even so, music journalists and much of Dylan's fan base remain highly intrigued by the question of just what Dylan makes of the events of the day. Cryptic comments made by Dylan at a Minneapolis concert the night of Barack Obama's election as president in 2008 were widely debated by Dylan followers on the Internet: did Dylan mean what he said when he remarked "it looks like there's going to be a change now," or was he gently mocking liberal exultation at Obama's victory?

Those comments became a primary focus of a September 2012 *Rolling Stone* interview on the occasion of the release of *Tempest*. Despite repeated prodding, Dylan refused to make any substantive comment about Obama's presidency, adding that if one wants an informed opinion about what kind of person Obama is, the journalist should ask Obama's wife. Dylan further added that he did not recall the election night comments of 2008, and was not sure what he was trying to say, though he did add that "I would hope that a change has in fact happened." Pressed by the interviewer for more clarity, Dylan finally replied in exasperation, "What the fuck do you want me to say?"[1]

That outburst can be understood as directed not only at the questioner, but at any and all who still, half a century after *The Times They Are A-Changin'*, have an impulse to look to Dylan to find "where it's at." A moment's reflection suggests the sheer absurdity of expecting Dylan to be a good source of expert insight about Obama or any specific aspect of contemporary politics.

Yet this is only part of the story. In that same *Rolling Stone* interview, Dylan made headlines by stating that slavery was a curse on American history, a stain that could never be erased.

> This country is just too fucked up about color. It's a distraction. People at each other's throats just because they are of a different color. It's the height of insanity, and it will hold any nation back—or any neighborhood back. Or any anything back. Blacks know that some whites didn't want to give up slavery—that if they had their way, they would still be under the yoke, and they can't pretend they don't know that....
>
> It's doubtful that America's ever going to get rid of that stigmatization. It's a country founded on the backs of slaves. You know what I mean? Because it goes way back. It's the root cause.[2]

While Dylan refused to endorse or otherwise be drawn into a substantive assessment of Barack Obama, the songwriter landed a far more devastating critique of American society and the pervasive legacy of racism. No wonder that Dylan never has and never will escape the "protest singer" label. He no longer goes in for topical songs about current events, or for writing songs out of newspaper stories. But his work continues to reflect an acute social conscience and a deep-seated critique of American history and contemporary society. Both his recent songs and his interviews show that Dylan remains attentive to what is going on now. As one of the characters in "Po' Boy" might put it, "the game is the same, it's just on another level."

Both *"Love and Theft"* and *Modern Times* display as a fairly consistent theme a deep concern and discomfort with social and economic conditions in the contemporary United States, as well as a consciousness of the deep injustices of American history. As has been widely noted, the very album title *"Love and Theft"* is a reference to scholar Eric Lott's 1993 book about the culture of minstrel shows in the early twentieth century, and Lott himself interprets the album as an extended reflection on themes related to the borrowing and theft involved in the cross-racial fusion of popular musical culture in the twentieth century.[3] *Modern Times* is not put in quotes, but that album title also calls to mind Charlie Chaplin's film of the same name, a critique and parody of the impact of the industrial era on the individual.[4] At the very least, these album titles are suggestive of what was on Dylan's mind in constructing these records.

Both Lott and Sean Wilentz[5] have pointed out the ways in which Dylan, in deploying a dazzlingly diverse array of cultural references, citations, and quotations, creates on these records a musical fusion in which past and present are continually intertwined. At one moment we are in the Civil War, the next moment we are in 2006, and then we are back in the 1930s.

A common view among some observers of the contemporary Dylan, observing the pastiche of half-borrowed melodies and lyrics on both of these albums and questions that have been raised about the veracity of *Chronicles*, is that in fact Dylan is simply the consummate "bullshit artist."[6] This is an understandable reaction for those puzzled by the lack of obvious political statements in the recent songs, troubled by the charges against Dylan of plagiarism, perplexed by Dylan's bizarre claim in his 2012 *Rolling Stone* interview that he had been "transfigured," and moved by the surface-level contradiction of Dylan being willing to tour China at the same time politically provocative artists like the sculptor Ai Weiwei are being persecuted by the Chinese government.[7]

It is not the purpose of this essay to defend Dylan against all such criticisms of his artistic integrity or political judgment, but I reject the claim that there is nothing coherent or compelling in Dylan's body of work. Writers like Wilentz have persuasively shown, first, that Dylan in fact has a powerful and well-educated mind honed not just by his personal experience but by wide, self-guided reading, particularly in American history; and second, that the deeper one goes into excavating Dylan's sources and quotations, the more coherent and compelling *"Love and Theft"* and *Modern Times* become.

Indeed, the most enduring political statement of these records, particularly *"Love and Theft,"* is the open engagement with the cross-racial fusion of American culture, the deliberate calling attention to minstrelsy and the practice of simultaneously appropriating African American culture while denigrating African Americans that has characterized white engagement with black culture. Expressing a consciousness of deep historic injustice is itself a political act, and a particularly important act with respect to race in the United States.[8] *"Love and Theft"* can be seen in the context of a long line of statements Dylan has made about race in virtually all stages of his career, statements that have continued with his 2012 *Rolling Stone* interview and the release of the powerful song "Pay in Blood" on *Tempest*.

At a surface level, Dylan (with one partial exception) does not include any obviously political songs on *"Love and Theft"* or *Modern Times*. There are no clarion calls here to end wars or change presidents. While social and political awareness forms part of the backdrop for Dylan's music on these records, explicit social commentary is scattered across numerous different songs in the form of one-off lines or isolated stanzas.

The absence of an explicit treatment of current political issues in these particular records does not mean Dylan lacks an analytical frame for assessing the political condition. On the contrary, the mature Dylan has not been shy about articulating a theory of political life and, implicitly, the state of current politics. While every Dylan record is unique, none are self-contained creations to be heard in a vacuum; in interpreting their meanings, it is both reasonable and necessary to hear each album in light of previous work.[9]

With respect to politics, to make sense of where Dylan is coming from we need to return to his 1989 album *Oh Mercy*. On that album, Dylan provided arguably the most definitive statement of his views about politics and the tragic flaws of human nature, particularly in the songs "Political World," "Everything Is Broken," and "Man in a Long Black Coat." Interestingly, the sessions for *Oh Mercy* also included a song (unreleased until 1994), "Dignity," which by using an upbeat melody and series of amusing vignettes to paint a wistful picture that is by turns hopeful and somber, is a precursor to the kind of songwriting often found on *"Love and Theft"* and *Modern Times*.

Oh Mercy's opening song, "Political World" announces that we live in a "political world," where "love don't have any place." But this is just the beginning of the indictment. As the song goes on we find that we live in times when crime does not have a face; wisdom is thrown into jail; and mercy and courage are absent. The world is a "stacked deck" we can all see and feel—that is, it is unjust. The latter part of the song turns to how individuals confront this damaged world in which "peace is not welcome at all," a world said to lack three of the four cardinal virtues (wisdom, courage, justice). "As soon as you're awake you're trained to take, what looks like the easy way out," sings Dylan, a verse signaling that individuals in this society are subject to a socialization process intended to secure compliance with an unjust order. Dylan thus restates, in more compact and coherent version, a theme of social critique dating back to "It's Alright, Ma (I'm Only Bleeding)." Society is fundamentally unjust, and those who recognize this fact become alienated from it (and perhaps suicide candidates); the only recourse available is to "climb into the frame and shout God's name," but even this is an uncertain enterprise.

This critique of society is thoroughly radical, and it follows in the footsteps of radical skeptics of the received order from Thrasymachus (the skeptical character in Book One of Plato's *Republic*) to Karl Marx. The key point is not simply that the world is unjust; it is that this "political world" also has mechanisms in place intended to secure consent and disguise the unjust character of the existing power structure. Unlike a figure such as Thrasymachus, however, Dylan does seem to insist that there are things such as wisdom, courage, justice, and peace that have real meaning—but that these virtues are scarcely present in our world.[10]

If we take this account of what it means to "live in a political world" as a statement of Bob Dylan's mature theory of the polis, we can quickly see why it might seem redundant for later songs to bother to talk about specific wars or other political evils. Dylan's mature critique is not aimed at ephemeral surface-level events, but rather at the deep structure of society and its perennial tendencies. Equally important, this critique is not generated from a reading of the newspaper or other short-term events. There is little reason to think that, if Jimmy Carter and Walter Mondale had been president in the 1980s instead of Ronald Reagan and George H. W. Bush, the content of Dylan's assessment of the political (and human) condition would have been significantly different.

Other songs from the *Oh Mercy* sessions speak to related themes, including most obviously "Everything Is Broken," the meditation on human sin that is "Disease of Conceit," and searching self-examination in "What Good Am I?" The jaunty anthem, "Dignity," describes "dignity" as utterly elusive.

These songs collectively reflect an understanding of politics shaped strongly by the Christian doctrine of Original Sin: not the strident fundamentalism of his earlier "Christian" period but rather the views that a) politics consist most fundamentally of systems of domination, and b) due to the prevalence of egoism in human nature, particularly with respect to political questions, there is no "political" solution to the problems and suffering produced by domination. This conception of politics is consistent with the views of influential neo-orthodox twentieth-century Christian theologians such as Reinhold Niebuhr (1932), who harbored harsh critiques of the existing political and economic order while simultaneously regarding as hubristic any claim that these orders could be overturned and replaced with a fully just order.[11]

Dylan's having delivered a veritable political treatise on *Oh Mercy* helps us understand why he saw no need to "repeat the past" in subsequent records. But there is a sense in which *Oh Mercy* should be understood as the beginning of the "mature" period of Dylan's work. Starting with *Oh Mercy*, Dylan begins (artistically) inhabiting the role of world-weary veteran who has seen it all. Some of the playfulness evident in both *"Love and Theft"* and *Modern Times* comes from the way Dylan's elder statesman persona insists there is still a young man inside him who can show all comers—perhaps even Alicia Keys—a whopping good time. Dylan himself has encouraged this periodization by describing *Oh Mercy* in his autobiofictional *Chronicles* as the start of an artistic rebirth and through the 2008 release of the box set *Tell Tale Signs*, which treats the entire period from 1989–2006 as a coherent phase of Dylan's work.

Social and political commentary in the more recent records thus should be read against the backdrop of *Oh Mercy*. The existence of injustice and human cruelty for Dylan is no surprise, and so deeply embedded in the human condition (and in the specifics of American history) that it is foolish to expect that any specific corrective action will uproot these evils.

What kind of commentary, then, do we find on *"Love and Theft"* and *Modern Times*? Four recurrent themes can be identified.

THE EXISTENCE OF SUFFERING

First, we find relatively broad statements of social empathy demonstrating awareness of the reality of widespread suffering. At times, Dylan goes so far as to suggest that he has reached a place where he has, if not the chosen-one/prophetic-vision attributed (by others) to some of his earlier work, at least a pretty good vantage point into suffering and the human condition: "I can see what everybody in the world is up against" ("Sugar Baby"). More often, though Dylan treats this suffering as obvious for all with eyes to see; its endemic nature is a fundamental part of the human condition.

> In this earthly domain, full of disappointment and pain ("When the Deal Goes Down")

> Time is pilin' up, we struggle and we scrape
> We're all boxed in, nowhere to escape ("Mississippi")
>
> The suffering is unending
> Every nook and cranny has its tears ("Ain't Talkin'")
>
> Everybody got to wonder what's the matter with this cruel world today
>   ("Thunder on the Mountain")

In three of these examples, Dylan points to suffering, disappointment, struggle, and cruelty in matter-of-fact asides, in the course of songs whose focus lies elsewhere. Importantly, Dylan indicates that this cruelty and suffering are not things one simply sees, but also things one inevitably experiences and participates in. Denial of the reality of suffering is akin to the denial of the reality of our own lives. This is not really up for debate, Dylan seems to say.

Dylan gives the theme of suffering and struggle his most sustained attention in "Ain't Talkin'," the closing song on *Modern Times* and undoubtedly the album's magnum opus. The song can be understood with more confidence than usual as Dylan speaking not as a character but for "himself" (or at least, for the character called "Bob Dylan"). Because "Ain't Talkin'" captures many of the critical themes Dylan is voicing on these albums, I will consider the song in more detail later in this essay.

POVERTY AND DEPRIVATION

A second recurring motif on these two albums is poverty. Poverty and material deprivation appear in two forms: first, as a result of some specific catastrophe, and second, as a result of hard economic times.

Catastrophe-induced poverty is referenced in "The Levee's Gonna Break" in an apparent nod to the events of Hurricane Katrina (which struck the Gulf Coast just six months before the album was recorded), as well as in the earlier "High Water."

> Some people on the road carrying everything they own
> Some people got barely enough skin to cover their bones ("The Levee's Gonna Break")

High water risin', the shacks are slidin' down
Folks lose their possessions—folks are leaving town ("High Water")

The flood of "High Water" is likely better understood as a metaphor for times being tough than a reference to a particular event. Succeeding verses of the song tell us that there's "Nothing standing there," "It's tough out there," "Things are breakin' up out there," "It's rough out there," and—skipping to the final stanza—"It's bad out there."

What is metaphorical in "High Water" is far more explicit in "Workingman's Blues #2." The song, commonly regarded as one of the strongest on *Modern Times*, speaks in a visceral way to hunger, redundancy, and loneliness, set against a context in which "the buying power of the proletariat's gone down" and "money's getting shallow and weak." The narrator here inhabits the role of the down-and-out, economically marginalized person who is determined to carry on with the help of companionship and an ability to "live off rice and beans."

It does not seem likely that Bob Dylan has spent a large amount of time poring over economic data demonstrating the stagnation of working-class incomes in the United States and widening economic inequality since the 1970s, but this song makes clear that he is aware of what is going on. Laments about capitalism have occasionally popped up throughout Dylan's career, from "North Country Blues" to "Union Sundown" to "Heartland" (1993, with Willie Nelson) to his comments on behalf of displaced American farmers at Live Aid in 1985. "Union Sundown" is the most explicit of these efforts, telling us that "capitalism is above the law / . . . 'it don't count unless it sells'" and that "this world is ruled by violence but I guess that's better left unsaid." The impact of that song, however, was dampened by both clunky lyrics and the ambiguity about whose "greed" it was that "got in the way" (corporate greed, or union corruption, or both?).

"Workingman's Blues #2" takes another tack, inhabiting the character of a down-and-out person trying to fend off hunger and express his love for a companion and determination to keep right on living. For the narrator of this song, the proletariat's buying power going down is just a fact, a "reality" that "they" say we must accept in order to "compete abroad." As in "Union Sundown," there is no hint that this is anything but inevitable—this is the way capitalism works—but here the focus is on how a person can survive and try to create or preserve meaning within that context. "Po' Boy" operates similarly: the repeated references to humble economic circumstances set a stage for the story, but the focus is on the story. If Dylan here is engaged in protest against poverty and economic inequality, it is at first glance a muted protest; but a deeper look suggests the radical implications of Dylan inhabiting, humanizing, and drawing sympathetic attention to the lives of people with limited economic means—an age-old strategy of literary critics of American capitalism like John Steinbeck. And as with Steinbeck, whose writing made a large impression on the young Dylan,[12] Dylan's character does not shy away from articulating class resentment and from accusing the privileged classes of ignorance: "Some people never worked a day in their life / don't know what work even means" ("Workingman's Blues #2").

POWER, POWERLESSNESS, CORRUPTION

Dylan's lyrics on these records also point to inequities of power, and a moral universe in which there are enemies to be confronted. These themes are again seen most clearly in "Workingman's Blues #2." Part of the workingman (narrator's) experience is what political theorist Iris Marion Young (1990) terms "marginalization"—the experience of being on the fringe of society, excluded from the mainstream, regarded as lacking in value.

"Sometimes no one wants what we got / Sometimes you can't give it away": Those lines are sung by a narrator who plans to "sleep off the rest of the day." For the marginalized, the day is something to be survived. Interestingly though, Dylan also has the narrator assert that he will "feed [his] soul with thought" prior to sleeping off the day. On the one hand, the narrator likely would prefer to fill his stomach with food before filling his soul with thought. On the other hand, the references to "soul" and the narrator's thinking capacities are an assertion of the workingman's dignity, humanness, and intelligence in the face of a society that has cast him off as "sometimes" worthless.

Yet at other times, the workingman works. In this line Dylan seems to invoke the idea of what Young terms "powerlessness"—the inequity in power and respect in the workplace across class lines. "Now they worry and they hurry and they fuss and they fret / They waste your nights and days": This striking quatrain also helps flesh out the subjective experience of the narrator. That character's experience of the world is not just one in which hunger is an ever-present threat, but in which one's existence is shaped by the decisions of others. The account of those who worry, hurry, fuss, and fret likely refers not to "the boss," the actual capitalist, but rather to the harried but privileged professional class, the managers with whom one is in direct contact during the work day. The fact that the narrator can dismiss the worriers by forgetting them further indicates that they are accessories to power, not power itself.

The situation is different in other lyrics in this song, in which the narrator speaks of those with real power—permanent enemies who are inclined to use physical force, and who must be confronted with physical force as well: "I'll drag 'em all down to hell and I'll stand 'em at the wall / I'll sell 'em to their enemies." The assertion that there are permanent enemies that one cannot simply (and simply cannot) reason with is central to class-based politics. These "foes" have the power to reduce one to utter poverty and ruin, and must be reckoned with one way or another (whether one chooses to confront them or hang back). Moreover, despite the fantasy of dragging them all to hell, the song as a whole makes clear that the foes are not going anywhere. Contrary to one of Dylan's earlier songs, the ship is not coming in, and Goliath is not about to be conquered.

The theme of heartless opponents capable of crushing life creeps up elsewhere on these records. "Cry a While," for instance, speaks of people that "ain't human, they got no heart or soul." "Ain't Talkin'" amplifies these themes, and like "Workingman's Blues #2" speaks openly of violent confrontation with enemies: "If I catch my opponents ever sleepin' / I'll just slaughter them where they lie."

A key question to be considered is who "they" are in each of these songs. Presumably people of wealth and power who do not even have to be named in any specific sense: in any given situation or circumstance, we know the agents of wealth and power pull the strings. But at times Dylan does name names so to speak, through depictions of heartless characters—the captain of "Lonesome Day Blues," for instance, who does not care how many of his pals he has killed, as well as a certain "Mr. Goldsmith" described in "Cry a While" as "a nasty, dirty, double-crossin', backstabbin' phony I didn't wanna have to be dealin' with." Wealth, power, and heartlessness seem to be the toxic combination.

MORAL CORRUPTION

Finally, Dylan on these records frequently points to the ways in which it is *difficult to be a good person* in the context of social breakdown and the ubiquity of sin. "Well, they burned my barn, they stole my horse / I can't save a dime": "Workingman's Blues" makes the simple point—reiterated by Dylan himself in a 2008 interview—that moral rectitude and sustained poverty do not go hand in hand. "America is in a state of upheaval," said Dylan. "Poverty is demoralizing. You can't expect people to have the virtue of purity when they are poor."[13]

The "virtue of purity" is not easily achieved by the more comfortable, either. Consider Dylan—now presumably speaking for himself—in "Ain't Talkin'": "They say prayer has the power to help / So pray from the mother / In the human heart an evil spirit can dwell." This is one of the great verses of Dylan's recent work, and his gravelly vocalization comes off as simultaneously spooky, timeless, and profound. It is one thing to confess sin to God, but presumably much harder to confess to one's mother. Whether Dylan had in mind his actual mother (deceased for five years at this point) or used the line metaphorically, this is an expression of moral helplessness: an inability to overcome the evil spirit in one's own heart, and an inability despite good intentions to act as one ought.[14] Indeed, sometimes good intentions are thwarted, or even backfire, as in "Lot of things can get in the way when you're trying to do what's right" ("Honest with Me") or "Try to make things better for someone, sometimes, you just end up making it a thousand times worse" ("Sugar Baby").

The "things" that get in the way of doing what is right might be the opposition of others, the practical costs of doing the right thing, or the resistance of one's own heart. The use of the term "trying" in both this lyric and five years later in "Ain't Talkin'" is of interest. Dylan might mean that he has given it his best faith effort, but that it still falls short; or he might mean that he had the *intention* of doing what was right, but as soon as he got started and saw what doing right actually entailed he found complications, rationalizations, and so forth, which prevented him from following through. Both thoughts are variations on the theme of "What Good Am I?" from *Oh Mercy*, in which the narrator has "had every chance and yet still fail[s] to see," is fully conscious of human pain but still fails to act.

Yet good intention is no guarantor of good result. This is another frustration of the moral life, voiced in the couplet from "Sugar Baby." It would be easy to read Dylan's complaint here as cynicism, as a justification for not engaging since the results are uncertain and quite possibly perverse. But this line must be read in the context of other places in Dylan's recent work where he faults himself for inaction and failure to love, and by the important qualifiers "someone, sometimes." Some people can be helped, but perhaps some cannot. Sometimes attempts to help may help, but sometimes they backfire dramatically, for reasons that may be entirely independent of the quality of one's intentions. Indeed, this is the risk of a morally engaged, loving-your-neighbor life: sometimes your engagement will lead to heartbreak, and sometimes you will feel as if it would have been better not to engage at all. But, as other lyrics from Dylan point out, moral disengagement from the reality of suffering is not a satisfying option either. Read together, Dylan's lines on the dangers of both inaction and action illustrate something tragic and inescapable about the human condition. Good intentions may be an improvement over moral obliviousness, but they are no guarantee of effective action.

HOW THEN SHOULD WE LIVE?

What then, for Dylan, *is* the best response to the reality of human suffering, poverty, power struggles, and corrupted virtue? It has long been clear that Dylan rejects what might be called Baez-ism (unreconstructed 1960s pacifism) as an adequate response. Indeed, in a striking and humorous bridge from "Moonlight," Dylan invokes Baez-ism and speaks of deploying it as an effective courtship strategy: "Well, I'm preaching peace and harmony/ ... Yet I know when the time is right to strike." This passage is not unambivalent—while it suggests a cynical stance toward the preaching of peace and harmony, at the same time Dylan is more than happy here to be with someone (a woman) who responds well to preaching of that kind. Baez-ism is not Dylan's own view, but perhaps he still admires it in others.

As for himself, Dylan at different points offers four kinds of responses to the problem of how one is to live amidst the backdrop of profound suffering. The first *is making an effort to live a life of moral integrity* as an individual, although as we have seen, Dylan's writing casts some doubt on this kind of response taken alone. Even so, at times Dylan seems determined to practice compassion and do justice:

> The sun keeps shinin' and the north wind keep picking up speed
> Gonna forget about myself for a while, go out and see what others need
>   ("Thunder on the Mountain")

> I'm gonna spare the defeated, boys, I'm going to speak to the crowd
> I am goin' to teach peace to the conquered
> I'm going to tame the proud ("Lonesome Day Blues")

Of course, neither of these examples is unambivalent. Particularly in the musical context of "Thunder on the Mountain," Dylan could be heard as wanting to out and see what others need out of boredom with one's self, as a form of stress release, or just because it seemed like a good thing to do on a sunny, windy day. In any case, this self-forgetting is only expected to last "for a while." Likewise, in the line in "Lonesome Day Blues," the operative word is "conquered"—the justice and kindness the narrator plans to dish out comes from a position of strength, after the conflict has already been won. Indeed, teaching peace to the conquered and taming the proud are good ways to consolidate one's own hegemony.

Second, Dylan seeks out and praises *companionship* as a kind of response—not just romantic companionship, but comradely companionship, with the two at times seemingly fused together, as in "Workingman's Blues #2." Affection for "those who've sailed with me" and for "loyal and much-loved companions" are also a theme in, respectively, "Mississippi" and "Ain't Talkin."

Third, and perhaps most surprising, Dylan validates the honor and necessity of *collective social struggle*—even though he no longer seems to hold promise that it likely to be successful. In "Summer Days," social struggle is referenced in a sardonic context: "What good are you anyway if you can't stand up to some old businessman?" (echoing, perhaps, the first verse of "All Along the Watchtower"). It appears as an aside in "Honest with Me": "I'm not sorry for nothin' I've done / I'm glad I fought—I only wish we'd won"; as a fantasy of rebellion in "Thunder on the Mountain": "Gonna raise me an army, some tough sons of bitches / I'll recruit my army from the orphanages"; or, more earnestly, in the refrain of "Workingman's Blues #2," in front-line struggle: "You can hang back or fight your best on the front line." The image invoked here is that of a labor struggle (a strike, or a march of the unemployed, or a simple act of resistance at work), a struggle that is somehow connected to both the narrator and the person being sung to. The struggle does not offer solution or salvation, but it is there as backdrop and is presented as an honorable (though perhaps futile) thing to participate in. At the same time, Dylan is not here critiquing "hanging back"—refraining from direct engagement—as an invalid course of action. Ultimately, what is important is that whether one hangs back or fights their best, they need to "sing a little bit of these workingman's blues."

The most developed response, however, and one that incorporates aspects of the previous three, is found in "Ain't Talkin.'" The key line here is that the narrator is not talking, but is *walking—no matter what*. No matter that efforts to practice virtue have fallen short, that he is practicing a faith that has long been abandoned, or that he has to use a walking cane, or that he cannot let go of revenge fantasies, that he is worn out from weeping, that he cannot forget the gal he left behind, or for that matter get you yourself out of his miserable brain. The narrator will keep on walking as long as his heart is yearning and burning, through cities of plague and endless woe, all the way out of sight unto the "last outback at the world's end." It's tempting to think Dylan's "mystic garden" will be a place of refuge, but this is not the case either: at the start of the song, the narrator is "hit ... from behind" in the garden; at the end he returns to find that the "gardener is gone."

What are we to make of this? The loneliness of Dylan's walk immediately comes to mind, despite his talk of his loyal companions. Shout-outs are given to both (departed?) parents, to ancient enemies, long lost loves, but in the end the narrator is very much alone with his thoughts and his walking. One cannot accuse Dylan of simply being selfish here—at least he has tried to love his neighbor, even if it has not gone well. What Dylan seems to be getting at is the importance of simply carrying on, despite the condition of the world, and despite one's flaws. Where there is yearning and burning, there is still life, and still value in walking—or as Dylan put it in a previous era, in trying to "keep on keeping on."

Taken as a whole, these records suggest that Dylan still has an acute social conscience, and is inclined to see the world in terms not just of individual "sin" but of structural conflict between the more and less powerful. Beyond these general points, Dylan also consistently articulates the idea that America is a society on the brink, one in a "state of upheaval," a time in which (to quote an alternative version of the 1989 song "Dignity") "the soul of a nation is under the knife." The film *Masked and Anonymous*, released between *"Love and Theft"* and *Modern Times*, makes this explicit, with its depiction of a dystopian version of the United States that has taken on the characteristics of a Third World society—gaping poverty, continual politically motivated violence, political dictatorship—with some familiar echoes of our own society (use of the media and celebrity as an instrument of diversion and political control). So too do recent interviews, and "Workingman's Blues #2."

Nonetheless, one would be hard pressed to claim that Dylan's fundamental aim on these records is to call attention to specific social problems, much less current events. Instead, Dylan is telling us what he sees, and making it clear that human suffering and cruelty to others is an important part of that picture. Likewise, while Dylan does not call on his listeners to take any particular action, he does call on them to think deeply—everybody *does* have to wonder what is going on with this cruel world today.

Here we can finally come full circle and make good on the claim that a concern with race is central to Dylan's music in *"Love and Theft"* and *Modern Times*, and reconsider why we should be singing a little bit of the working man's blues. Charley Patton, Alicia Keys, and Nettie Moore all make appearances on these records, all allusions to African American experience and to black culture. Who is it in American culture that might teach us how to persevere, live with dignity, and create meaningful, even beautiful lives, while facing up squarely to the reality of human suffering and profound injustice? Singers of the blues. In this rich and compelling part of black culture—exemplified by Charley Patton, Blind Willie McTell, and many others—we find the most compelling answer on offer concerning how to make one's way through a cruel world. To recognize this point, and to pattern one's own life (musically and/or morally) after the bluesmen and women, is an act of both love and theft.[15]

Singers of the blues took for granted a backdrop of racialized brutality and oppression, a backdrop Dylan's recent songs, movie, and interviews have referenced in various ways. Few would contest Dylan on the claim that America is a deeply troubled society, but Dylan's invocations of America's racial history also offers something deeper than the recent antiwar, anti–fat cat songs of Neil Young and Bruce Springsteen. The point of Eric Lott's *Love and Theft*, for instance, is not simply to demonstrate how the minstrel shows offered a potent way to exploit blackness for pleasure and profit while furthering an ideology of racial supremacy. The politically consequential point is that the racial borrowing/mocking involved in minstrelsy was *constitutive* of the cultural identity of the white American working class, and helped redirect the social resentments of white workers away from their bosses and instead toward African Americans. What is at stake, then, is ultimately the ability of elites to keep power through the development of distinctively white cultural identity that white workers will (in the main) place a higher value on than class identity, thus sharply reducing the likelihood of fundamental challenges to the power structure. This is an analysis Dylan absorbed and brilliantly articulated as early as "Only a Pawn in Their Game," his hardest-hitting civil rights song.[16] To understand this point is to understand a crucial feature of the deep structure of American politics—and to understand why acts of historical and cultural recovery are political acts, especially in the context of a society determined to forget this history.

Dylan in his later years seems determined not to let us forget—hence his 2012 interview comments on slavery, and hence also the signature song off *Tempest*, "Pay in Blood." A full analysis is beyond the scope of the present work, but the song can be plausibly interpreted not only as a graphic account of human bondage but as a rageful dialogue between slave and master, accentuated by commentary from a third narrative voice.[17] On this interpretation, the slave tells his master (or ex-master), "You lousy bastard, I'm supposed to respect you?" In the closing verse, the narrator then reports that "our nation must be saved and freed / you've been accused of murder, how do you plead?" Dylan's precise meaning here is uncertain, but it is plausible that he is articulating, again, the need to save and free the nation from the burden and living legacy of past historical crimes.

This is a much bigger project than simply electing or reelecting an African American president. When Dylan deflected interview questions about Obama's first term in his 2012 *Rolling Stone* interview by saying real change begins in the heart, he was not simply voicing a truism, nor was he being apolitical. He is best interpreted as saying the full magnitude of America's original sin of slavery and racial oppression must be grappled with in the heart and gut if the country is to get anywhere, and that this is more important and more difficult than voting for Obama. It is worth noting that, in the end, Dylan did in fact—in a slightly roundabout way—endorse Obama from the concert stage on the eve of the 2012 election. Perhaps conscious of the debate over his 2008 remarks, Dylan also had his representatives take to Facebook to restate the gist of the comment to the audience (a statement that he had told his band they had to play well because the president had just been there, followed by a prediction that Obama would win reelection easily, and a warning not to believe the media to boot). It is entirely understandable that at a certain moment during the campaign, Dylan came to the conclusion that reelecting the first African American president would, in the large sweep of history, be a big deal and much better than the alternative, and felt a need to get himself clearly on the record on this point.

At the same time, it is implausible to suppose Dylan believes that Obama's elections mean the nation has been "saved and freed." Presidents can be elected without hearts changing and without the full force of history being addressed. Modern times continue to be times of hunger and desperation for many, suffering continues to be unending, and claims that "It's All Good" are either the products of self-deluded elites or sick jokes. Against this backdrop, Dylan recognizes the impulse to struggle and scrape, to fight for change, but has only limited confidence such change will be successful. Those with wealth and power, who have never worked a day in their lives, do not give in so easily.

NOTES

1. Gilmore, "Bob Dylan Unleashed," n.p.
2. Gilmore, "Bob Dylan Unleashed," n.p.
3. Lott, "Love and Theft in 'Love and Theft.'"
4. Alternatively, Dylan might be quoting his own liner notes for *World Gone Wrong*, in which he refers to "these modern times" as the "New Dark Ages."
5. Lott, "Love and Theft in 'Love and Theft'"; Wilentz, *Bob Dylan in America*.
6. Dylan borrows melodies and sometimes lyrical phrases from an astonishing range of sources, but almost always put his own distinctive stamp on the final product, musically and lyrically.
7. Maureen Dowd, "Blowin' in the Idiot Wind," *New York Times*, April 9, 2011.
8. Lawrie Balfour, *Democracy's Reconstruction: Thinking Politically with W. E. B. DuBois* (New York: Oxford University Press, 2011).
9. Put another way, Dylan's oeuvre can be considered a cumulative body of work. Each new record does not have to tell us that "the answer, my friend, is blowin' in the wind" or that "the times they are a-changin'"; those ideas have already been established, and still carry validity even when new ideas or observations have been grafted on top of them. The assumption here is that Bob Dylan can be described as a single artist whose work can be viewed as an evolving whole. This is the case, in my view, even though it is also the case that almost no artist has engaged in continual reinvention and deliberate (or accidental) presentation of a multitude of personas as well as musical idioms, and even though there is reason to think that Dylan's angle of vision has evolved and shifted multiple times over the course of his long career.
10. For extended analysis of Dylan's invocation of virtues and vices throughout his career, see Ricks, *Dylan's Visions of Sin*.
11. To this very day, Dylan frequently closes his concerts with "Blowin' in the Wind," which I interpret neither an accident nor as (or not simply as) an effort to please his audiences. Whereas earlier audiences often heard the song (especially when sung by Peter, Paul and Mary) as a kind of call to arms, the mournful, stately manner in which Dylan performs the song today invites listeners to hear simply a series of plaintive questions with no clear answer, motivated by an awareness of unnecessary and wasteful human suffering that seems to have no end in sight.
12. Bell, *Time Out of Mind*.
13. Alan Jackson, "Interview with Bob Dylan," *New York Times*, June 2008.
14. How "ought" we to act, according to Dylan? As the lyric from "Ain't Talkin'" suggests, moral action for Dylan here means to "love my neighbor and do good unto others."
15. In Eric Lott's book, it is fairly clear that both "love" and "theft" involve white appropriation of black culture, repackaged in the minstrel shows. The embrace of blues culture by both early white rock 'n' roll artists and the folk revival also had an obviously racialized dynamic, albeit one that could have a liberating impact (in both directions). Yet it would probably be a mistake to assume that Dylan's homage to the blues singers is aimed at only his white listeners (just as it would be utterly false to assume, despite the demographics of most of his contemporary concertgoers, that Dylan only has a white audience). Recalling

the blues singers of eighty and ninety years ago is an act of cultural recovery with relevance for all listeners.

16. Mike Marqusee, *Chimes of Freedom: The Politics of Bob Dylan's Art* (New York: New Press, 2003); Avery Kolers, "Who Killed Medgar Evers?" in *Bob Dylan and Philosophy: It's Alright Ma (I'm Only Thinking)*, Peter Vernezze and Carl Porter, eds. (Peru, IL: Open Court, 2005), 29–39.

17. I take this interpretation from http://johannasvisions.com/great-song-pay-in-blood-by-bob-dylan-a-land-built-on-slavery/. For a theologically oriented interpretation of the song based on the view that the blood that is paid with is Christ's, see Kees de Graff's extensive effort at www.keesdegraaf.com/media/Misc/8620p17fre4ggh1kcifeh8501s1iagg1.pdf.

WORKS CITED

Abbott, H. Porter. *The Cambridge Introduction to Narrative*. New York: Cambridge University Press, 2002.

Alex, Ben. *Søren Kierkegaard: An Authentic Life*. Kelowna, British Columbia: Northstone, 1997.

Anon. "Prayer at lying down." *The New England Primer: A Primary Source*. http://cdlrsandbox.org/neprimer/versiononepages/page19.html.

Arnold, Kokomo. "Mean Old Twister" (1937). *MaxiLyrics*. Retrieved October 6, 2012, from http://www.maxilyrics.com/kokomo-arnold-mean-old-twister-lyrics-19a2.html.

Avery, Todd. *Radio Modernism*. Hampshire, UK: Ashgate, 2006.

Bakhtin, Mikhail. *The Dialogic Imagination: Four Essays*. Michael Holquist, ed. Carly Emerson and Michael Holquist, trans. Austin: Texas University Press, 2000.

Balfour, Lawrie. *Democracy's Reconstruction: Thinking Politically with W. E. B. DuBois*. New York: Oxford University Press, 2011.

Barker, Derek, ed. *ISIS: A Bob Dylan Anthology*. London: Helter Skelter, 2004.

———. *The Songs He Didn't Write: Bob Dylan Under the Influence*. New Malden, UK: Chrome Dreams, 2008.

Baudrillard, Jean. "The Spirit of Terrorism." In *The Spirit of Terrorism and Other Essays*. London and New York: Verso, 2002. 3–34.

Bauldie, John, ed. *Wanted Man: In Search of Bob Dylan*. London: Penguin, 1992.

The Beatles. *Sgt. Pepper's Lonely Hearts Club Band*. Compact disc, Capitol/EMI Records CDP 7464422, 1967.

Becker, Howard S. *Art Worlds*. Chicago: University of Chicago Press, 1982.

Bell, Ian. *Once Upon a Time: The Lives of Bob Dylan*. Edinburgh: Mainstream, 2012.

Blake, William. "The Tyger" (1794). *The Poetry Foundation*. www.poetryfoundation.org/poem/172943.

Bourdieu, Pierre. *Outline of a Theory of Practice*. Cambridge, UK: Cambridge University Press, 1977.

Bouton, Jim. *Ball Four, Plus Ball Five: An Update, 1970–1980*. New York: Stein and Day, 1981.

Bowden, Betsy. *Performed Literature: Words and Music by Bob Dylan*. Bloomington: Indiana University Press, 1982.

Boym, Svetlana. *The Future of Nostalgia*. New York: Basic Books, 2001.

Brake, Elizabeth. "You can always come back, but you can't come back all the way: Freedom and the past in Dylan's recent work." In D. Boucher and G. Browning, eds., *The Political Art of Bob Dylan*. Upton Pyne, UK: Imprint Academic, 2009. 184–206.

Bratus, Alessandro. *Bob Dylan. Un percorso in sedici canzoni*. Milano: Carocci, 2011.

Burroughs, William. *Naked Lunch*, New York: Grove Press, 2009.

Cameron, James, dir. *Titanic*. Paramount Home Video, 1998.

Campbell, Gregg M. "Bob Dylan and the Pastoral Apocalypse." *Journal of Popular Culture* 4 (1975): 696–707.

Carrera, Alessandro. *La voce di Bob Dylan. Una spiegazione dell'America*. Milano: Feltrinelli, 2001.

Carroll, Lewis. *Alice's Adventures in Wonderland and Through the Looking-Glass*. New York: Barnes and Noble Classics, 2004.

Charles, Larry, dir. *Masked and Anonymous*. Sony Picture Classics, 2003.

Cossu, Andrea. *It Ain't Me, Babe: Bob Dylan and the Performance of Authenticity*. Boulder, CO: Paradigm, 2012.

———. "Localizing Dylan: Political and Musical Narratives in Italy." In Eugen Banauch, ed. *Refractions of Bob Dylan: Cultural Appropriations of an American Icon*. Manchester, UK: Manchester University Press, 2015. 36–50.

———. "Poetry, Politics, and America: Awards and the Memorialization of Bob Dylan." *Celebrity Studies* 4(2) (2013): 235–37.

Cott, Jonathan, ed. *Bob Dylan: The Essential Interviews*. New York: Wenner Books, 2006.

Culler, Jonathan: "Why Lyric?" Cornell Cast, www.cornell.edu/video/index.cfm?VideoID=619.

Dällenbach, Lucien. *Le récit spéculaire. Essai sur la mise en abyme*. Paris: Seuil, 1977.

Dalton. David. *Who Is That Man?: In Search of the Real Bob Dylan*. New York: Hyperion, 2012.

Danner, Mark. *Stripping Bare the Body: Politics Violence War*. New York: Nation Books, 2009.

Dayan, Daniel, and Elihu Katz. *Media Events: The Live Broadcasting of History*. Cambridge, MA: Harvard University Press, 1992.

de Graaf, Kees. "Bob Dylan's 'Ain't Talking'—The Old Testament revisited—An analysis by Kees de Graaf—Part 1." www.keesdegraaf.com/media/Misc/3293p16bfeaap41ckroqq1hsdqmn19441.pdf.

DeNora, Tia. *Beethoven and the Construction of Genius: Musical Politics in Vienna, 1792–1803*. Berkeley: University of California Press, 1995.

DeRosa, Aaron. "Literature after 9/11." *MFS Modern Fiction Studies* 57(3) (2011): 607–18.

Derrida, Jacques. "Autoimmunity: Real and Symbolic Suicides—A Dialogue with Jacques Derrida." In *Philosophy in a Time of Terror: Dialogues with Jürgen Habermas and Jacques Derrida*. Giovanna Borradori, ed. Chicago and London: University of Chicago Press, 2003. 85–136.

Di Lauro, Frances. "Living in the End Times: The Prophetic Language of Bob Dylan." In *Buddha of Suburbia: Proceedings of the Eighth Australian and International Religion, Literature and the Arts Conference*. Carole M. Cusack, Frances Di Lauro, and Christopher Hartney, eds. Sydney: RLA Press, 2005. 186–201.

Dowd, Maureen. "Blowin' in the Idiot Wind." *New York Times*, April 9, 2011.

Dylan, Bob. *Blonde on Blonde*. Compact disc, Columbia 5123522, 1966.

———. *Blood on the Tracks*. Compact disc, Columbia 5123502, 1975.
———. *The Bootleg Series, Vol. 8: Tell Tale Signs—Rare and Unreleased 1989–2006 [Deluxe Edition]*. Compact disc. Columbia/Legacy 735797, 2008.
———. *Christmas in the Heart*. Compact disc. Columbia 88697596142, 2009.
———. *Chronicles, Volume One*. New York: Simon and Schuster, 2004.
———. *Desire*. Compact disc, Columbia 5123452, 1976.
———. *John Wesley Harding*. Compact disc, Columbia 5123472, 1967.
———. "Love and Theft." Compact disc, Columbia 5123576, 2001.
———. *Lyrics, 1962–2001*. New York City: Simon and Schuster, 2004.
———. *The Lyrics: Since 1962*. Edited by Julie Nemrow, Lisa Nemrow, and Christopher Ricks. New York: Simon & Schuster, 2014.
———. *Modern Times*. Compact disc, Columbia 82876883062, 2006.
———. "Musicares Person of the Year Award Acceptance Speech." *Rolling Stone*, 9 February 2015. Web. 24 July 2015.
———. Official Bob Dylan Site. www.bobdylan.com/us.
———, dir. *Renaldo and Clara*. Circuit Films, 1978.
———. *Saved*. Compact disc, Columbia CK-36553, 1980.
———. *Shadows in the Night*. Compact disc, Columbia 88875057962, 2015.
———. *Tempest*. LP, Columbia 88725457601, 2012.
———. *Time Out of Mind*. Compact disc, Columbia 4869362, 1997.
———. *Together Through Life*. Compact disc, Columbia 88697516972, 2009.
Eccleston, Danny. "New Dylan Album: The First In-Depth Review." *Mojo*. April 17, 2009.
Eisenstein, Sergei, dir. *Battleship Potemkin*. London: Tartan Video, 2007.
———, dir. *October*. London: Tartan Video, 2007.
———, dir. *Strike*. 1925. London: Tartan Video, 2007.
Eliot, T. S. *Selected Prose of T. S. Eliot*. New York: Farrar, Straus and Giroux, 1975.
Ennis, Philip. *The Seventh Stream: The Emergence of Rock and Roll in American Popular Music*. Middletown: Wesleyan University Press, 1992.
Epstein, Daniel Mark. *The Ballad of Bob Dylan: A Portrait*. New York: Harper Collins, 2011.
Erlwine, Steven Thomas. Review of *The Times They Are a-Changin'*. www.allmusic.com/album/the-times-they-are-a-changin-mw0000202344.
Estrin, James, and Josh Haner. "The Renowned, Unknown Bruce Davidson." *New York Times*, June 28, 2010.
Expecting Rain. www.expectingrain.com/discussions/viewtopic.php?f=2&p=1250514&sid=5aedde2bf43eb91209f964474939b778.
Faithfull, Marianne. *Faithfull: An Autobiography*. New York: Cooper Square Press, 2000.
Farinaccio, Vince. *Nothing to Turn Off: The Films and Video of Bob Dylan*. n.p., 2007.
Fine, Gary A. *Difficult Reputations: Collective Memories of the Evil, Inept, and Controversial*. Chicago: University of Chicago Press, 2001.
———. "Reputational Entrepreneurs and the Memory of Incompetence: Melting Supporters, Partisan Warriors, and Images of President Harding." *American Journal of Sociology* 101(5) (1996): 1159–93.
Flanagan, Bill. "Bob Dylan Interview with Bill Flanagan." *The Telegraph*. April 13, 2009.

---. "Interview with Bob Dylan." *Mojo* 189 (August 2009): 51–52.
Frankl, Victor. *Man's Search for Meaning*. Boston: Beacon Press, 1991.
Frith, S. *Performing Rites: On the Value of Popular Music*. Cambridge: Harvard University Press, 1996.
Frost, Robert: *Complete Poems of Robert Frost*. New York: Holt, Rinehart and Winston, 1964.
Fryer, Judith. *Felicitous Space: The Imaginative Structures of Edith Wharton and Willa Cather*. Chapel Hill: University of North Carolina Press, 1986.
Gates, David. "Dylan Revisited," *Newsweek*, October 7, 1997.
Geller, Stephen A. "Were the Prophets Poets?" *Prooftexts* 15(1) (2007): 211–21.
Giamo, Benedict. "Bob Dylan's Protean Style." In *Refractions of Bob Dylan: Cultural Appropriations of an American Icon*. Eugen Banauch, ed. Manchester, UK: Manchester University Press, 2015. 69–82.
Gilmore, Mikal. "Bob Dylan." *Rolling Stone*, November 22, 2001.
---. "Bob Dylan." *Rolling Stone*, December 6–13, 2001.
---. "Bob Dylan on His Dark New Album, *Tempest*." *Rolling Stone*, August 1, 2012. www.rollingstone.com/music/news/bob-dylan-on-his-dark-new-album-tempest-20120801.
---. "Bob Dylan: The Rolling Stone Interview." *Rolling Stone*, October 27, 2012: 42–51.
---. "Bob Dylan Unleashed: A Wild Ride on His New LP and Striking Back at Critics." *Rolling Stone*, September 27, 2012.
Gilmour, Michael J. *The Gospel According to Bob Dylan: The Old, Old Story for Modern Times*. Louisville: Westminster John Knox Press, 2011.
---. *Tangled Up in the Bible: Bob Dylan & Scripture*. New York: Continuum, 2004.
Gooding, Cynthia. "Folksinger's Choice," New York, WBAI-FM, 11 March 1962, transcription available at expectingrain.com/dok/int/gooding.html
Gray, Michael. *The Bob Dylan Encyclopedia*. London: Continuum, 2008.
---. *Song and Dance Man III: The Art of Bob Dylan*. London: Continuum, 2004.
Griffey, Adam Clay. *Dylan's Apocalypse: Country Music and the End of the World*. Master's thesis, Appalachian State University, 2011. http://libres.uncg.edu/ir/asu/listing.aspx?id=8227.
Gundersen, Edna. "Dylan is positively on top of his game." *USA Today*, September 10, 2001. www.usatoday.com/life/music/2001-09-10-bob-dylan.htm.
Halliwell, Martin, and Catherine Morley. *American Thought and Culture in the 21st Century*. Edinburgh, UK: Edinburgh University Press, 2009.
Hardy, Thomas. *The Complete Poems*. James Gibson, ed. Houndmills: Palgrave, 2001.
Harvey, Todd. *The Formative Dylan: Transmission and Stylistic Influences 1961–1963*. Lanham, MD: Scarecrow Press, 2001.
Hayward, Susan. *Cinema Studies: The Key Concepts*, 2nd ed. London: Routledge, 2004.
Heylin, Clinton. *Revolution in the Air: The Songs of Bob Dylan 1957–1973*. Chicago: Chicago Review Press, 2009.
---. *Still on the Road: The Songs of Bob Dylan Vol. 2: 1974–2008*. London: Constable, 2010.
Hilburn, Robert. "Rock's Enigmatic Poet Opens a Long-Private Door." *Los Angeles Times*, April 4, 2004.
Hong, Howard V. "Trying to Do the Right Thing," *Reece Report* 7(1) (January 1992): 9, 18.

Howard, Mark: "Life with Bob Dylan, 1989–2006." *Uncut*. February 25, 2015. www.uncut.co.uk/bob-dylan/life-with-bob-dylan-1989-2006-feature.

Howard, Theresa. "Dylan ad for underwear generates lingering buzz." *USA Today*, May 16, 2004. http://usatoday30.usatoday.com/money/advertising/adtrack/2004-05-16-victoria-secrets-dylan_x.htm.

Huels, Mitchum. "Foer, Spiegelman, and 9/11's Timely Traumas." In *Literature after 9/11*. Ann Keniston and Jeanne Follansbee Quinn, eds. New York City: Routledge, 2008. 42–59.

Jackson, Alan. "Interview with Bob Dylan." *The Times*, June 2008.

Jackson, Andrew. "Farewell Address. March 4, 1837." *The American Presidency Project* www.presidency.ucsb.edu/ws/?pid=67087.

Janssen, David, and Edward Whitelock. *Apocalypse Jukebox: The End of the World in American Popular Music*. Berkeley: Soft Skull Press, 2009.

Kepler, Thomas S., ed. *The Fellowship of the Saints: An Anthology of Christian Devotional Literature*. Nashville: Abingdon-Cokesbury Press, 1948.

Kermode, Frank, and Stephen Spender. "The Metaphor at the End of the Funnel." In *The Dylan Companion*. Elizabeth Thomson and David Gutman, eds. New York: Da Capo, 2001. 155–62.

Kierkegaard, Sören. *Kierkegaard's Writings*. Princeton: Princeton University Press, 1978–1998.

———. *Journals and Papers*. Bloomington: Indiana University Press, 1967–1978.

Kolers, Avery. "Who Killed Medgar Evers?" In *Bob Dylan and Philosophy: It's Alright Ma (I'm Only Thinking)*. Peter Vernezze and Carl Porter, eds. Peru, IL: Open Court, 2005. 29–39.

Lee, Hermione. *Double Lives*. New York: Vintage International, 1989.

Leeder, Murray, and Ira Wells. "Dylan's Floods." *Popular Music and Society* 32(2) (2009): 211–27.

Lethem, Jonathan. "The Genius and Modern Times of Bob Dylan." *Rolling Stone*, 7 September 2006. www.rollingstone.com/music/news/the-genius-and-modern-times-of-bob-dylan-20060907.

Leung, Rebecca. "Dylan Looks Back." cbsnews.com. December 2, 2002.

Light, Alan. "Dylan as Performer." In *The Cambridge Companion to Bob Dylan*. Kevin J. H. Dettmar, ed. New York: Cambridge University Press, 2009. 55–68.

Lott, Eric. "Love and Theft in 'Love and Theft'." In *The Cambridge Companion to Bob Dylan*. Kevin J. H. Dettmar, ed. Cambridge, UK: Cambridge University Press, 2009. 167–73.

———. *Love and Theft: Blackface Minstrelsy and the American Working Class*. Oxford, UK: Oxford University Press, 1993.

Love, Damien. "Bob Dylan: *Tell Tale Signs* Special—Mark Howard." *Uncut*. www.uncut.co.uk/bob-dylan/bob-dylan-tell-tale-signs-special-mark-howard-interview.

———. "Bob Dylan: *Tell Tale Signs* Special—Interview with Chris Shaw." *Uncut*. www.uncut.co.uk/bob-dylan/recording-with-bob-dylan-chris-shaw-tells-all-interview.

———. "Recording with Bob Dylan: Chris Shaw Tells All." *Uncut*, November 2008. www.uncut.co.uk/features/recording-with-bob-dylan-chris-shaw-tells-all-37854.

Marcus, Greil. *Bob Dylan by Greil Marcus: Writings 1968–2010*. London: Faber, 2010.

———. *Invisible Republic: Bob Dylan's Basement Tapes*. London: Picador, 1997.

———. *Like a Rolling Stone: Bob Dylan at the Crossroads*. New York: Public Affairs, 2006.
———. *The Old, Weird America*. New York: Picador, 2011.
Marqusee, Mike. *Chimes of Freedom: The Politics of Bob Dylan's Art*. New York: New Press, 2003.
———. *Wicked Messenger: Bob Dylan and the 1960s*. New York: Seven Stories Press, 2011.
Marshall, Lee. "Bob Dylan and the Academy." In *The Cambridge Companion to Bob Dylan*. Keven J. H. Dettmar, ed. Cambridge, UK: Cambridge University Press, 2009. 100–109.
———. *Bob Dylan: The Never Ending Star*. Oxford, UK: Polity, 2007.
McCarthy, Cormac. *All the Pretty Horses*. New York: Vintage International, 1992.
———. *The Road*. New York: Vintage, 2006.
McGilchrist, Megan Riley. *The Western Landscape in Cormac McCarthy and Wallace Stegner*. New York: Routledge, 2010.
Michael, Magali Cornier. "Writing Fiction in the Post-9/11 World: Ian McEwan's *Saturday*." In *From Solidarity to Schisms: 9/11 and After in Fiction and Film from Outside the US*. Cara Cilano, ed. Amsterdam and New York: Rodopi Press, 2009. 25–51.
Muir, Andrew. *Razor's Edge: Bob Dylan and the Never Ending Tour*. London: Helter Skelter, 2001.
———. *Troubadour: Early and Late Songs of Bob Dylan*. Bluntisham, UK: Woodstock Publications, 2003.
Muzzioli, Francesco. *Scritture della catastrofe*. Roma: Meltemi, 2007.
Negus, Keith: "Living, Breathing Songs: Singing Along with Bob Dylan." *Oral Tradition* 22(1) (March 2007): 71–83.
———. *Bob Dylan*. Bloomington and Indianapolis: Indiana University Press, 2008.
Newman, Andrew Adam. "Hey, Mr. Escalade Man." *New York Times*, November 4, 2007. www.nytimes.com/2007/11/04/automobiles/04DYLAN.html/partner/rssnyt?pagewanted=print&_r=0.
Nichols, Bill. *Introduction to Documentary*. Bloomington and Indianapolis: Indiana University Press, 2001.
Niebuhr, Reinhold. *Moral Man and Immoral Society*. New York: Charles Scribner's Sons, 1932.
Nielsen, A. L. "Crow Jane Approximately: Bob Dylan's Black Masque." In *Highway 61 Revisited: Bob Dylan's Road from Minnesota to the World*. C. J. Sheehy and T. Swiss, eds. Minneapolis: University of Minnesota Press, 2009. 186–96.
Örnek, Nilay. *Haber Türk*. www.haberturk.com/kultur-sanat/haber/519935-en-pahali-bob-dylan-konserini-turkler-izledi.
Pareles, Jon. "A Wiser Voice Blowin' in the Autumn Wind." *New York Times*, September 28, 1997.
Pascal, Blaise. *Pensées*. New York: Dutton, 1931.
Pearson, Chris. "Slavery and Dogs in the Antebellum South." In *Sniffing the Past: Dogs and History*. http://sniffingthepast.wordpress.com/2012/02/23/slavery-and-dogs-in-the-antebellum-south/.
Pennebaker, D. A., dir. *Dont Look Back*. New York: New Video Group, 2006.
———, dir. *Bob Dylan—Dont Look Back (65 Tour Deluxe Edition)*. USA: Sony BMG, 2007.
Pepys, Samuel. *Diary, Volume 41: January/February 1665–66* (January 2nd). www.gutenberg.org/ebooks/4163.mobile.

Peterson, Richard A. *Creating Country Music: Fabricating Authenticity*. Chicago: University of Chicago Press, 1997.
Pickering, Michael, and Emily Keightley. "The Modalities of Nostalgia." *Current Sociology* 54(6) (2006): 919–41.
Poe, Edgar Allan. "The Philosophy of Composition." In *Poe's Poems and Essays*. London: Everyman's Library, 1969.
Polito, Robert. "Bob Dylan's Memory Palace." In *Highway 61 Revisited: Bob Dylan's Road from Minnesota to the World*. C. J. Sheehy and T. Swiss, eds. Minneapolis: University of Minnesota Press, 2009. 140–53.
Reginio, R. "Nettie Moore: Minstrelsy and the Cultural Economy of Race in Bob Dylan's Late Albums." In *Highway 61 Revisited: Bob Dylan's Road from Minnesota to the World*. C. J. Sheehy and T. Swiss, ed. Minneapolis: University of Minnesota Press, 2009. 213–24.
Ricks, Christopher. *Dylan's Visions of Sin*. New York: Ecco, 2004.
Rilke, Rainer Maria. *Letters to a Young Poet*. Stephen Mitchell, trans. New York: Modern Library, 2001.
Rings, Steven. "A Foreign Sound to Your Ear: Bob Dylan Performs 'It's Alright, Ma (I'm Only Bleeding) 1964–2009.'" *Music Theory Online* 19(4) (2013). www.mtosmt.org/issues/mto.13.19.4/mto.13.19.4.rings.php.
Rosowski, Susan. "Willa Cather and the Fatality of Place: *O Pioneers!*, *My Antonia*, and *A Lost Lady*." In *Geography and Literature: A Meeting of the Disciplines*. William E. Mallory and Paul Housley, eds. Syracuse: Syracuse University Press, 1987. 81–94.
Ruiz, Teofilo F. *The Terror of History: On the Uncertainties of Life in Western Civilization*. Princeton and Oxford: Princeton University Press, 2011.
Schechner, Richard. *Performance Theory*. New York: Routledge, 1988.
Scorsese, Martin, dir. *No Direction Home: Bob Dylan*. Hollywood: Paramount Home Video, 2005.
Shakespeare, William. *The Tragedy of Hamlet, Prince of Denmark*. New York: Washington Square Press, 1992.
———. *King Lear*. Quoted in *Shakespeare Uncovered: King Lear with Christopher Plummer*. PBS. January 30, 2015.
Shaw, Chris. "Life with Bob Dylan, 1989–2006." www.uncut.co.uk/bob-dylan/life-with-bob-dylan-1989-2006-feature.
Shedd, Matt. "Bob Dylan's Folk Poetics in the Later Albums: Telling the Story of America in Ruins in Simple Poetic Language." In *Rupkatha Journal on Interdisciplinary Studies in Humanities* 3(2) (2011). rupkatha.com/V3/n2/07_Bob_Dylan_Folk_Poetics.pdf.
Shelley, P. B. "Ode to the West Wind." *The Norton Anthology of Poetry*. New York: Norton, 1983. 620–22.
Shirane, Haruo. "Performance, Visuality, and Textuality: The Case of Japanese Poetry," in *Oral Tradition* 20(2) (October 2005): 217–32.
Skorecki, Louis. "Dylan, emmett miller et moi." December 10, 2002. http://skorecki.blogspot.it/2010/12/im-56-dylans-not-60-yet.html.
———. *D'où viens-tu Dylan?* Nantes: Capricci, 2012.

Spargo, R. Clifton, and Anne K. Ream. "Bob Dylan and Religion." In *The Cambridge Companion to Bob Dylan*. Keven J. H. Dettmar, ed. New York: Cambridge University Press, 2009. 88–99.

Stensland, Lucas. "Scatter Shots: Reading Masked and Anonymous." *Montague Street. The Art of Bob Dylan* 1 (2009): 80–103.

Strindberg, August. *Easter*. Chicago: Aldine, 1962.

Tate, Greg. "Intelligence Data." *Village Voice*, September 25, 2001. www.villagevoice.com /2001-09-25/music/intelligence-data/.

Thomas, Richard F. "The Streets of Rome: The Classical Dylan." *Oral Tradition* 22(1) (March 2007): 30–56.

Thomson, James. *The City of Dreadful Night*. 1874. Project Gutenberg. www.gutenberg.org/ files/1238/1238-h/1238-h.htm.

Tolkien, J. R. R. *The Lord of the Rings*. London: Harper Collins, 2007.

Various Artists. *Lost Notebooks of Hank Williams*. Compact disc, Columbia/Sony 88697090102, 2011.

Versluys, Kristiaan. "9/11 as a European Event: The Novels." *European Review* 15(1) (2007): 65–79.

Vesely, Rainer. "Tangled Up in Blue." In *Bob Dylan: Five Songs: Lectures Accompanying the Exhibition Bob Dylan. The Drawn Blank Series at the Kunstsammlungen Chemnitz*. Ingrid Mössinger and Wilfram Ette, eds. Berlin: Kerber Art, 2008. 66–78.

Warmuth, Scott. "Goon Talk: 'The Scheme Is for Real.'" *Blogspot*. http://swarmuth.blogspot.no/.

———. "A Bob Dylan Bookshelf"; "A Tempest Commonplace."

———. "The Story of a Lie: Bob Dylan and Robert Louis Stevenson." *Pinterest*. www.pinterest .com/scottwarmuth/.

———. "Scam Truth Two." *Youtube*. www.youtube.com/channel/UCmjLqe2G5pxgkYOhlNooLZg.

———. *Twitter*. https://twitter.com/scottwarmuth1.

Wenner, Jann S. "Bob Dylan Hits the Big Themes, From Religion to the Atomic Age." *Rolling Stone* May 5, 2011. www.rollingstone.com/music/news/bob-dylan-hits-the-big -themes-from-religion-to-the-atomic-age-20110511.

———. *Bob Dylan in America*. New York: Doubleday, 2010.

Whittier, John Greenleaf. "Snow-Bound: A Winter Idyl." *The Poetry Foundation*. www .poetryfoundation.org/poem/174758.

Wilentz, Sean. "American Recordings: On 'Love and Theft' and the Minstrel Boy." In *Do You Mr. Jones? Bob Dylan with the Poets and Professors*. London: Pimlico, 2003.

Williams, Paul. *Bob Dylan: Performing Artist 1960–1973*. London: Omnibus Press, 1990.

———. *Bob Dylan: Mind Out of Time, Performing Artist 1986–1990 and Beyond*. London: Omnibus Press, 2005.

———. *Bob Dylan, Performing Artist, 1974–1986: The Middle Years*. London: Omnibus, 1992.

Wilson, Edward O. *Consilience*. New York: Vintage, 1998.

Yaffe, David. *Bob Dylan: Like a Complete Unknown*. New Haven, CT: Yale University Press, 2011.

Žižek, Slavoj. *Violence*. New York: Picador, 2008.

———. *Welcome to the Desert of the Real*. London and New York: Verso, 2002.

CONTRIBUTORS

Alberto Brodesco is research assistant at the Department of Sociology and Social Research, University of Trento, Italy. One of his main research interests concerns the audiovisual representation of the apocalypse. He is author of two books: *Una voce nel disastro. L'immagine dello scienziato nel cinema dell'emergenza* (Meltemi, 2008) and *Sguardo, corpo, violenza. Sade e il cinema* (Mimesis, 2014). Many of his publications are available on open access at http://unitn.academia.edu/AlbertoBrodesco.

James Cody is a professor at Brookdale Community College in Lincroft, New Jersey, where he teaches Composition, Research Writing, World Literature, American Literature, Shakespeare's Plays, and Short Story courses. He currently lives in New Jersey with his wife and three children.

Andrea Cossu teaches Sociological Approaches to Culture and Sociological Theory at the University of Trento, Italy. He is the author of *It Ain't Me, Babe: Bob Dylan and the Performance of Authenticity* (Paradigm, 2012).

Anne Margaret Daniel was born and raised in Virginia. She teaches literature at the New School University in New York City. Her articles, essays, notes, and reviews, covering topics from Oscar Wilde's trials to Bob Dylan and contemporary music, have appeared for the past twenty years in books, critical editions, magazines, and journals from the *New York Times* to *Hot Press* to the *Times Literary Supplement*. Anne Margaret has degrees in American history and English literature from Harvard (A.B.), Georgetown (M.A.), and Princeton (Ph.D.). Since the summer of 1988, she has heard Dylan in concert nearly a hundred times. She is currently finishing a book on F. Scott Fitzgerald. Anne Margaret lives in Manhattan and upstate New York with her husband and a small lovely dog named for the Hammond B3.

Jesper Doolaard graduated from Leiden University in 2014 with a M.A. degree in Literary Studies. His current research focuses on the changing roles of contemporary fiction and art in a digital world. As coeditor of the online magazine *DYLAN*, he is no stranger to the world of Dylanology.

Nina Goss is adjunct professor at Fordham University in New York. She earned her PhD and MFA at the University of Washington, and is coeditor of and contributor to *Dylan at Play* (Cambridge Scholars Press, 2011). She is also the founder and editor of the journal *Montague Street*, devoted to Bob Dylan's work.

Jonathan Hodgers has degrees from Queen's University, Belfast (English and History B.A., M.A. in Creative Writing) and Trinity College Dublin (Ph.D. in Musicology, 2014), where he is a lecturer in popular music. His research focuses on appropriations of Bob Dylan's music, the intersection of song lyrics and poetry, and album art.

Eric Hoffman is the author of over a dozen collections of poetry, the most recent being *Forms of Life* (Dos Madres Press, 2015) and *The Transparent Eye* (Spuyten Duyvil, 2016). Together with Dominick Grace he edited three volumes of the University Press of Mississippi Conversation with Comic Artists series, *Dave Sim: Conversations* (2013), *Chester Brown: Conversations* (2013), and *Seth: Conversations* (2015).

Jamie Lorentzen chairs the Friends of the Hong Kierkegaard Library at St. Olaf College. He is the author of *Becoming Human: Kierkegaardian Reflections on Ethical Models in Literature*; *Sober Cannibals, Drunken Christians: Melville, Kierkegaard, and Tragic Optimism in Polarized Worlds*; *Kierkegaard's Metaphors*; and is the editor of *Toward the Final Crossroads: A Festschrift for Howard and Edna Hong*.

Dr. Fahri Öz works at Ankara University. He teaches English and American poetry and literary history, writing articles on twentieth-century poetry. Among his translations into Turkish are books by Christina Rossetti, Jack London, Saki, William Burroughs, and Bob Dylan.

Nick Smart is professor of English at the College of New Rochelle and coeditor with Nina Goss of *Dylan at Play*. His writing on Dylan also appears in *Popular Music and Society*. He lives in New York City.

Thad Williamson is associate professor of Leadership Studies at the University of Richmond. He is author, coauthor, or coeditor of six books, including most recently *Property-Owning Democracy: Rawls and Beyond* (with Martin O'Neill) and *Sprawl, Justice, and Citizenship: The Civic Cost of the American Way of Life*. He has also served as director of the Office of Community Wealth Building for the city of Richmond, Virginia, an antipoverty agency. Williamson attended his first Bob Dylan concert in New Haven, Connecticut, in 1991, and is still blown away by the solo performance of "The Lonesome Death of Hattie Carroll" that evening.

INDEX

Acuff, Roy, 19
Adams, John Quincy, 16
Addison, Joseph, 116n20
"Adonais" (Shelley), 70
Aeschylus, 16
Agamemnon (Aeschylus), 16
Alchemist, The (Jonson), 66
Alias: Bob Dylan (Scobie), 6
All the Pretty Horses (McCarthy), 35, 37
Anthology of American Folk Music (Smith), 18
Ashley, Clarence, 50, 51, 55, 57
Astor, John Jacob, 69
Atlas the Dwarf, 20
Auden, W. H., 70
Auster, Paul, 16

Baez, Joan, 61, 169
Bakhtin, Mikhail, 146
Ball Four (Bouton), 16, 25n11
Bank of Montreal, 3
"Barbara Allen" (trad.), 49, 67, 144
Barnum, P. T., 20
Beale, Simon Russell, 30
Bearded Lady, 20
Beatles, 5, 111, 116
Berlin, Irving, 8
Big Bad Love (Brown), 29
Big Money, The (Dos Passos), 16
Billy the Kid, 23
Blanchett, Cate, 7, 15
Blood Meridian (McCarthy), 35
Boggs, Dock, 50, 55, 77

Bouton, Jim, 16, 25n11
Bowden, Betsy, 135
Brake, Elizabeth, 49
Bridges, Jeff, 14
Brown, Larry, 29
Burroughs, William S., 16, 24n9, 77, 80
Byron, Lord, 71

Cadillac, 4, 8, 24n3
Cage, John, 135
Cameron, James, 69, 116n22
Campbell, Larry, 13, 55
Camus, Albert, 5
Canterbury Tales, The (Chaucer), 40
Carnegie, Andrew, 65
Cash, Johnny, 26n27
Catchfire (1990), 15
Cather, Willa, 33, 39
Charles, Larry, 13
"City of Dreadful Night, The" (Thomson), 99
"Clean, Well-Lighted Place, A" (Hemingway), 35
Clinton, Bill, 7
Columbia Records, 46
Confessions of a Yakuza (Saga), 77
"Coo Coo Bird, The" (trad.), 52, 55
Cotton, Elizabeth, 56
Crossing, The (McCarthy), 35
Crowell, Rodney, 138
"Cuckoo, The" (trad.), 51
Culler, Jonathan, 137
Cyprian, 16, 25n12

189

Dahan, Olivier, 37
Dalton, David, 43, 102
Darkness, Jean, 20
Davidson, Bruce, 29
"Day in the Life, A" (Lennon and McCartney), 111
Death Is My Dancing Partner (Woolrich), 16
de Graaf, Kees, 142
Derrida, Jacques, 75–76, 78–80, 82
Dharma & Greg, 15
"Diamond Joe" (trad.), 23
DiCaprio, Leonardo, 69, 116n22
"Dixie" (trad.), 22–23
Dont Look Back (Pennebaker), 5, 14, 107
Dos Passos, John, 16
Douglas, Michael, 3
Duquesne Steel Works, 65
"Dust My Broom" (trad.), 51
Dylan, Bob
 apocalypse: as flood, 16, 94; as motif in songs, 13, 25n16, 28, 42, 43, 76–79, 81–82, 87, 91, 94; as theme in *Masked and Anonymous*, 16–20
 authenticity, 4, 8, 46, 48, 54–56, 58–59, 130
 and "Baez-ism," 169
 China, willingness to perform in, 160
 Christian-era music of, 7, 8, 87, 120, 131, 151
 City Center (New York), 2006 performance in, 101–2
 and commercialism, 3, 4, 8, 24n3, 152
 and composition methods: fragment and appropriation, 5, 15–16, 45, 50–52, 59, 77, 80, 110–14, 119, 160, 174n6; narrative style, development of, 5, 6, 9, 15, 17, 39, 86–87, 96, 103–15, 137–38, 141–43, 146–48; refrain, use of, 37–39, 41, 69–71, 93, 100, 111, 134–50; rhyme, use of, 39, 51–52, 63–65, 88, 91, 99, 104–5, 139, 141, 145–46
 and counterculture, 3–8, 14, 18, 19, 25n21, 45, 46, 50, 51
 and cultural memory, 29, 46–60
 and dystopianism, 17–19, 171
 and feminism, 7, 33
 folk revival, 5, 7, 51, 55, 59, 77–78, 123, 174
 Free Trade Hall performance, 6
 geography: comparison to McCarthy's use of landscape, 35–37; landscape as metaphor, 29–43; significance of US regions, 129–30
 Harbiye Cemil Topuzlu Amphitheatre (Istanbul), 2010 performance in, 136
 as "Jack Frost," 64, 108
 Live Aid (1985), 55–56, 165
 motorcycle accident, 6
 MusiCares Person of the Year Award speech (2015), 151–52
 Never Ending Tour, 14, 47, 50, 53, 54, 56, 58–60
 Newport Folk Festival, 5, 7
 as 1960s icon, 4, 5, 14, 18, 19, 25n21, 45, 46, 50, 51, 54, 56, 58–60
 Nobel Prize in Literature, 3, 11n1, 134
 Obama election, comments regarding, 158–59, 173
 Orphic imagery, 36–38
 pastoral imagery, 33, 34, 36
 as performer, 3, 8, 9, 10, 13, 16, 22, 23, 28–30, 46, 47, 50–62, 97, 101, 103, 128, 131, 134–36, 146–48, 149n12, 150n37, 155, 157, 174
 personas of, 4, 6, 7, 9, 45–47, 55, 86, 87, 92, 93, 98, 101, 103, 112, 163, 174
 politics, 5, 7, 17, 73, 77, 85, 86, 89, 90, 96, 130, 143, 158–73
 as prophet, 19, 25n21, 57, 73–83, 93, 138, 144, 147, 163
 and race and racism, 18, 21–22, 26n37, 110–11, 159, 160–61, 172, 173
 religiosity in work: biblical allusions, 40, 66, 68; as theme, 16, 25n16, 25n23, 78, 118, 120–21, 143
 Rolling Thunder Revue, 22
 romantic vs. divine love in work, 121–24
 September 11, 2001 (also 9/11): event, 4, 7, 42, 73, 74–84, 86, 93, 95, 117; 9/11 studies, 73–83

socioeconomic class as topic, 165–66
Supper Club performances, 8
Tom Paine Award, 5, 7
and traditional music: ballad, 51, 56, 59, 64, 67–69, 79, 87, 106, 110, 112–13, 139, 146; ballad and refrain, 137, 148n4; folk music, 4, 8, 18, 41, 46, 47, 51, 56, 57, 64, 87; role of folk lexicon in his songs, 46, 47, 50, 55, 59, 108, 120; and songwriting approach, 87, 146, 147
and violence, 31, 37, 76, 81–82, 85–102, 124–25, 165, 171
Works: "Ain't No Man Righteous, No Not One," 131; "Ain't Talkin'," 16, 20, 99–102, 139, 142–44, 164, 167–68, 170, 174; "All Along the Watchtower," 170; "All the Tired Horses," 145–46; *Another Side of Bob Dylan*, 31; "The Asia Series," 116n23; "Ballad of a Thin Man," 6, 21, 154; "The Ballad of Frankie Lee and Judas Priest," 58; "Ballad of Hollis Brown," 55, 59, 87; *The Basement Tapes*, 6, 7, 25n16, 48; "Beyond Here Lies Nothin'," 30–33, 41, 49; "Black Diamond Bay," 69, 105; "Blind Willie McTell," 17, 129–30; *Blonde on Blonde*, 5, 6, 105, 151, 152; *Blood on the Tracks*, 28, 87, 103, 106, 152, 157; "Blowin' in the Wind," 77, 86, 88, 109, 138, 149n12, 157, 174n9, 174n11; *Bringing It All Back Home*, 5–6, 28, 131, 138, 151; "Bye and Bye," 77, 78, 81, 83, 90, 105, 139; *Christmas in the Heart*, 10, 116n23; *Chronicles Volume One*, 6, 24n2, 25n21, 40, 103, 116n23, 117, 119, 129–30, 144, 154, 160, 163; "Cold Irons Bound," 17, 23, 126; "'Cross the Green Mountain," 99–100; "Cry a While," 92, 105, 139, 167; *Cutting Edge: The Bootleg Series Volume 12*, 3, 8; "Day of the Locusts," 32; "The Death of Emmett Till," 87, 102; *Desire*, 31, 106, 138; "Desolation Row," 8, 21, 28, 35, 58, 63, 85; "Dignity," 86, 161, 162, 171; "Disease of Conceit," 162; "Don't Think Twice, It's Alright," 41, 122; "Down Along the Cove," 139; "Down in the Flood," 13, 16–17, 22, 25n16; *Down in the Groove*, 8; "Drifter's Escape," 14; "Duquesne Whistle," 64–65, 91; *Dylan and the Dead*, 8; "Early Roman Kings," 67, 68, 153, 156; *Eat the Document*, 14; "Every Grain of Sand," 127; "Everything Is Broken," 161, 162; *Fallen Angels*, 10; "Floater (Too Much to Ask)," 79, 81, 90–91, 92, 105; "Forever Young," 4; "Forgetful Heart," 36, 37; "Fourth Time Around," 58; "Gates of Eden," 86, 131; "Golden Loom," 28; *Good As I Been to You*, 7, 19, 48; "A Hard Rain's A-Gonna Fall," 16, 76, 77; "Highlands," 132; "High Water (for Charley Patton)," 10, 16, 19, 47, 50–57, 59, 62n27, 92, 105, 140, 165; *Highway 61 Revisited*, 5, 6, 21, 28, 151, 152; "Honest with Me," 21, 80, 90, 92, 105, 119, 139, 168, 170; "If Dogs Run Free," 58; "I Feel a Change Comin' On," 39–40; "If You Ever Go to Houston," 38–39; "I'll Be Your Baby Tonight," 139; *Infidels*, 151, 153; "Is Your Love in Vain?," 41; "It Ain't Me, Babe," 41, 122; "It's All Good," 41–42, 173; "It's Alright Ma (I'm Only Bleeding)," 56, 57, 58, 59, 162; "John Brown," 59; *John Wesley Harding*, 7, 48, 87, 105, 139; "John Wesley Harding," 88; "Jolene," 43; "Just Like a Woman," 107; *Knocked Out Loaded*, 8, 153; "Lay Lady Lay," 37; "The Levee's Gonna Break," 16, 94, 107, 113, 137, 164; "Life Is Hard," 37; "Like a Rolling Stone," 6, 128, 129, 138, 154; "Lonesome Day Blues," 78, 81–82, 90, 91, 108, 114, 126, 139, 149n18, 167, 169–70; "The Lonesome Death of Hattie Carroll," 87, 102; "Long and Wasted Years," 62n27, 64, 67, 156, 157; *The Lost Notebooks of Hank Williams*, 116n23; "Love and Theft," 6–11, 15, 18,

19, 21, 45, 47, 48, 50, 56, 58, 64, 73–84, 86, 88–93, 94, 95, 96, 104, 105, 106, 108, 110, 113, 114, 115, 117, 121, 125, 135, 139, 140, 146, 148, 149n18, 152, 156, 159, 160–61, 163, 171, 172; "Love Sick," 4, 62n27, 142; "Man in a Long Black Coat," 161; "Masters of War," 87, 109, 154; "Mississippi," 37, 63, 76, 79, 84, 91, 124, 126, 130, 135, 139, 141, 142, 144, 164, 170; *Modern Times*, 6–11, 15, 18, 19, 32, 38, 50, 59, 64, 85, 86, 93, 94, 95, 96, 98, 103, 104, 105, 106, 107, 108, 109, 110, 113, 114, 116n16, 117, 121, 123, 125, 135, 137, 139, 140, 142, 146, 148, 149n18, 152, 159, 160, 161, 163, 164, 165, 171, 172; "Moonlight," 76, 81, 91, 100, 114, 152, 156, 169; "Mr. Tambourine Man," 6, 138; "My Wife's Hometown," 38; "Narrow Way," 67, 110, 113, 152, 153, 156; *Nashville Skyline*, 28; "Neighborhood Bully," 109; "Nettie Moore," 20, 36, 124, 126, 131, 139; "New Pony," 156; "North Country Blues," 87, 165; "Not Dark Yet," 17, 35, 58, 129; *Oh Mercy*, 8, 40, 130, 151, 153, 154, 161–63, 168; "One More Cup of Coffee (Valley Below)," 17, 138; "Only a Pawn in Their Game," 43, 172; "Pay in Blood," 67, 110, 111, 112, 156, 161, 172; "Po' Boy," 63, 83, 92, 104, 105, 108, 159, 165; "Political World," 161–62; "Positively 4th Street," 41; *Real Live*, 147; *Renaldo and Clara*, 15; "Ring Them Bells," 121; "Roll On John," 64, 70, 111; "Sad-Eyed Lady of the Lowlands," 6; "Sara," 105; "Scarlet Town," 49, 64, 67, 68, 113; *Self Portrait*, 7, 145; "Señor (Tales of Yankee Power)," 17, 22; "Series of Dreams," 128, 154; *Shadows in the Night*, 8, 10, 116n23, 152; "Shake Shake Mama," 43; "Shelter from the Storm," 29; "Soon After Midnight," 66, 156; "Spirit on the Water," 94, 114, 115n7, 120, 139, 149n18; *Street-Legal*, 28; "Stuck Inside of Mobile with the Memphis Blues Again," 63; "Subterranean Homesick Blues," 39; "Sugar Baby," 16, 76, 77, 78, 81, 92, 93, 94, 104, 121, 139, 163, 168; "Summer Days," 37, 90, 91, 105, 170; "Tangled Up in Blue," 36, 129, 147, 150n41; *Tell Tale Signs: The Bootleg Series Volume 8*, 10, 115n6; *Tempest*, 6, 9, 24n7, 63–71, 103, 104, 110, 111, 112, 116n16, 116n22, 121, 152–57, 158, 161, 172; "Tempest," 69–70, 113, 149n18; *Theme Time Radio Hour*, 50; "Things Have Changed," 3, 8, 62n27; "This Dream of You," 32, 34–37; "Thunder on the Mountain," 16, 93, 95, 105, 106, 121, 125, 156, 164, 169–70; *Time Out of Mind*, 4, 8, 10, 43, 45, 48, 73, 104, 107, 114, 142, 151, 152, 154; *The Times They Are a-Changin'*, 151, 154, 157n1, 159; "The Times They Are a-Changin'," 3, 4, 77, 78, 86, 174n9; "Tin Angel," 67, 68, 69, 113; *Together Through Life*, 9–11, 28–43, 26n32, 113, 116n16; *Triplicate*, 10, 116n23; "Tweedle Dum and Tweedle Dee," 88–89, 92, 93; *Under the Red Sky*, 28; "Union Sundown," 109, 165; "Visions of Johanna," 150n37, 154; "What Good Am I?," 62, 168; "When the Deal Goes Down," 123, 139, 163; "Where Are You Tonight? (Journey through Dark Heat)," 36; "Who Killed Davey Moore?," 43, 87, 95; "Workingman's Blues #2," 20, 35, 94, 106, 108–9, 165, 166–67, 170, 171; *World Gone Wrong*, 7, 19, 48, 133n30, 139, 174n4

"Dylan and the Academy" (Marshall), 155
Dylanologists, The (Kinney), 85

Easter (Strindberg), 16
Ecclesiastes, 68
Eccleston, Danny, 34, 35, 39, 41, 43
Eisenstein, Sergei, 107
Eliot, T. S., 35, 152
Ella the Fortune Teller, 20, 24n9
El Mundo, 20

Emergency Civil Liberties Union, 5
Epstein, Mark Daniel, 39
Erener, Sertab, 17
Estes, Sleepy John, 26n26
Everly Brothers, 57

Faerie Queene, The (Spenser), 66
Faithfull, Marianne, 116n19
Faulkner, William, 32
Fitzgerald, F. Scott, 49
Flanagan, Bill, 32, 34, 40–42
Foxfire books, 64
Frankl, Viktor, 126
Freud, Sigmund, 75

Gandhi, Mahatma, 20
Garcia, Jerry, 17, 22
Garnier, Tony, 13
Gilmore, Mikal, 63, 116n22
Ginsberg, Allen, 4
Globe Theater, 64
Gooding, Cynthia, 21
Goodman, John, 13
Gospel of Matthew, 16
Grateful Dead, 8, 68
Gray, Richard, 74
Great Depression, 52
Green, Peter, 9
Greenwich Village, 55
Gregory, Robert, 70
Grooms, Red, 118
Grossman, Albert, 60n4, 61n6
Guthrie, Woody, 6, 119
"Gypsy Davy" (trad.), 68

Harris, Ed, 21
"Harrison Bergeron" (Vonnegut), 42
"Having Myself a Time" (Holliday), 77
Hawks, 6, 56
Haynes, Todd, 6, 15
Hearts of Fire (1984), 14–15
Hemingway, Ernest, 35
Hendrix, Jimi, 14
Herron, Donnie, 55, 64

Heylin, Clinton, 51
Hicks, Bill, 3
Hidalgo, David, 39, 64
"Highway 51" (trad.), 57
Hilburn, Robert, 51, 116n12
Hong, Howard, 127
Hopkins, Lightnin', 50
Hopper, Dennis, 15
House, Son, 26n26
"House Carpenter" (trad.), 51
Hunter, Robert, 116n23
Hurricane Katrina, 70

IBM, 3, 8
"I Look into My Glass" (Hardy), 143
I'm Not There (2007), 6, 15
Invisible Republic, The (Marcus), 20, 21, 23
Iran Contra, 7
Iraq War, 7
"I Saw the Light" (trad.), 26n23

Jackson, Andrew, 16, 24n8
Janssen, David, 16, 19
Jefferson, Blind Lemon, 18, 19
Joel, Billy, 14
John Paul (pope), 20
Johnson, Blind Willie, 19
Johnson, Robert, 19, 50, 119
John the Baptist, 20
"John the Revelator" (Blind Willie Johnson), 19
Jonson, Ben, 66
Journal of Albion Moonlight, The (Patchen), 16
Juvenal, 26n32

Kaiser Permanente, 3
Keats, John, 70
"Keep on the Sunny Side" (trad.), 25n23
Keightley, Emily, 49
Kermode, Frank, 146
Kierkegaard, Søren, 9, 117–33
King, Edward, 70
King James Bible, 40, 66, 68
Knopfler, Mark, 153

Lange, Jessica, 14
Lanois, Daniel, 154
Lead Belly, 56
Lee, Hermione, 33
Lennon, John, 70–71
Lethem, Jonathan, 11
"Let Me Rest on the Mountain" (trad.), 26n23
Letter to Donatus concerning God's grace (Saint Cyprian), 16
Levy, Jacques, 106
Lincoln, Abraham, 20
Lincoln County War, 23, 28
"Lord Darnell" (trad.), 68
Los Angeles Times, 51
Los Lobos, 64
Lott, Eric, 37, 159–60, 172, 174n15
Love and Theft (Lott), 159–60, 172, 174n15

Magnum Photos, 29
"Mannish Boy" (Waters), 68
Marcus, Greil, 4, 18, 147
Marlowe, Christopher, 36
Marquand, Richard, 14–15
Masked and Anonymous (2003), 9, 13–23, 24nn8–10, 25nn11–13, 171
"Matchbox Blues" (Jefferson), 18
McCarthy, Cormac, 35–36, 37, 43
McCartney, Paul, 14
McTell, Blind Willie, 20
"Mean Old Twister" (Arnold), 95
Michelet, Jules, 41
Miller, Emmett, 21
Milton, John, 70
minstrelsy: aural minstrelsy, 50, 152; blackface, 21–22, 50, 55; in culture, 160, 172; references to in song lyrics, 110
Moon Palace (Auster), 16
Moore, Nettie, 172
Muddy Waters, 68
My Own Love Song (2010), 37

Naked Lunch (Burroughs), 16
Negus, Keith, 138–39, 140, 147, 148, 149n12

Nehemiah, 40
Nelson, Willie, 3, 165
New York Times, 11, 29
Niebuhr, Reinhold, 162–63
Nixon, Richard M., 7, 18
Noah, 70
No Direction Home (2005), 6
Nolan, Bob, 51

"Ode to the West Wind" (Shelley), 145
Orbison, Roy, 119
Oswald, Lee Harvey, 5
Outside Inside (Davidson), 29
Ovid, 9, 146

Pascal, Blaise, 127, 132n22
Pasteur, Louis, 26n26
Patchen, Kenneth, 16
Pat Garrett and Billy the Kid (1973), 7, 15
Patton, Charley, 9, 19, 50, 52
Peckinpah, Sam, 7, 15
Pepsi, 4
Pepys, Samuel, 67
Peter, William, 70
Pickering, Michael, 49
Plato, 93, 162
"Play Lady Play" (*Dharma & Greg* episode), 15
Poe, Edgar Allan: "The Philosophy of Composition," 137; "The Raven," 113, 137
Presley, Elvis, 5
"Pretty-Peggy O" (trad.), 51
"Pretty Polly" (trad.), 55

Quasimodo, 20

"Raggle Taggle Gypsy, The," 68
Rainey, Ma, 9
Randall, Martin, 74
Reagan, Ronald, 7
Ream, Anne, 77
Recile, George, 13
Ricks, Christopher, 138
Rilke, Rainer Maria, 119–20

Rimbaud, Arthur, 6
Road, The (McCarthy), 35, 37, 43
"Road Not Taken, The" (Frost), 141
Rolling Stone, 11, 63
Rosen, Jeff, 61
Rourke, Mickey, 14
Rubber Girl, 20
Rush, Otis, 49

Saga, Junichi, 9, 77
Samedi, Baron, 68
Sartre, Jean-Paul, 5
Satires (Juvenal), 113
Schechner, Richard, 135
Scobie, Stephen, 6
Scorsese, Martin, 6, 128
Seeger, Pete, 61
Seventh Seal, The (1957), 97
Sexton, Charlie, 13
Shakespeare, William, 7, 26n26, 30, 31, 33, 38, 41, 63–71, 85, 89, 92; *Antony and Cleopatra*, 69; *As You Like It*, 33, 41, 66; *Coriolanus*, 67, 68; *Hamlet*, 65, 66, 70, 85, 89; *Henry V*, 65; *King Lear*, 30, 31, 66; *Macbeth*, 7, 92; *Measure for Measure*, 63; *The Merchant of Venice* 66; *A Midsummer Night's Dream*, 65, 67; *Much Ado About Nothing*, 67; *Othello*, 67; *Romeo and Juliet*, 63, 68; "Sonnet XIX," 68; *The Tempest*, 63, 65, 66, 70–71
Shedd, Matt, 140
Shelley, Percy Bysshe, 70
Sinatra, Frank, 11, 152
Sir John Oldcastle (anon.), 66
Skorecki, Louis, 21, 25n13
Smith, Harry, 18, 19
"Snow Bound: Idyll" (Whittier), 116n17
Sony, 3, 10
Spargo, Clifton, 77
Spender, Stephen, 146
Spenser, Edmund, 66
"Spirit of Terrorism, The" (Baudrillard), 80
Springsteen, Bruce, 14, 18, 26n27, 158

Stanley, Ralph, 55
Stanley Brothers, 56
Steidl, Gerhard, 29
Sting, 14
Strindberg, August, 16, 24n10
Stripping the Body Bare (Danner), 86–87
"Sugar Baby" (Boggs), 77
Super Bowl, 4

Tate, Greg, 73
Tatum, Stephen, 36
Terror of History: On the Uncertainties of Life in Western Civilization, The (Ruiz), 97–99
Thomas, Richard F., 146, 147
Through the Looking Glass and What Alice Found There (Carroll), 88
Timrod, Henry, 9, 49
Tin Pan Alley, 5, 47
Titanic (film, 1997), 69–70, 116n22
Titanic (ship), 69–70
Tolkien, J. R. R., 109
Tom Petty and the Heartbreakers, 56
"Tradition and the Individual Talent" (Eliot), 153
"Tumbling Tumbleweeds" (Nolan), 51
Turner, Big Joe, 50
"Tyger, The" (Blake), 111–12

Versluys, Kristiaan: "9/11 as a European Event: The Novels," 74; *Out of the Blue*, 74
Vesely, Rainer, 147
Victoria's Secret, 4, 24n3
Vietnam War, 7
Vonnegut, Kurt, 42

"Wake Up Little Susie" (Everly Brothers), 57
Warmuth, Scott, 116n23
"What'll I Do?" (Berlin), 8
Whitelock, Edward, 16, 19
Whittier, John Greenleaf, 110, 116n17
Who Is That Man? In Search of the Real Bob Dylan (Dalton), 102

Wilentz, Sean, 29, 43, 47, 152, 160
Willa Cather: Double Lives (Lee), 33
will.i.am, 4
Williams, Hank, 26n23
Williams, Paul, 135
Wilson, Luke, 18
Wonder Boys (2000), 3
Woodstock, 14, 18
Woolrich, Cornell, 16
"World Can't Stand Wrong, The" (Acuff), 19
"World Is Going Wrong, The" (Mississippi Sheiks), 19
Wright, David, 40
Wurlitzer, Rudolph, 7

Yeats, W. B., 70
Young, Iris Marion, 166
Young, Neil, 158
Youtube, 13

Žižek, Slavoj, 81, 96

www.ingramcontent.com/pod-product-compliance
Lightning Source LLC
Chambersburg PA
CBHW030624230426
43661CB00053B/2130